Watching

Alex Horne co-created, writes and co-hosts the BBC4 comedy quiz *We Need Answers*. He is widely renowned among critics, comics and audiences as a thoughtful and original stand-up, writer and solo performer and has many TV and radio credits under his belt. Alex's first book *Birdwatchingwatching* was published by Virgin Books. www.alexhorne.com.

By the Same Author

Birdwatchingwatching *(also available from Virgin Books)*

One Man's Quest for
LINGUISTIC IMMORTALITY

Word
Watching

ALEX HORNE

For Mum and Tom

1 3 5 7 9 10 8 6 4 2

First published in 2010 by Virgin Books

This edition published in 2011 by Virgin Books, an imprint of Ebury Publishing
A Random House Group Company

The Random House Group Limited Reg. No. 954009

Addresses for companies within the Random House Group can be found at
www.randomhouse.co.uk

A CIP catalogue record for this book is available from the British Library

The Random House Group Limited supports The Forest
Stewardship Council® (FSC®), the leading international forest
certification organisation. All our titles that are printed on
Greenpeace approved FSC® certified paper carry the FSC® logo.
Our paper procurement policy can be found at
www.randomhouse.co.uk/environment

Typeset in Swift-Light by Palimpsest Book Production Limited,
Falkirk, Stirlingshire

Printed and bound in Great Britain by CPI Bookmarque, Croydon, CR0 4TD

ISBN 9780753515754

To buy books by your favourite authors and register for offers visit
www.randomhouse.co.uk

Et semel emissum volat irrevocabile verbum.

'Once released, the word flies irrevocably.'

Horace, *Epistles,* I.XVIII.71

THE BEGINNING

Sometimes it seems as if a new word has about as much chance of developing into a permanent addition to our vocabulary as a single sperm has of fertilizing an egg and developing into a fully grown human.

Predicting New Words, Allan Metcalf

I love words.

It's difficult to write that sentence without sounding chillingly pretentious or worryingly trite. But I don't mean that I love using long, complicated or zany words; I don't love reading obscure modern poetry and I don't mind when someone uses an apostrophe in the wrong place.

It's certainly not a reciprocal love either. Words don't come particularly easily to me. My brain doesn't lob up the perfect adverb for my tongue to volley home as Stephen Fry's seems to. I wouldn't have known that I suffer from onomatomania had a more learned friend not told me so. I've used Microsoft's thesaurus function twice already and I've barely started. What I mean is I love *playing* with words, mucking about with them, building them up and breaking them down like Lego.

My first word was 'mama', which is not a particularly inventive choice. All across the world babies of every race say 'mama', 'dada' and occasionally 'papa' before anything more interesting; they (well, we) are apparently pre-programmed to utter these soft repetitive sounds first, and it's thought by some that adults (well, we) took words like 'mummy' and 'daddy' from our offspring, rather than the other way round; we turned their primal noises into words. It was a baby who invented the word 'mum'.

But I like to think that my 'mama' was rather more of a conscious choice as it's from my mum that I've gained my love of words. She is a wordwatcher. It's a subtler hobby than bird-watching as no binoculars betray the pursuit, rather it is the odd spoonerism here and the odd anagram there that gives her away as a worder. She collects teapots too, but that's a side-project, a diversion, not an obsession. My older brother was shown birds by my dad and he still follows them today. I was shown words by my mum. They're now my passion.

It all started when, instead of books about spies or wizards, she got me reading joke books. Traditionally these are perched somewhere near a toilet to lighten the tedium of our daily ablu-tions, or tucked away on a shelf next to the dictionaries and thesauri for reference when writing a speech or settling an argu-ment. But my joke books were stacked up next to my bed and I read them one by one, from cover to cover.

Unfortunately my mum didn't pass on her remarkable memory so I could never remember more than a few jokes at a time. My mind, I worry, is like my mobile phone – it can only store so many messages at once, then, when it's full, I have to delete some information before starting again. As I read these books, I jotted down my favourite jokes so I could unfurl them later, at family events. In fact, I found that I could always remember punchlines, even if the set-ups deserted me. So Christmas for me was all about the crackers. I prided myself on knowing the solution to every joke equation. I rarely failed. The satisfying logic of the set-up and punchline made sense to me.

When I'd read and scribbled on every joke book she could find me, my mum got me on to harder stuff. While my brothers wolfed down stories by Roald Dahl, J. R. R. Tolkien and Gerald Durrell, I read and re-read a slim blue book called *Palindromes and Anagrams* by a less celebrated writer called Howard W. Bergerson. Again, I scribbled asterisks and exclamation marks next to my favourites and again I stowed away the few my memory was able to cope with. To my more patient friends I'd occasionally say things like, 'Did you know that "dirty room" is an anagram of "dormitory", a "canoe" can be made out of "ocean" and "the classroom" from "schoolmaster"? Isn't that fantastic?!' I'd even try to slip in short anagrammatic sentences like 'kleptomaniacs task policeman', 'the detectives detect thieves' or 'this ear, it hears'. I don't think I was trying to be clever and I certainly didn't realise quite how pompous I must have sounded. I may have been showing off, but it was an innocent exhibition. I had discovered these amazing things and wanted to share them with my friends.

I was genuinely fascinated by the neatness of the best examples. I was entranced by the fact that 'moonstarers' became 'astronomers', that 'eleven + two' equalled 'twelve + one' and that 'one hug' was 'enough'. Yes, I thought, 'an aisle' 'is a lane'! Sometimes 'the answer' just 'wasn't here'! I started looking for my own anagrams and palindromes around the house; 'Siemens' was my 'nemesis', both 'Evian' water and 'Nivea' skin cream were for people 'naive' enough to buy them. This was how I relieved the 'boredom' in my 'bedroom'. Wordplay was my thing. Like the double-jointed kid in my class, this was the peculiar trick I could pull off. In my Bergerson book next to 'testament' and 'statement' I scribbled 'men attest'.

I found the palindromes hypnotic, maybe because both my mum and my dad are palindromic people; from flawless classics like Leigh Mercer's 1948 hit, 'a man, a plan, a canal – Panama' to the current master, J. A. Lindon's modern responses, including, 'a dog, a pant, a panic in a Patna pagoda' and the more realistic, conversational, 'Did I do, O God, did I as I said I'd do? Good, I did!', 'Marge lets Norah see Sharon's telegram' and 'pull up, Eva, we're here, wave, pull up'. 'I'm Al, a salami', I scrawled underneath, desperate to join in.

Then there were the lesser known word games such as

pangrams – all twenty-six letters of the alphabet in as short a sentence as possible: 'the quick brown fox jumps over the lazy dog' or, my attempt, 'Alex Horne's big five jokey word impact quiz' – and charades – not the 'parlour game' which, irritatingly, doesn't involve any words, but a form of anagram in which the order of the letters remains the same while the meaning changes: 'amiable together' becomes 'am I able to get her?' or, one of my early attempts, a short story about a girl gardening: 'Amanda rescues pot sand; Mandy in gloves', which becomes the more dramatic snooker-themed love story: 'A man dares, cues, pots and man, dying, loves'. I became addicted to letters and started seeing hidden messages all around me, from the mysterious instruction 'Nation, Alex, Press!' in National Express, to the true motto of Iceland (the supermarket, not the country): 'Food You Can't Rust'.

As I say, it was my mum who entrusted me with Bergerson's anagrammatic bible. It's not the sort of thing a kid would be naturally drawn to in a library or borrow from another kid, but my mum was keen to share her passion for words. As a child she'd been given her own blue book called *Primary English* by D. W. Walters, a progressive grammar packed full of linguistic puzzles and palindromes which she treasured then and treasures still. Now I too could play with language like a toy.

To my mum words represented a true pastime. While dad pointed out kestrels, she spent family trips teaching us word games she'd learnt from Walters's book: could we find the boys' names hidden in sentences like, 'They had either to charge or get killed' or 'The giant groaned "How ill I am"'? Could we change 'gold' to 'bell' or 'fire' to 'mark', altering one letter at each step and forming another word each time? I was entranced by these simple brainteasers. Again and again I would ask her to tell me the stories that ended with the spectacular sentences: 'There is not enough space between Vanstone and and and and and Sons' or 'James, though Jones had had "had", had had "had had"; "had had" had had the examiner's approval'.[1]

The peculiarities of language were a constant source of amusement for us both. She would always slip in a spoonerism when one suggested itself: 'I'm going to break some bed,' she'd say before baking. Horace the cat would scarper through the 'flat cap'. My bed would always have its 'shitted feet'. I was never sure whether these were deliberate or if, like Dr Spooner himself, she created them unwittingly. Either way, they were second nature to her and I started knowing my blows, fighting liars and chipping flannels too.

The shifting of a single letter could delight us. One Christmas my grandmother sent my brother Chip a gift consisting of an ornate pen from Russia and a card, inside which she'd written the apparently innocent message: 'Chip, Much love from Granny – The pen is from Russia'. Unfortunately for Granny, she had written the words 'is' and 'pen' extremely close together. So close, in fact, that it actually read, 'Much love from Granny – The penis from Russia': a small charade but one that made a lasting impression.

Chip

Much love

from

granny

The penis from Russia

---

1 The first describes an unsatisfactorily spaced shop sign reading 'H. VanstoneandSons', the second an exam in which Jones had written 'had' as an answer, and James 'had had'. 'Had had' was correct.

My mum and I would always do *The Times* crossword together over breakfast and would almost always share the victor's spoils after a family game of Balderdash (a terrific and highly recommended word-based board game). I was always amazed by how much she so modestly knew – an obscure word like 'noop' or a Czech composer, six letters.[2] 'Oh no,' she would say when complimented. 'You should see *my* mum doing the cryptic. Now that's impressive.'

When revising for my A-levels we'd watch *Countdown* with a cup of tea together every afternoon to break up the day; I told myself it was good for the brain, she didn't disagree. On leaving school I applied for a place at Cambridge University, so got a job in the local Budgens (the logical choice) while preparing for the interview. Again, I'd be home by a quarter past four every afternoon so we could both sit down in front of Richard and Carol before I hit the books.

It was whilst working at this supermarket that I wrote my first ever joke. As Deputy Head of Dairy (there were only two of us in the department) I received monthly copies of *Check Out*, the in-store magazine, and was excited to find a competition in the Christmas edition to see which Budgens employee could write the best Christmas cracker joke. This was my big break, I thought. I'd done my research. I had to win. So, after about a week's tinkering I whittled down a number of joke ideas to the following single quip (try to imagine someone reading this out at the Christmas table):

> Monday, Tuesday, Wednesday, Thursday, Friday,
> Saturday, Sunday – those were the days.

I appreciate it's not necessarily the funniest joke in the world. If even one person laughed out loud while reading it in their

---

2 The sharp point of the elbow and Dvořák.

head I'd be pleasantly surprised. But that's not the point of Christmas cracker jokes. All they require is a nod, a groan and, perhaps, a knowing, 'I see what they've done there'. What's more, this maiden joke was enough to win that year's competition, and the prize, an open spot at the local comedy club in Chichester, was a life-changing one.

My five-minute spot at the club was spectacularly subdued. I told that joke and several others of a similar ilk but when you're onstage, a nod, a groan and a knowing, 'I see what they've done there' are far less satisfying than sitting round the Christmas dinner table. Even so, despite the staring faces, conscious coughs and a round of applause whose claps I could count on my fingers, I loved it. I was hooked.

I also managed to get into Cambridge, more specifically into a small, friendly college called Sidney Sussex where I would follow in the footsteps of famous alumni like Oliver Cromwell and, more impressively to me, Carol Vorderman. Here I studied Latin and German. For six weeks. Then I left. Unfortunately, most of my fellow linguists had spent their gap year immersed in their chosen languages, rather than the milk aisle of Budgens, and I was out of my depth. I did know one German palindrome: *'nie fragt sie: ist gefegt? Sie ist gar fein'*, a poignant portrait of a modern woman that translates as, 'She never asks: has the sweeping been done? She is very refined', but that, apparently, was not enough.

Thankfully, once allowed into the hallowed corridors of an Oxbridge college it's very hard to get out again. I was granted permission to take a few months off, learn the Greek alphabet and come back to study Classics instead, so I embarked on my second gap year, this time working on the *West Sussex Gazette* as People's Correspondent, writing stories about dead donkeys (just the one, actually, but I really did have to write an obituary for a deceased mule) and attempting to get to grips with alpha, beta and the rest in my lunch break.

That word 'Classics' may need some qualification. It's a strange, all-encompassing name, as grandiose as The United Kingdom or *The One Show*. The degree itself isn't limited to classic works of fiction, nor does it include classic cars or the classic BLT. Instead, it represents a period in antiquity, the classical Greco-Roman era, in which a whole load of what can only be described as classic stuff got done. So I was to study Latin and Ancient Greek, with some archaeology, philosophy and linguistics thrown in.

I used to be uncomfortable admitting this. When I got my hair cut back home in Midhurst I was more comfortable saying I still worked in the local supermarket than that I was off to study Classics at Cambridge. I was embarrassed by it. Latin has such connotations of elitism, public-school education and moneyed pointlessness, saying I studied it *by choice* seemed like an act of showing off that could only arouse suspicion and contempt. Arranging yogurts for ten hours a day seemed a far nobler pursuit.

Over the years, however, I have accepted that I *did* study Latin and what's more, I enjoyed it. I can now talk about it without shame. We'll return to the subject throughout this story but all I'm trying to say now is, please don't let the very idea of Latin put you off. Give Latin a chance. Thank you.

I was never an outstanding student, ending up with a respectable but undistinguished 2:1, but during my three years at Cambridge I wrote at least three things that would shape the rest of my life. First, I dashed out more newspaper articles, this time for *Varsity*, the official Cambridge newspaper with lofty ideas way above its station. I liked the thrill of being published, especially in such a ridiculously pompous but admirably ambitious publication, but despite a dearth of dead donkeys I still couldn't take the news seriously, and soon realised that I didn't want to become a journalist.

Second, I eventually completed a dissertation about wordplay in the Golden Age of Ancient Rome. I did contemplate including it as the opening chapter to this book but realised it might be just too diverting for the average reader. (I sent a copy to my mum at the time. She said she'd read it and enjoyed it although I now realise she may have exaggerated both those claims.) Suffice to say that my early fondness for wordplay was strengthened and legitimised when I learnt that anagrams (*ars magna* – 'the great art') were invented by the Greek poet Lycophron in 260 BC (he turned ΠΤΟΛΕΜΑΙΟΣ – the Egyptian King Ptolemy – into ΑΠΟ ΜΕΛΙΤΟΣ – meaning 'from honey', and ΑΡΣΙΝΟΗ – Arsinoe, the name of both Ptolemy's wives, the second of whom was also his sister – into ΙΟΝ ΗΡΑΣ, meaning 'Hera's violet'), while a satirist in the same country and century called Sotades of Thrace created palindromic verse (he is believed to have re-written the whole of Homer's *Iliad* in palindromic form). Thousands of years ago people like me liked sentences that read the same forwards and backwards. God! A red nugget! A fat egg under a dog! On their fountains the Greeks wrote ΝΙΣΠΟΝ ΑΝΟΜΙΜΑΤΑ ΜΙ ΜΟΝΑΝ ΟΠΣΙΝ (meaning 'wash the sin as well as the face'), while the Romans wrote of moths '*in girum imus nocte et consumimur igni*' (meaning 'we enter the circle after dark and are consumed by fire'). During one of our lengthy breaks between terms I sent this palindromic postcard home:

In the course of my studies I learnt that people have been mucking around with words, just as I had, for as long as speech has existed. It's a natural thing to do. In fact, it's an honourable thing to do. Leaping forward to the seventeenth century and across the channel to France, King Louis XIII appointed his own Royal Anagrammatist, a man called Thomas Billon, who was specifically employed to entertain the court with his anagrams of famous people's names. If such a job had been available when I finally left university I'm sure I would have found employment far sooner than I was able to.

Third, finally, besides the articles and essays, I wrote more jokes. There was a three-year hiatus between that first Budgens-inspired open spot and the next time I told jokes to strangers, but I did eventually pluck up enough courage to attend an audition for 'Footlights', the Cambridge equivalent of a stand-up comedy club. Every few weeks, the society would host a 'Footlights smoker', at which anyone could perform three minutes of material in front of a judgemental crowd of self-confident students. Here I tried out my own puns and gags. It was an excellent, if sometimes painful, training ground.

Now, ten years after writing my very first joke, I'm officially a comedian, of sorts. For me, it's the best job in the world because I get paid to tinker with words *and* watch *Countdown* every single day. There are very few jobs that can incorporate *Countdown* into the working day, especially now it starts at the earlier time of 3.25 p.m., so I feel incredibly lucky.

Currently I'm a little busy writing this book so am spending less time 'on the road' and more time 'at home with my chickens', but until recently I spent most of my time driving to far-off places and telling jokes, usually involving simple wordplay, to strangers. One- or two-liners like:

> My dad used to work in a tiddly-wink factory, but he said it was counter-productive.
>
> I've felt very lonely ever since someone told me I was about as tall as a tall flightless bird. I just felt very ostrich-sized.
>
> My grandmother was recently beaten to death. By my grand-father. Not with a stick. He died first.

This last is my current favourite. It's a simple pun on the word 'beat' but it changes the meaning of the sentence dramatically, transforming a sad story about my grandmother dying into a sad story about my grand*father* dying – although not *as* sad because in the second version he hasn't (necessarily) been bludgeoned to death by his spouse.

So that's how I am where I am now. Unimaginative journalists often ask comedians if they always knew they wanted to 'do comedy', to which they either explain that they were the jokers in the class at school, or one of the quiet ones who read a lot, watched a lot and wrote things down. I was in the latter, silently ambitious, camp but like to throw in the Budgens story so I don't sound too dull or earnest. My real, even more pretentious-sounding answer, however, is that I became a comedian because I love words.

But one afternoon, at approximately 4.05 p.m., I realised that writing jokes wasn't enough. By now I was twenty-seven years old and my comedy career was progressing steadily (when somebody stands still they can be described as very steady indeed). After a handful of years on the circuit I finally accepted that wordplay, and puns in particular, were now regarded as old-fashioned. A punchline like 'ostrich-sized' very rarely got what could accurately be described as a 'laugh'.

In fact, puns have been sneered at for centuries. In Dryden's *Defence of the Epilogue*, he classed them 'the lowest and most grovelling kind of wit', while in Ambrose Bierce's *The Devil's Dictionary*, they are dismissed mercilessly as 'a form of wit, to which wise men stoop and fools aspire'. Regardless of whether I have spent much of my life stooping or aspiring, I hope that's not true. I have always thought puns are a part of life in Britain that we should be proud of, like birdwatching and cricket, an innocent diversion to some, an all-consuming passion to others. But even though I loved creating these jokes, they now felt lightweight compared to other comedians' targets of sex and drugs and politics. I wasn't satisfied with my lot. I wanted more recognition. And just after four o'clock one afternoon, it was *Countdown*, more specifically, Sidney Sussex's Carol Vorderman who stirred me into action.

Just before the first advert break in what I thought was a normal episode of my beloved programme, Carol displayed typically stylish numerical dexterity by revealing to her viewers an equation with which they might work out how many *days* old they were on that particular day. It's a tricky figure to come up with, one's exact age in days, what with leap years and multi-length months, but thanks to Ms Vorderman's mental arithmetics Countdowners across the land could instantly (well, fairly quickly) find out their tally and say something like, 'Gosh, who'd have thought?' But my reaction was a little stronger than that, my exclamation a little fruitier. Being less than thirty, I was almost certainly dragging down the average age of the audience by several decades, but when I worked out that I was 9,945 days old, I suddenly felt incredibly old myself. I was just fifty-five days away from my ten-thousandth day on earth. 'Oh f***.'

Saddled, as we are, with our Gregorian calendar, we often forget about this particular birthday. But one's ten-thousandth day, one's 'tkday' to give it its official name, is an immensely important occasion. It's a turning point, a true coming-of-age moment. By the time you've reached your tkday, you've flown past the one- and ten-day marks, whizzed on beyond a hundred then a thousand days and raced up to the ominous five-figure checkpoint at which you will remain for the rest of your life (unless you live to be 274 years old, which is unlikely even considering today's advances in science). So a tkday is one of life's key landmarks. It represents the moment when you have unequivocally reached adulthood. There's even a website (www.tkday.com, helpfully) which will calculate your tkday for you and, if you desire, send you a cake on the relevant date, because it's a date worth marking. Sure, when you're sixteen you can get married (but only if you're straight, of course), when you're eighteen you can buy a beer to celebrate (and if you're not straight, *now* you can get married too!) and when you're twenty-one you're legally old enough to do everything else everyone else is doing; but in practice you've still got a lot to learn. When you're ten thousand days old, about twenty-seven years and four months old, you should be *able* to do everything else everyone else is doing and, what's more, you should know what it is you *want* to do.

But as I sat in front of *Countdown*, scribbling away on my designated *Countdown* notepad during the adverts for stairlifts and cruises, I realised that my life wasn't quite heading in the direction I'd intended. I had always wanted to leave my mark on the world, to do something memorable, to achieve something remarkable, but it had become increasingly apparent that my innocent, dare I say it, childish wordplay wouldn't furnish me with the immortality I desired. Yes, I might get over 75 per cent of the *Countdown* teatime teasers, often before the very first advert was over, but all of a sudden that didn't seem enough. In less than two months I would hit that ten-thousand-day mark and meekly join the rest of the aged population in the five-figure camp. I didn't fancy this obscurity. It was time to set myself a tougher challenge. So inspired by my mathematical muse, I immediately hatched a plan to devise a project that would ensure I left my linguistic mark on the world.

I would create a new word.

That was it! At once I felt young again, full of vigour and hope. Yes! I would invent my own word! More simple than a joke but also more complete! A joke is a fun, frivolous thing, cheap and disposable. But a word ... a word seemed to me a wholly more satisfactory creation. A word must be the ultimate legacy to leave any offspring I might be lucky enough to spring off (they might well prefer a car, a house or just some more sporty DNA, but imagine, a word!). My own word would be the ultimate achievement, something that would give meaning to an otherwise playful life. I would win a place in the only record book that really mattered: the dictionary.

An enduring and treasured feature of *Countdown* is 'Dictionary Corner', a desk in the studio manned by an eminent lexicographer and that week's celebrity guest who suggest their own words and verify the contestants' efforts by consulting the *New Oxford Dictionary of English*. Since first appearing on the show in 1992, Oxford graduate and former employee of the Oxford University Press Susie Dent has made the 'Guardian of the Dictionaries' role her own. Alongside Carol, she is both televisual and lexical royalty. One day, I promised myself, she would look up a word in *Countdown*'s 'Dictionary Corner' and see my word, with my name cited underneath.

Because getting a word *in the dictionary* had to be the aim of this project. Ever since the heavyweight lexicographer Samuel Johnson completed his pioneering dictionary on 15 April 1755, these mighty books have safely housed our language. For the first time in history, he'd attempted to comprehensively document the English lexicon, single-handedly collating each of its words and illustrating its meaning with quotations from literature. Now, for me to feel satisfied, my verbal creation had to end up in one of today's respected dictionaries, ideally the *Oxford English Dictionary* of course, but any recognised dictionary really, just as long as others could one day look it up and discover its meaning in an official reference book.

Anyone can invent a word; 'ghuid' – there, I just did that by shutting my eyes, shifting my hands along a bit and typing. 'Ghuid'. I guess it means something like 'a wise Welsh woman'. Yes, something like that. And if I say a 'ghuid' means a wise Welsh woman then, in a way, it does. But it doesn't really, does it? If a few other people start using 'ghuid' instead of 'wise Welsh woman' then it might start to mean it. But until 'ghuid' is actually *in the dictionary*, it won't really count.

And getting a word *in the dictionary* isn't easy. You can't just write to the dictionary authorities and say,

Dear Richard[3]
    I've got a new one for you: 'ghuid' – meaning 'a wise Welsh woman'.
    My pleasure,
    Alex

It's not that easy.

It used to be that easy. Shakespeare is arguably our finest inventor of words, with about 1,700 to his name (we'll come back to this figure and that name later on), but I can't help thinking he just happened to be in the right place at the right time. Because the Bard is said to have coined words like 'eyeball' and 'elbow'. So before that, if you got 'elbowed' in the 'eyeball' you'd only have been able to say, 'He did that in my thing and it hurt,' miming the affected body parts and

---

3 'Richard' is eighteenth-century slang for dictionary. To quote Francis Grose's 1811 *Dictionary of the Vulgar Tongue*, 'A country lad, having been reproved for calling persons by their Christian names, being sent by his master to borrow a dictionary, thought to shew his breeding by asking for a Richard Snary.' That's my sort of pun.

getting frustrated both by your inability to explain the situation and the considerable ocular pain. Then Shakespeare came along, observed such a fracas and thought to himself, 'Well, there's a gap in the market here, I'll label those body parts right up!' Now, the body is fully labelled up (even the point of the elbow has its own name) and it's a lot harder to come up with new words.

But if a word is used enough it will still end up in the dictionary, thanks largely to the work of Sir James Murray, the man behind the first edition of the *Oxford English Dictionary* (*OED*), who once claimed to be fluent in Italian, French, Catalan, Spanish and Latin, 'tolerably familiar' with Dutch, German, Danish, not bad at Portuguese, Vaudois and Provençal, pretty good at Anglo-Saxon and Moeso-Gothic and able to read Slavonic, Russian, Hebrew, Aramaic, Arabic, Coptic, Phoenician and a little Celtic in an (unsuccessful) application for a job at the British Museum. Beginning work on 12 May 1860, he was determined that, unlike all previous lexicons, his would have no limits. He would settle for nothing less than an exhaustive collection, the complete dictionary, documenting the entire English language.

Murray therefore embarked on an unimaginably arduous quest to pin down and define every English word ever spoken, relying on the public's interest in the language to plug every gap and drawing up a great team of learned helpers (including his own eleven children and one J. R. R. Tolkien, who worked as an assistant editor in 1919 and whose 'hobbit' made it into the final dictionary) who themselves collected data from correspondents across the world.

By the time the *OED* was published in 1928, seventy years after its inception, Murray had been dead for thirteen years. So meticulous was his research, so thorough his approach and so unswerving his principles, that one cannot imagine his legacy will ever be forgotten. He didn't just list the words, he traced each one as far back in linguistic history as possible and explained where and when it was first used. The *Oxford English Dictionary* really is The Dictionary.

Today, thanks to Murray's original ethos and enthusiasm, it is still possible to get new words into the dictionary. The *OED* is still very much alive, with editors and volunteers working round the clock to keep it up to date; a total of 90,000 new words were collected in the twentieth century. That works out at two and a half words coined every single day. These are encouraging numbers.

In the year of my tkday, the exotic word 'bootylicious' (meaning 'shapely, voluptuous, especially with reference to the buttocks') was one of those allowed into the exclusive club thanks to poet, writer and, well, pop star, Beyoncé Knowles. She may not actually have invented the word itself (it was featured in an intriguing song from 1992 by Dr Dre, called 'F*** wit Dre Day (and Everybody's Celebratin)', but it was Beyoncé whom the dictionary heralded because in 2001 it was she who wrote a top-selling single of the same name for her band Destiny's Child. So Beyoncé invented the word 'bootylicious'. It is definitely possible to get a word in the dictionary.

Irksomely, Beyoncé herself was unimpressed by her achievement, telling *TV Hits* magazine, 'I wish there was another word I could have come up with if I was going to have a word in the dictionary.' One day, I am sure, Miss Knowles will understand the enormity of her achievement, a triumph surely more long-lasting and more satisfying than any of her many Grammies, Brits or MTV music awards. In the meantime, I have named one of my two chickens after her, partly in honour of her feat but also to remind myself exactly how possible it is every time I look down from the window by my desk at my bootylicious poultry.

Because back in 2006 I felt that if Beyoncé could do it, I could do it. (That's not normally a mantra for my life. I don't always compare myself with her – she is, after all, a truly outstanding dancer.) With my childhood spent playing with words and this current determination to invent my own, I felt sure that I could at least match her in this arena.

It wasn't just Beyoncé either. In my optimistic frame of mind I reasoned that I was as qualified as anyone else anywhere else to invent a word. For despite being a magnificent feat, the birth of a word, like the birth of a baby, is something that happens all the time. Every single word we speak must, at some point, have been spoken by someone first. They may seem to emerge indistinctly from the fog of history, but all words must have first come from one mouth. Indeed, in the course of telling my own story I shall describe how many others have coined their own words, while every word with an asterisk can also be traced directly back to a single human being whose own tale of linguistic innovation can be found in The Wordwatcher's Dictionary at the back of the book.

Yes, I was attempting to follow in the mighty footsteps of Shakespeare, Chaucer and even Virgil, literary[*4] genii who shaped the language we all speak today, but I would also be following in the rather less daunting tread of Ian Dowie, George W. Bush and Jasper Carrott, all of whom, like Beyoncé, have got words in the actual dictionary.

The last of these extraordinary men is just one of several comedians who managed to coin their own words in the eighties and early nineties, at a time when I hung off every one of those they said. Mike Harding is credited with first writing 'wazzock' in his 1984 book *When the Martians Landed In Huddersfield*, Hale and Pace re-popularised the old Scottish word 'stonk' during 1991's *Comic Relief*, and it was Carrot who brought 'zits' over from American slang in his song of the same name. While Lenny Henry's 'spon-

---

4 For all asterisked words, please see The Wordwatcher's Dictionary, page 299.

ditious' (meaning 'fabulous') failed to survive the eighties, Harry Enfield's 'wad' did become common slang for 'cash' and his catch-phrase 'loadsamoney' is still repeated twenty years on. I could join this merry band. This, I believed, would be my attainable ticket to immortality, my shot at fame, my destiny.

I therefore delved (to quite a shallow level, at first) into the world of dictionaries and discovered that to be let into the club, to become a recognised word, a new verbal idea, a neologism, must have been used several times over a prolonged period of time by a variety of people. As the helpful website of the *OED* explains,* lexicographers need evidence:

> A new word is not included in the OED unless it has 'caught on' and become established in the language. Words that are only used for a short period of time, or by a very small number of people, are not included. To determine whether a word has caught on, we normally require several independent examples of the word being used, and also evidence that the word has been in use for a reasonable span of time. The exact span of time and number of examples can vary from word to word: a word may be included on the evidence of only a few examples, if these are spread out over a long period of time. Conversely, a large number of examples collected over a short period of time can show that a word has very quickly become established.

They need, to use their own word, a 'corpus' of examples, hard proof that a word has widespread and long-lasting usage. So a corpus I resolved to create. A hundred and fifty years before James Murray and twice that before me, Samuel Johnson had allotted himself three years to write our language's first true dictionary. I would take the same amount of time to create just one entry. In about a thousand days I would get a word into that dictionary.

*

Almost as soon as I'd resolved to invent a word I christened the project 'Verbal Gardening'. Such an endeavour needed a title and this, I thought, summed up the task perfectly. My wife Rachel and I were then living in a ground floor flat in Kensal Green, London, that boasted the smallest of outdoor spaces: a few slabs of sandstone surrounded by three troughs traditionally known as 'flower beds' but which contained no flowers and were nothing like beds. They were more like 'weed baths'. I'd planted a few bulbs here and a couple of bushes there, but none was flowering. A tomato plant had struggled to produce four of the tiniest tomatoes ever seen and an ambitious chilli plant had blurted out at least three respectable fruits, but this was not one of west London's most impressive gardens.

Nevertheless, I loved the whole gardening business. I was in charge of the digging, planting and watering so it was I who'd made those tomatoes and chillies. I had created something. I had made a difference. The beds/baths might not have been over-flowing with colour quite yet but these were early days. Whilst I was in charge, anything might emerge the following spring. I was the boss.

In just such a way the phrase 'Verbal Gardening' summed up my hopes for this linguistic project. I was the boss. Anything might emerge. In the preface to his seminal book, Samuel Johnson acknowledges the horticultural metaphor, writing, 'No dictionary of a living tongue can ever be perfect, since, while it is hastening to publication, some words are budding, and some falling away.' I had to pray that my words would flower at just the right time to be plucked by a future dictionary editor.

I therefore resolved to plant a whole packet of Verbal Seeds, at least some of which would subtly mature underground then bravely poke their heads up into the public eye and gradually grow stronger before triumphantly sending their own seeds out into the world. I didn't want to produce a flashy short-lived word like a pansy or a passion flower. My word had to stand the test of time like an oak, or bear fruit each year like an apple tree, so it had to be worth scattering a handful of hopeful candidates out onto the land. These Verbal Seeds would be my attempt to start life, and I would be on hand to nurture that life for as long as it might take.

But, unlike my actual garden, I couldn't tend this Verbal Garden all on my tod. I would need help. For instead of a three-metre square patch of land, I would be casting my seeds over the entire country, indeed over the entire world. I might start with some fairly localised Verbal Gardening, testing out new ideas on friends, bestowing phrases on my family, but the goal was to implant a word in the English language, as used by 375 million people across the planet.

In 1959 a committee called the 'Ten Rare Men' (more formally, the British Birds Rarities Committee or the BBRC) was established to decide whether sightings of rare birds by amateur observers were authentic. Inspired by such neat bureaucracy, I decided this was exactly the sort of body needed both to look out for sightings of my budding new words in print or conversation *and* to confirm that these usages were genuine; that the word was being used in the right context meaning what it was supposed to mean. So I set about forming my own group of Ten Rare Men. If deemed admissible by this jury, any quote would go into our corpus.

But far more crucially than this assessment, my own Rare Men would be involved in the innovation and development necessary in a bid to get a word in the dictionary. This was a project far too large for one man, so I resolved also to ask my Rare Men to help me come up with some words themselves. The more collective thought that went into the selection of our seeds, the more chance they would have to germinate. After nominating their own words, these men, I hoped, would then help to spread them. As well as being my eyes and ears, looking and listening out for the words, they would be my mouth, passing the words on. My Rare Men would be the face of Verbal Gardening (except for the nose, which isn't relevant to the story).

Bearing all this in mind, I selected ten friends who were best placed to tackle what was going to be a tricky job. The members of the current birding committee include statisticians, an archivist and a museum consultant, an appropriately administrative bunch. Mine was drawn from the world of communication and the arts in particular, a place whence words are cast far and wide and would, I hoped, be heard by many.

Despite having stated its desire to be made up of members representing 'all age ranges and both sexes',[5] all sixty-seven people who have served the BBRC have been male. Mine were too. I did consider asking my mum for help, but decided that this time I would find my wordy way independently, from her at least. When my own verbal invention had fledged I would show her what I'd done and how far I'd come. But until then, it was time for me to do the nurturing.

Unfortunately, I can't reveal the names of my committee members; as you shall see as the story progresses, experimenting with the English language is a dangerous business. People get angered and enraged (two more anagrams) if you muck around with their tongue. So, in order to protect my friends, my frontline, I have given them codenames. This, I can assure you, is in the spirit of linguistic innovation. All the great anagrammatists use pseudonyms, with Viking, Traddles and Verdant Green among my favourites. As a nod to these illustrious linguists and, I hoped, as an appropriately wordy gesture, I named my Rare Men after my favourite fonts (we all have favourite fonts, don't we?). So here are my men, in their respective styles of writing:

---

5 BBRC report for 1999, page 513.

Mr Bodoni – a theatre director
Mr Bookman – an actor
Mr Elephant – a poet
Mr Garamond – a teacher
Mr Goudy-Stout – a radio producer
Mr Matisse – a hotel Health and Safety inspector
Mr Palatino – a playwright
Mr Rockwell – a journalist
Mr Roman – a nightclub promoter/magazine editor
◖▨☐   ✦⟨▨Ŋ♭♌⟨▨Ŋ♭✦ (Mr Wingdings) – a comedian

You may notice Mr Matisse's profession standing out amongst the other more media-related roles. I must admit that his inclusion was mainly to extend the age range of my Rare Men. Without him their average age, when the project began, was twenty-seven. With him, that leaped up to the far more mature thirty. For those of you not as good at maths as Carol, that makes him fifty-seven years old and our senior adviser.

The eleven of us would make up the Verbal Gardening team, with me in the role of player-manager like Kenny Dalglish in Liverpool's glory days. And it was to these ten potential team-mates that I sent my first Verbal Gardening missive on 7 December 2005, exactly fifty days before my tkday, explaining my plan and asking for their help and support.

Replies came in thin and slow. Mr Rockwell was the first to respond with a positive, 'I'm intrigued and excited by the project.' Mr Roman soon followed with a simple; 'I'm in.' After a couple of days Mr Bookman agreed ('you can trust me to be covert') as did the more enigmatic Mr Wingdings ('I think this is a red radish of an idea,' he wrote, which I took to be a good thing) and the mature Mr Matisse ('I do apologise for the tardiness of my response, but I only returned last evening from a twelve-day trip to the Middle East where I was giving various hoteliers (forty-eight) a hard time with regards to the Health and Safety standards in their hotels').

Ten days after the original invitation Messrs Palatino, Garamond and Goudy-Stout also replied to say yes. Eight down. A few days later I received an email from Mr Elephant, who really set the tone for all his future correspondence by writing: 'I'm in your divvy thing about words.' Ninety per cent had agreed to take part; I was waiting only for Mr Bodoni; it was time to start creating the words.

Picking a brand-new word is a daunting task. If you are to be responsible for a mint item in the English lexicon you want to make it a good one. It's like naming a baby. You need to get it right, otherwise you'll have to spend the rest of your life introducing it to other people with embarrassment. As I've said, I don't like wacky, flashy, glitzy words. I wouldn't call my children Sage Moonblood, Blue Angel or Jermajesty (names chosen by Sylvester Stallone, The Edge and Jermaine Jackson respectively). As I thought about what seed I wanted to plant I began to understand why Beyoncé had been defensive about hers. She's now stuck with 'bootylicious', which is far from a terrible example, but also not that sophisticated an adjective. That's why I got my Rare Men to help. Between us we were bound to come up with something more respectable. I instructed them each to nominate three verbal ideas they wanted to add to the language. From this heap of suggestions, we would vote for the five best.

I should also say that our emphasis was never on these words being particularly funny. I was interested only in success. I was desperate to get a word in the dictionary and anything that might decrease the chances of that happening had to be discounted. The outstanding American comedian Rich Hall has created many hilarious 'sniglets' ('any word that doesn't appear in the dictionary but should'), similar to the contents of Douglas Adams and John

Lloyd's *The Meaning of Liff*, in which characterful place names become a 'dictionary of things that there aren't any words for yet'. In 1998, *Viz* first published its mighty reference book, *Roger's Profanisaurus*, which lists and defines thousands of ingenious obscenities with both wit and skill. But, as amusing as these collections are, they haven't actually changed the language. People laugh at these new words and their sharp meanings, but they rarely take them on board and use them themselves. None of their 'words' are now in the dictionary. We couldn't afford to be so entertaining.

Taking this into consideration, I now present the words that the committee and I eventually decided upon and with which, for three years, I attempted to infiltrate the English language. But just before revealing them I should also report that on the day before the Verbal Election, Mr Bodoni, the tenth Rare Man, did also give his full support with a hastily thumbed text message:

Hello* Mr Farmer, looking forward to this word gardening!

For some reason, having reported this message to the rest of the team, the title 'Farmer' stuck. From then on, in all communication, I was The Farmer. That was my codename throughout this whole covert operation. So now you know the back-story to Verbal Gardening, here, at last, are our five brave new words:

bollo (adj) 1. Unsatisfying and disappointing. *That's bollo, Beckham!* 2. A cry of disgust. *Bollo! My tomatoes have died.*

games (adj) Really rubbish and a little bit pretentious. *Learning Arabic? That's properly games.*

honk (or hoot) (noun) Money, especially cash. *He paid me a pile of honk for that job.*

mental safari (noun) When someone goes mad for a few moments, or does a series of rash acts. *When I was on my gap year I went on a complete mental safari and got an earring and a tattoo of a lizard.*

pratdigger (noun) 1. Pickpocket. *Just be careful on the Ramblas, watch out for those crafty pratdiggers.* 2. That friend of yours who always has a rubbish girlfriend everyone has to put up with, or a crap best mate from school they always ask out with you, or the person who finds the most obnoxious person at a party and exposes everyone to them. *Apparently that pratdigger Mary's going to the party so it's bound to be full of awful people.*

I was more than happy with the eventual seed selection. I was very happy. I sent the list over to my Rare Men on the eve of my tkday, then, on 25 January 2006, Verbal Gardening proper commenced.

PART ONE

It is rare indeed to find a single individual altering the character of a language's lexicon.

Words Words Words, David Crystal

1

Of our five new words, 'bollo' seemed the most straightforward, its meaning most apparent. So it was 'bollo' that I set about spreading first, in conversations with friends and family, whenever the subject matter would allow it. 'This is bollo,' I muttered at the traffic lights. 'What a bollo man!' I shouted after a bus driver who'd cut me up.

Naturally there were many early occasions during which the Rare Men and I felt the urge to describe something as 'unsatisfactory'. Mr Bookman sent an email to his colleagues about a creative writing course: 'A day out in Brighton but the standard's usually a bit bollo.' Mr Palatino emailed everyone in his address book to say: 'I had my old phone nicked. Bollo. What's your number please?' Mr Matisse noted that the view from his latest hotel room was 'decidedly bollo'. Mr Wingdings even played with the usage of the word, introducing the melodious phrase 'swallow the bollo', meaning 'to allow oneself to be deceived' or 'to show great tolerance'; 'This guy rang me and told me I'd been specially selected for a prize. Like I was going to swallow the bollo and get excited,' he told his wife. 'My sister's a real pratdigger and her boyfriend's staying for the weekend so I'm just going to have to swallow the bollo,' he told his mates.

With this sort of encouragement, it wasn't long before 'bollo' became a recognised word amongst a small social circle that, I hoped, would soon rub circly shoulders with other circles and pass it on like cogs in a well-oiled machine. Indeed, just a few weeks after the word was invented, I received a text message from someone entirely unrelated to the project saying he thought a sitcom recently screened was 'disappointingly bollow'. I couldn't believe it. Already one of our words had taken flight. We were off.

It's worth addressing this issue of spelling right away. It's not a problem. Despite the original five-letter 'bollo', this new 'bollow' was fine. 'Bollo' is a word designed to be spoken out loud, to be yelled even, so if it's spelt differently but pronounced the same, the job still gets done. I'd even take 'bolo' (which, by the way, is the name of a type of necktie, the 'Bolo Tie' being the official neckwear of Arizona since 1971) as long as it doesn't rhyme with 'polo'.

Some of the greatest Verbal Gardeners in history have been famously liberal with their spelling. Both William Shakespeare and Sir Walter Raleigh spelt their own names in several different ways but not once the way we do now. Even dictionary king Samuel Johnson let some misspellings slip into his great book, with the long-term result that 'deign' is now the opposite of 'disdain' and 'immovable' the reverse of 'moveable'. Rather than anything negative, variety in spelling is proof that a word is being used. If a word can be seen to mutate and evolve it must be alive.

As well as spreading via conversation, my early theory for the propagation of language was that if someone writes something somewhere, someone else will, eventually, see it. And if that something is eye-catching enough, it will settle in that other someone's subconscious and they, eventually, will pass it on to another person, who in turn will impart it to someone else, and so on and so on (and soon and soon). I therefore plastered 'bollo' all over the various websites I'm linked with ('I know the colour scheme is a little bollo,' www.alexhorne.com; 'I'm a bit of a bollo man when it comes to social situations,' www.facebook.com; and all five words and definitions on a specific Verbal Gardening MySpace site, www.myspace.com/verbalgardening). More desperately, whenever I failed to complete *The Times* crossword* on trains or tubes, I started scribbling the word 'bollo!' above the incomplete puzzle before placing it as conspicuously as possible on my seat. If I conquered the puzzle I wrote 'I am the bollo!' neatly across the top of the page and again left it for a stranger to find and take in.

Proof that this method could work to some extent at least came when Mr Elephant and I arrived in Chester to perform a comedy show one month into the project. Within minutes of walking into the venue a charming young American lady introduced herself as Julia.

'Oh, hello,' I said, awkwardly. 'Sorry if I'm a bit awkward. I'm not good at this sort of thing. Well, any sort of social thing, really . . .'

'It's OK,' Julia interrupted. 'I've seen your status on Facebook. I know, you're a bollo man when it comes to social situations.'

I was so excited to hear another person (a foreign person!) using the word that we'd come up with. 'It works!' I thought (and said, actually – she didn't mind, she knew I was a bollo man socially). People *would* adopt our words. Indeed, checking the Verbal Gardening MySpace page when we got home that night I found a message from a new 'friend', Aleks from Connecticut, who had promised to do his bit to help:

yo, send me a couple of words that you want to spread and i'll work on them, maybe even graffiti them on something. Just tell me what you want them to mean as well so i can get a good style for them. Aight, aleks.

This was an excellent start; I felt both internationally productive and a little bit cooler. Aight.

It was 'bollo' too that I used for the first time on stage, at a gig in New Cross, south-east London. It's a strange experience, deliberately using made up words in public, but one I highly recommend. In fact, please do experiment with our words yourselves. If you're on a train, tell the conductor your ticket cost a lot of honk, if you're in bed tell your partner you went on a mental safari today, if you're at a party, well, stop reading this book and go and enjoy the party. Whatever you're doing, try to slip in a 'bollo' in the company of your friends and see how they (and you) react. You'll be surprised how daring it feels.

At the mic I chickened out twice. 'I've never been very good with . . . money,' I stuttered. 'I can't order a cappuccino without feeling g-g-g . . . pretentious.' I stammered. But then, when I'd finally gained some momentum, I closed an impassioned rant about *Sky Sports News* by describing the channel as 'bollo'. '*Sky Sports News* is bollo!' were my exact words. I even repeated the key one: 'Bollo!' I bellowed. No one seemed to mind; no one seemed to laugh very much either but that wasn't the point. No one questioned the word's meaning. I had planted the word and the world was still turning.

As well as dropping 'bollo's onstage from then on, I tried to use my job as a comedian to my advantage in other, more subtle ways. In addition to watching *Countdown* every day, my job enables, indeed forces, me to visit our country's fine service stations on a similarly regular basis. Keen to maximise every possible gardening opportunity, I therefore decided that whenever I frequented one of these delightful establishments I would sow a tiny seed.

The plan was simple. Every time I passed a service station I would stop and visit the toilet area. Inside a cubicle I would then pose the question, 'Is graffiti bollo?' on the back of the door. This might sound like wanton vandalism but I also vowed only to do this on pre-graffitied walls with a non-permanent pen, the ink from which I would then wipe away with white spirit (as well as any other unwanted writing I might find) the next time I dropped in. I was actually doing a good thing.

And so, whilst the project was still in its early stages I buried a 'bollo' deep within the Newport Pagnell Motorway services, like a hyacinth bulb, primed to flower the following year. There were eighty-three motorway service stations in the UK when I started the project; I was fairly sure I could impregnate well over half and not only spread, but receive feedback on 'bollo'.

Over in the United States*, my first ever graffiti artist 'friend' Aleks was also beavering away. 'Yo,' he addressed me, 'bollo is going very well, I tagged a 6ft tall bollo on a downtown street building so that everyone can see it. Not vandalism-style, but artstyle. My friends don't use it yet, but I try to use it.'

This was amazing news. Suddenly, thanks to our little Verbal Gardening project, the good people of Wallingford, a peripolitan town in Connecticut, 3,384 miles away from the Verbal Gardening hub, were walking past a 'bollo' as big as me every day, some of them probably muttering 'bollo' under their American breath. And because it was 'artstyle' rather than 'vandalism-style' I didn't even feel too guilty. True, I didn't want to break the law or deface other people's property myself, but if someone in Connecticut volunteered to do something 'artstyle' on a 'downtown street building', who was I to stop him?

I was confident that 'bollo' would be understood by the general public on both sides of the pond. Not only is it a fairly self-explanatory word, but 'bollo' had also been rigorously road tested by its proposer, Mr Wingdings, soon after its creation.

Wingdings had spent Christmas with his family, which included two younger sisters whose presence meant that swearing in the family home was discouraged. This, clearly, is a difficult thing to adhere to at Christmas time; a happy time, yes, but also the time in which family members want to swear most often. It's just the way it is. Keep a large family indoors for a day and someone will want to swear. So after a couple of outbursts, on Mr Wingding's suggestion, the family agreed on 'bollo' as their acceptable familial cry of disgust.

'There's going to be a blizzard?* Absolute bollo!' cried Mr Wingdings Snr. 'What a bollo man he turned out to be!' expounded Mr Wingdings Snr's wife after a festive film.

The feisty 'bollo' settled comfortably into the Wingdings family life over this jolly period and with a little push was now branching out into the wider world with ease. This is a common way for language to develop; families adopt a word without thinking and gradually, with a little luck and support, other people start using it too. In my own home, the word 'rootle' was used throughout our childhoods to mean 'any sort of pudding-y food found in the fridge', a natural development of the verb coined by Mum. 'What's for pudding?' we'd ask. 'Have a rootle in the fridge,' she'd reply. 'A rootle' therefore came to mean 'a yogurt' or any other delights that lived in the fridge. When I finally left home I couldn't believe no one else had a rootle after supper. In fact a few people thought I was referring to something else altogether.

But a nascent word has to have the right feel to cross the boundaries of the family kitchen, and 'bollo' seemed to be perfect, echoing the upbeat frustration of 'golly' and 'gosh' but with a harsher edge. While it does, of course, resemble the start of a coarser word, that similarity only adds to the functionality of the word. When you use 'bollo' it feels like you're going to swear, your mind presumes you're going to swear, so you still feel you've got something off your chest when it's out: 'Bollo!' It's a satisfying exclamation. But that Christmas Mr Wingdings and his family definitely weren't swearing because 'bollo' wasn't in the dictionary, unlike all our officially 'vulgar' words. Until it received a formal classification 'bollo' could, in theory, mean anything.

One of my most abiding school memories was looking up the language's most offensive members in the dictionary, cheered on, I would now like to reveal, by a certain Latin teacher. 'Isn't language wonderful!' he would cry. 'The "F-word" has so many uses! Isn't language amazing!' And so we would indeed look up* the 'F-word' and try out every single usage of the word; as a verb, a noun, an adjective, an exclamation, it really is a most versatile* lexeme. You can F-up, off, about and around, give or not give one, be a F-up, or know F-all. It's brilliant. My favourite example of the word in the *OED* was in the term 'windfucker', defined, surprisingly, as 'a species of hawk' or 'a name for the kestrel' (as used by Thomas Nashe, inventor of the word 'balderdash',* in the sentence, 'The kistrilles or windfuckers that filling themselues with winde, fly against the winde euermore'). I always felt that was a great thing to know. It was also used 'as a term of opprobrium' in the early seventeenth century (Ben Jonson, for example, asked, 'Did you euer heare such a Windfucker, as this?') but if you ever spy a bird of prey hovering above a motorway you can look up and quite legitimately cry, 'Wow, what a windfucker', citing the *OED* as your source.

Despite this wayward encouragement on the part of my favourite teacher, I always knew the F-word was also 'a bad word', mainly because I had never heard either of my grandmothers use it. My grannies would never use such language. That was until another grandparent-related incident.

The grandmother in question (not the Russian penis this time) would usually express herself most politely, her most extreme curse being the remarkable phrase 'go and boil your head!', the impracticality of which always seemed to outweigh the sheer horror of it actually happening. Then one morning a few years ago, my mum was visiting, hoping, I imagine, for a cup of tea. She knocked on the door. A few seconds later my grandmother opened the door. Instead of her usual 'Hello dear', my grandmother chose the following words with which to open their morning exchange:

Have you seen this fucking weather?

My mother was stunned and after a somewhat rushed cup of tea phoned me to share the news. I too was shocked. Why would my grandmother suddenly choose to break her usual verbal habits in such a dramatic way? Was she also embarking on some ambitious linguistic project?

It was a couple of weeks later that I came up with what I still believe to be the right answer. There is a theory in comedy that if you're going to swear onstage, whether you're performing an hour-long show or a twenty-minute set, you should only use the F-word once so it has maximum impact. It's a theory I subscribe to and which I've followed in this book (except for the windfucker, which I've now mentioned five times). But I think my grandmother may have taken this to the next logical step. I think she decided to use that word once in her *entire life*. I think she made up her mind that her usage of the 'F-word' would be truly powerful, that she wouldn't just carelessly fling it about, that people would notice the splash it made when she chucked it in. And notice it my mum did.

Unfortunately I can't help thinking my grandmother might have wasted her one chance. I'm worried that in the end, with time inevitably ticking by, she panicked,* thought to herself, 'Well, I've got to use it once, here goes!' and blurted it out blindly. Because my mum said the weather really wasn't that bad. 'It was drizzly, yes, but no need for that sort of language.'

Bollo would have been far more appropriate.

2

It won't have escaped your attention that 'mental safari' is not a word. It's two words. But that doesn't make it any less valid a candidate for this project. There are several thousand two-word lexical items in the dictionary, and I was confident 'mental safari' could join this throng mainly because, like 'bollo', its appearance in a sentence was unlikely to arouse too much suspicion.

Invented by the tardy Mr Bodoni, the vague sense of the phrase is comprehensible without question. We all know what 'mental' means, we all know what 'safari' means, so it's not hard to guess roughly what they might mean placed side by side. My job, therefore, was to spread the expression so wide that it warranted its own definition in the dictionary. I needed 'mental safari' to become as familiar as a hot dog*, the Big Bang* or, at the very least, a monkey wrench. The two words 'mental safari' had to warrant their own single inclusion in the Book.

With facebook and MySpace proving such happy haunts for 'bollo', I launched 'mental safari' in a similar area, focusing specifically on the digital equivalent of the public toilet door: the Internet forum. As a twenty-first-century Verbal Gardener, for me the Web* was always going to be a logical starting point. Thanks to its democratic usability, the birth and movement of new words can now be announced and tracked more swiftly than ever before, and while this easy access does make it a more superficial medium than the likes of books or newspapers, it also makes the Web the perfect training ground for verbal activists. Dictionary authorities might be less impressed by an appearance of a word on a website than in more official physical publications, but any appearance online is still proof that words are in use. And if they're used on an Internet forum, like the door of a public toilet, people are bound to see them. My plan was simply to leave a 'mental safari' lying around and see if it tripped anyone up. I felt sneaky but excited.

My first target was what I guessed would be a most reputable website, the debate section of the Associated Board of the Royal Schools of Music's Internet home. For me, this grand title conjured up images of mature bassoonists discussing semitones and quavers or articulate percussionists typing rhythmically away about metronomes and zzxjoanws. After registering as a new member with my codename 'Farmer', however, I discovered that it was mainly used by schoolchildren. This made me feel a bit odd. I guess the word 'Schools' in the title should have been a clue. Nevertheless, I knew that children are the future, I wanted my words to be spoken in (or by) the future, so I pressed on (instead of off), determinedly ignoring any feelings of inappropriateness.

Luckily, I soon came across a debate, initiated at 6.51 a.m., whose title was distracting enough to banish any doubts:

Does anybody else *really* like to whistle?

My my. There's a question to demonstrate just how far back the Internet is pushing the boundaries of communication. Ignore the maverick* asterisks, that is a brilliant topic for consideration. You just don't find that level of curiosity in the broadsheets. I certainly like to whistle, I thought to myself, but do I *really* like to whistle? I had to follow this thread.

The originator of this poser was a poster with the nickname 'all ears' who played (let's hope still plays) the flute and provided what I think is called 'the flautists' conundrum' alongside her question:

Did I choose flute because I like to whistle, or do I like to whistle because I play the flute???

Gordon Bennett!* That is a poser. Everything about the post I liked – the queries themselves, the triple question mark, the fact that 'all ears' felt the need to seek other people who also *really* like to whistle before seven o'clock in the morning, everything.

It was four and a half hours before anyone answered. But then a saxophonist* (presumably), calling him or herself 'saxophonist', wrote with raw honesty:

I cant stop whistleing!!!!! on the way home from school Im always whistling the piece im playing or the theme from that film I watched the night before. it drives my friend mad.

Audacious spelling and punctuation again, but mostly a clear demonstration that this person also *really* liked to whistle. In fact, they couldn't stop whistling. That's how much they liked it. They always whistled in the car, even though it had an adverse effect on their friend's sanity.

Mercifully this eased the mind of the troubled flautist who that same afternoon logged on to write, 'Whew! So at least the art hasn't died out completely yet!' While whistling is not, strictly speaking, an art and has never shown any signs of dying out, I was glad to sense her relief in that first, possibly invented word 'Whew'.

For the next forty-eight hours, the discussion rumbled on. But then, as abruptly as it started, it stopped. For almost a whole year nobody told anybody that they *really* liked whistling. Nobody had any further opinions on the matter. It was time for me, aka the 'Farmer', to try to fan the embers of the whistling chat back to life:

Farmer   Feb 6 2006, 05:08PM   Post #9

I know this thread came to a bit of a halt a while ago but I really wanted to write something because I've recently really got into whistling!

Last year I was getting really frustrated with my French horn – sometimes it just won't behave itself – and in the end I just started to whistle what I wanted to play instead.

I then went on a bit of a mental safari, not practising the horn, whistling in orchestra, that sort of thing, and I'm now pretty much addicted to whistling!

I just can't stop!
Is this fine?

This wasn't a complete lie. I did try to learn the French horn at school, attracted to the instrument not by its glamorous 'G' shape but by its name, so nearly the same as mine. I liked the idea of Alex Horne playing the horn. It was sort of a joke. But I wasn't musical and I did once hum in orchestra – not quite the same as whistling but sounding more similar to a horn.

It took just one hour for the debate to start raging again. A recorder player called 'recorderzrule' first chipped in with, 'I'm always whistling! My mum tells me not to because I'll get wrinkles!!' – a terrific rumour presumably started by recorderzrule's mother. Further messages of support came rolling in. One user wrote, 'I cannot whistle at all! My dad tried to teach me but ...' which I found a bit sinister, while katyjay cheerfully added, 'I think I rather surprised my singing teacher with the volume at which I can whistle,' presumably meaning she could whistle either very loudly or very quietly; she didn't say what the volume was, just that it was a surprising one.

In fact, the topic went on to take up three whole pages of the forum, more than tripling in size after my mental safari prompt (helped on one occasion, I should admit, by me asking katyjay if she thought she 'could whistle louder than a harmonica'), and not once did anyone question our Verbal Seed. It was accepted unflinchingly. Another seed had been planted.

But, like 'bollo's welcoming reception, this wasn't a surprise. 'Mental safari', invented by Mr Bodoni, is a safe phrase, more of a novel metaphor than a brand-new word. What's more, as well as being instantly understandable and easy to slip into a conversation, it looks and sounds good. 'Safari' was exported to English from Swahili and has glamorous roots that can be chased back to the Arabic word *safar*, meaning 'a journey'. It's an exotic flourish after the surest of starts. For 'mental', despite enjoying fresh urban credibility with the un-PC slang sense of 'amazing' (as in, 'did you hear the rain last night, it was mental'), is, of course, of Latin origin, coming directly from the word *mens*, meaning 'mind'.

You can always rely on Latin. For both language and linguists it provides the finest of foundations, with thousands of everyday words handed directly to us by the Romans. If you've ever watched a *video* or listened to an *album*, you've effectively spoken Latin. If you're driving a *Volvo*, that's the Latin for 'I roll'. Perhaps you're rolling with your *posse*; they take their name from the Latin phrase, *posse comitatus*, 'the force of the country'. Sometimes the language of the classroom can help you learn the language of the street.[6]

While my school Latin teacher had shown me the darkest secrets of the dictionary, my university Latin teacher, I discovered, had one of his own. Hoping for some support as a fellow Latin fan, this academic (who shall remain mostly anonymous) was one of the few people I told about the Verbal Gardening project. I knew I shouldn't have. It was meant to be an assignment shared only by me and my Rare Men. But there is a trust among Latinists, an unwritten code. In many ways, we're like the Masons, with just a shade less creepiness. So I knew I could count on Rob.

'Interesting,' he said with a smile. 'But I've already got a word in the dictionary.' At this point he took a step back to admire my reaction.

'What do you mean?' I asked, incredulous, jealous and excited all at once.

'Well,' he whispered, 'it's not an English word. I actually invented a *Latin* word and got it in the dictionary. You see, I was the editor of the latest *Penguin Latin Dictionary* and I couldn't resist. I snuck the word *lexicographus* in there with the meaning "writer of dictionaries, harmless drudge", a reference to . . .'

'Yes, I know, to Samuel Johnson. Excellent work,' I sighed admiringly.

It was a little like cheating, but coming up with a new word for an apparently dead language was impressive. If you happen

---

6 It doesn't quite fit into this urban theme but one of my favourite secret Latin words is 'Hovis', the great British bread brand. The term was concocted by a student called Herbert Grimes, itself a wonderful name, who won twenty-five pounds and everlasting fame by winning a competition to name a patent flour set by bakers S. Fitton & Sons Ltd in 1890. He made 'Hovis' from the Latin *hominis vis*, meaning 'the strength of man'.

to have the *Penguin Latin Dictionary*, look *lexicographus* up. It's there. He did it.

Two thousand years ago, many native Latin-speakers did it too. The following might not be classed as 'ordinary individuals' like you or me, but they too spawned words that made it into Murray's *OED* millennia later. 'Volcano', for example, is named after the Roman god Vulcan, who was unusually skilled in smelting and smithery, 'cereal' comes from Ceres, a female deity in charge of growing plants, not words, and you can blame 'insomnia' on Somnus, the god of sleep. Jupiter himself, the chief of these distinctive divinities, spawned our word 'jovial', thanks to his pseudonym 'Jove', and his occasionally cheerful attitude. On a more mortal level, a character called Sipylus in Ovid's *Metamorphoses* inspired the coining of 'syphilis' in Italian poet Girolamo Fracastoro's 1530 poem '*Syphilis sive morbus gallicus*'[7] ('Syphilis or the French disease'); not necessarily the word you'd choose to be for ever associated with, but a word nevertheless.

But some dictionary-approved words that seem to have come from Latin aren't quite what they seem. Everyone knows that a *vomitorium* is where the Romans went to be sick after gorging on too many grapes and sparrows. But everyone is wrong. *Brave New World* author Aldous Huxley invented that meaning back in 1923. Whether he made the error intentionally or not is unclear, but either way, everyone believed him and the Romans are for ever cast as an over-indulgent over-eating nation. A *vomitorium* was actually a passage behind the seats in an amphitheatre out of which the crowds could 'spew' after watching the latest show. The Colosseum in Rome, for example, could empty its stomach of 50,000 people in just fifteen minutes.

---

7 According to Fracastoro's poem, his protagonist Syphilus was the first man to contract the disease as a punishment for angering the god Apollo. The poet then used the name to refer to the disease in his medical text *De Contagionibus* ('On Contagious Diseases') and the title stuck.

There is also a story of personal invention behind the word 'quiz', a great and inspirational story, almost certainly untrue but which I love so will include here without further qualification. 'Quiz' looks rather like *quis*, a Latin word meaning 'who'. It also looks like *quid*, which means 'what' (or a pound, of course). But 'quiz' itself is definitely not a Latin word. Oh no. It was invented by perhaps the most efficient Verbal Gardener of all time; a man called Daly (which, by the way, is my mother-in-law's maiden name; undeniable proof that I too am destined one day to create my own word).

In 1791, James (or Richard, nobody knows for sure) Daly (or Daley), a Dublin theatre manager (or pub landlord), was challenged to a typically alcohol-fuelled bet. In order to win the metaphorical and literal punt, he had to introduce a new word to the language in one (or two, again, it's all a bit murky) day (or days). As soon as the curtain had fallen on that evening's performance he therefore hired a group of street urchins to write 'Q-U-I-Z', a previously unseen sequence of letters, on walls around the Irish city. These young vandals* worked hard, and within a day (or so) the word was the talk of the town. A newspaper ran a competition asking people to say what they thought it meant. That competition itself became a 'quiz'. The word became common currency.

Daly's tale might just be true. The word 'quiz' was already around; a lady called Fanny Burney (who also invented 'tea party', 'grumpy' and 'shopping' in her 1778 novel *Evelina*) wrote it in her diary on 24 June 1782, and a yo-yo-like toy of the same name was popular around 1790, but the meaning of 'interrogation' or 'entertaining questioning' can't be attached to anything any more concrete.

For me, the factual or fictitious nature of the story is irrelevant. What is far more significant is that the tale exists at all. The anecdote first emerged in Benjamin's Stuart's book *Walker*

Remodelled, published in 1836, with the most detailed account appearing in F. T. Porter's *Gleanings and Reminiscences* (an appropriately vague title) almost a century later in 1875. If it didn't actually happen then someone, possibly Daly himself, must have gone to the trouble of inventing the story and so made a name for himself that way instead. Somehow the legend got passed along from town to town and from generation to generation, and I'm more than happy to continue spreading the news. Helped by its Latin appearance, 'quiz' is now part of our linguistic establishment. Could I do the same for 'mental safari'?

3

'Pratdigger' also has history. It was Mr Rockwell who suggested it after exhuming what he thought might be treasure on the *Oxford English Dictionary* online archives. The two-word phrase 'prat digger', he discovered, was once used on the streets of Britain to describe petty criminals. 'Prat', and this was news to me, is a nineteenth-century word for 'buttocks', hence 'pratfall' meaning 'a fall on one's arse'. 'Prat digging' implied the act of rummaging around in someone's back pocket but, inexplicably, fell out of use and so not into the dictionary. The noun 'para-bore' is still defined by the *OED* as 'a defence against bores', but neither 'prat digger' nor 'pratdigger' has a listing. Yet.

Inspired by the very sound of the words, Mr Rockwell set about them like a verbal alchemist, uniting the separate halves into a brand-new portmanteau term and mixing in the twenty-first-century sense of 'attracting prats'. Thus 'pratdigger' was born, the old pickpocketing idea still burning alongside the modern extra meaning. I was sure he had created gold. Surely few could deny that 'pratdigger' is an eye-catching word. Who wouldn't want to brighten up their vocabulary with such a sparkler?

This word 'portmanteau', by the way, is a linguistic term refer-ring to a single word that combines two meanings and was itself invented by Lewis Carroll to explain his word 'slithy' in the tale of Humpty Dumpty. Just as a portmanteau suitcase keeps things together in its two separate halves, so 'slithy' contains the senses of 'lithe' and 'slimy' in one single adjective. Not that Humpty (a great first name, by the way – Humpty Horne, that's tremendous) believed in explanations. 'When I use a word ... it means just what I choose it to mean, neither more, nor less,' he said to Alice. Quite right, Mr Dumpty. I just hope the dictionary authorities see it that way too.

Despite this first association with an essentially nonsensical word, the process of portmanteau soon became widespread, with 'animatronics', 'brunch'* and 'bootylicious' just a few modern examples. One should never underestimate essentially nonsensical words. They can penetrate the language as deeply as any technical terms. Take 'chortle' and 'galumph', two established verbs that Carroll used before anyone else, also in *Through the Looking-Glass*. Or 'pretend', the modern playful sense of which was also created by Carroll and has since usurped the more formal previous meaning of 'making a false claim'. In *Alice In Wonderland* he put the phrase 'mad as a hatter' into wide circulation, thrusting it far ahead of its competitor 'mad as atter', with 'atter' being the Saxon word for a snake (the words originally meant 'poisonous as a viper' when first coined). So Carroll undoubtedly achieved what I was attempting to do.

Another jabberer[8] was a man called Theodor Geisel, or more often, Dr Seuss, his pen name. Like Doctors Fox and Dre, Seuss was not a real doctor. He was, however, a cartoonist as well as a children's author, and worked for the little-known animation department of the US Army during World War II.* But it was in his 1950 book *If I Ran A Zoo* that he coined his dictionary-breaking word, the outstanding noun, 'nerd'. Much like Edward Lear's

---

8 Used not pejoratively, but with a nod to 'Jabberwocky', the poem Carroll wrote inside *the Looking-Glass*. 'Jabber' itself is an old alliterative word. 'Gibberish' is almost certainly echoic too, although some claim it was coined by explorers describing the unintelligible speech of Gibraltar residents in the eighteenth century.

'runcible spoon' (which found its way into the 1926 edition of the *OED*), this was originally a fanciful word, one of many imaginary animals that inhabited his hypothetical zoo.

Seuss's 'nerd' was the first use of the word in print, but so memorable and quotable were his verses that within a decade it had been passed on from little brothers to bigger brothers who in turn smoothed its path into common American slang.[9]

Unsurprisingly there are some who claim that Seuss's 'nerd' was an altogether different 'nerd' to the 'nerd' we think of today, and one might well wonder why his 'nerd' succeeded while the 'preep's, 'proo's and 'nerkle's all failed. These doubters point instead to the ventriloquist Edgar Bergen's dummy Mortimer Snerd, or the initials N.E.R.D. printed on the shirts of engineers at Northern Electric Research and Development, or, rather desperately, to the word 'drunk', spelled backwards (and tinkered with somewhat) as the true origin of the word. It's impossible to say who's absolutely right. In all likelihood 'nerds' are a mixture of all these things; some people knew Seuss's poem, some the dummy, others the drunk, and a very few those geeky engineers. But no matter who first invented it, enough people started using the term for various reasons at about the same time and 'nerd' rose into public view. And now that 'nerd' is such an established part of the language, all I can say for sure is that Dr Seuss has the earliest recorded usage so, until someone can find an antecedent, he also has the biggest and best claim on the word. Dr Seuss invented the word 'nerd'.

It was exactly this sort of verbal innovation that gave me hope: despite appearing ridiculous, words like 'nerd', 'galumph' and 'pratdigger' can triumph.

*

---

9 Ironically, Seuss used no more than fifty of the commonest words to write his most famous story, *Green Eggs and Ham* after being dared to do so by his editor Bennett Cerf.

So back to this 'pratdigger'. Despite referring to something illegal, it's a fun word, cheeky but harmless, playful and amusing. Throughout history, the criminal world has provided a rich seam of such mischievous slang, with 'pickpocket' itself tripping off the tongue impishly, 'swindling' sounding so satisfying, 'burgling' ridiculous and even 'mugging' rather appealing; like hugging, only softer: 'Mmm, mug me, mmm, then give me a nice big sloppy Glasgow kiss.'

In Jonathon Green's exhaustive study *Slang Down the Ages* you'll find the following cheerful words, all meaning 'thief': 'pudding-smammer', 'snick fadger', 'international* milk thief', 'knickers bandit', 'ark-ruffian', 'flimper', 'bung-napper', 'billy buzman', 'dipping bloke', 'landpirate', 'snaffler', 'smugger' and 'snabbler'. Of course it's a relief our streets are now largely free from such swindlers, but I can't help wishing a few more of these phrases had endured.

But some common words and phrases have succeeded thanks to their criminal links. 'Jack the lad', for example, refers to one Jack Sheppard, a petty thief who managed to break out of jail four times in 1724. Because his image was one of 'crafty scamp' rather than 'violent thug', he managed to bestow his name on to every future cheeky hoodlum,* before being hanged at London's Tyburn in November that year. That's quite a consid-erable cost but it shows that some misdemeanours do pay. By being naughty, Jack Sheppard coined his own phrase. As well as drawing from this fund of criminal language, therefore, I was also inspired by transgression itself. I too would have to bend some rules. And my gentle graffiti of motorway service stations and infiltration of a private music-based chat room was surely defensible as a means to a linguistic end.

I'm not saying that any crime is justified if the perpetrator is trying to get a word in the dictionary. There is always a thin line between the acceptable and the pernicious; if you visit a good friend's house I think you can help yourself to a banana or a pear. That's fine. In Indonesian it would come under the umbrella of *mencomot*, a useful word meaning 'stealing things of small value such as food or drinks, partly for fun'. A 'funcrime', if you will. But taking the TV couldn't be excused as such. That's very rarely fine. Perhaps walking away with a book from their shelf is hovering over that line; it would seem a bit odd, not quite the done thing, but probably no one would mind that much. As long as I stayed the right side of that line, a little verbal flimping was acceptable.

Phrases like 'The Farmer is a pratdigger' therefore began to appear alongside the 'bollos' in several bogs, and I began to plan more daring ways of challenging the traditional word order.

4

Despite being far less intuitive than these first three Verbal Seeds, it soon became apparent that 'honk' (meaning 'money') was going to be easier to spread further than these initial inscriptions. Being little more than a noise, 'honk' could be slipped effortlessly into conversation and was consistently accepted as the slang term we wanted it to be. As well as several BBC Internet forums, I swiftly managed to sneak it onto the BBC Manchester website (in an interview I said that after the Edinburgh festival, 'you come home and start preparing and saving up all your hard-earned honk for the next one'), and into a hard-fought game of Monopoly with three other monopolists at Belsize Park. ('Ha! I've got loads more honk than you! Look at all my honk!')

But more significant even than this board-game banter was the inclusion of 'honk' in a magazine, the first ever appearance of a Verbal Gardening word in print. This historic occasion was brought about through the diligence of honk's creator, Mr Roman, who managed to get me an interview with a national magazine, where my answers would be printed without tampering by any meddling editors. By making the most of (certainly not abusing) his position on the publication, 180,000 copies of *Itchy*, the handy guide to the social side of Britain's cities, were distributed across Manchester, Liverpool, London, Birmingham, Glasgow and Edinburgh, each featuring an article in which I was quoted as saying:

> It's stupid, but I'm really scared of . . . *not making enough honk as a comedian and ending up having to get a job in an office.*

Our corpus was swelling.

In my haste to get the project going I have to admit that I hadn't done exhaustive research into which words might work and which almost certainly wouldn't. I'd drawn up some basic principles but really I jumped in, head first, without paying too much attention to the swimming pool rules.

Mr Roman, on the other hand, studied linguistics at Cambridge University. He now edits magazines and runs nightclubs in London but back then he'd done his homework, and the Verbal Gardening project was a chance for him to show off:

> While I was at home, I dug up some of my linguistics notes and books from uni, and even found an essay on neologisms that I wrote in my second year. So here are a few thoughts:
>
> I've tried to be subtle. The stuff I learned doing linguistics really helped with this. What they taught us is that the science of new words is a mysterious and unpredictable one. Sometimes existing words in a language change their meaning a bit (gay used to mean happy), this is called semantic shift; sometimes a word is borrowed from another language to mean the same or something similar as the original (zeitgeist, khaki, curry etc); very, very rarely is an entirely new word is coined that goes into general usage; if they do make it, they tend to be technical or specialist (laser, quark etc).
>
> Totally new coinings are much more likely to enter into general usage if they're compounds (bits of other existing words) or phrases. Some examples are: spin doctor, weapons of mass destruction, workaholic etc, although again, these tend

to come from specialist areas first (i.e. politics), and then spread in use to other areas of life and language.

So, having mulled that lot over for a while, and wanting this project to have the best chance of succeeding (I think getting in the dictionary has to be the gold medal), I've steered away from foreign language borrowings and totally new words (no point trying to get a word like 'zoing' into the English language) and decided to focus on using an existing word in a new way.

Hence honk.

If you glance back at the original list of new words (you don't have to. You could just take my word for it), you'll see that Mr Roman originally suggested 'honk' *and* 'hoot' to mean money, 'a neologistic pincer movement' with which to attack the dictionary. For now, however, it was 'honk' that was making all the moves.

With the benefit of hindsight, I have to applaud Mr Roman's judgement. 'Honk' hits the mark for a variety of reasons. First, it's a short sharp simple word, like 'cash', 'dosh' (either a mixture of 'dollars' and 'cash' or an African word for a backhander according to other wordwatchers – take your pick), 'dough' or even 'wonga'. It's easy to say, easy to hear, easy to copy. It even echoes its youngest relation, 'bling', flashy or ostentatious jewellery, that was introduced to the language in 1998 by a rapper calling himself BG (represented by the Cash Money Records label, appropriately enough) in a song called 'Bling Bling' the first word of which was, yes, 'bling'. Just four years later, the phrase 'bling bling' made it into the fifth edition of the *Shorter Oxford English Dictionary* and is now regarded by contemporary rappers as too mainstream for their own use, a true indication of how far the word has come. Unlike Beyoncé, BG knows the significance of his achievement, saying (or rapping, I suppose), '"bling bling" will never be forgotten. So it's like I will never be forgotten,' in an interview with *MTV News*. Too true, BG. He may, however, have overestimated the monetary value of the word: 'I just wish that I'd trademarked it, so I'd never have to work again,' he continued. I may have been optimistic in hoping to infiltrate the dictionary in three years, but I never thought such a feat would yield any physical honk for myself.

Second, 'honk' is currently an underemployed word. Its first, main meaning is the noise a goose makes. Geese were the first to say 'honk'. Then, in the early twentieth century, it was borrowed by humans to represent the noise of a car horn (the two are now pretty much interchangeable; if your horn breaks, grab a goose, and vice versa). During the early 1900s the word 'honky' became a derogatory term for Caucasians, deriving from 'hunky' or 'bohunk', both offensive terms for the Hungarians (and Poles and Slavs) who'd come to America to work in the stockyards of Chicago.[10] A few decades later it evolved into a verb meaning 'to smell strongly'. A pungent stilton, for example, might be said to honk. But these later slang meanings, in this country anyway, aren't especially prevalent. Honk hasn't been overused. It's perfect for the role of 'cash', and, with a push, I was sure we could reinvent it, give it a new lease of life just as words like 'gay' and 'cool' have been granted in the recent past.

Third, money is a massive target at which to aim. Since its invention money has always been talked about. Slang is the language of the street and throughout history the four most popular topics of street talk have been alcohol (or drugs), crime, sex and money. What that says about society I'm not sure, but

---

10 Although other theories suggest it might stem from the practice of white males honking their car horns to attract African-American prostitutes in the 1920s, or from the patrons of 'honky-tonk' saloons in the Wild West. As is so often the case, the origin is murky, but I'm putting my honk on the immigrant theory.

being a socially awkward sort of chap myself, money was the ideal choice, the least uncomfortable of this quartet for me to discuss. By inventing a new word for cash I was joining a club with a long and healthy heritage.

Countless forerunners to 'honk' have cropped up in the past: actual, ballast, scratch (which can also mean 'to kill' or 'to write'), crackle, cake, lettuce, moolah,* spondulics, beans and trump. All these were once used every day by people to refer to money. Some pecuniary slang terms have had fairly obvious relations to money itself: 'rivets' hold things together, as does cash; 'sugar' sweetens life, 'bread' is necessary, 'green' the same colour as dollar bills; 'dead presidents' refers to the pictures on them. 'Bling' supposedly reflects the sparkle of the diamonds BG and his colleagues were so fond of, although it does also sound a bit like a telephone.* Others make less sense: 'gravy' makes things taste better? A 'rhino' is a bit scary? So while 'honk' has no direct connection with coins or notes, a derivation could be forced if required. 'It reflects the loud, brashness of cash,' we might say. 'It probably comes from the rudeness of City bankers.' Whatever the etymology we chose to use, there's no doubt the financial semantic field was a fertile one.

So it was no surprise when honk began to show early form. It was, however, surprisingly stirring to see 'honk' in an actual magazine. (You might not have heard of it, but *Itchy* is a genuine publication. I promise.) After my postman had handed me the package containing the magazines, I laid them out on the kitchen table and stared at them with huge satisfaction. If we were to succeed, these would one day be highly significant documents, the original examples of English words. I had one of my words in print. This was just one (quite large) step away from being in the dictionary.

For the very act of printing breathes life into a word. While butterflies have to die before being pinned into books, sounds are immortalised on the page, frozen not killed, preserved for the future. It was a businessman from Kent called William Caxton who produced England's first printing press in the fifteenth century (the German goldsmith Johannes Gutenberg is credited with actually inventing it around 1439), taking the opportunity to introduce words like 'brutish' and 'ample' himself in the process. Both were subtle adaptations of French words, and by allowing ordinary people to read literature he cleared the way for these new words to travel up and down the country more speedily than ever. Printing had the same effect on words as cars would on people a few centuries hence. And nearly all the means by which I would attempt to spread my own words – newspapers, magazines, radio, television, the Internet and, indeed, books – were all made possible through Caxton's innovation.

It was he, for instance, who first printed Geoffrey Chaucer's *The Canterbury Tales*, which were themselves crucial in shaping all future European writing. It is thanks to Caxton that Chaucer is often described both as the founder of the English vernacular tradition and the father of modern English literature. An asteroid and a lunar crater have both been named in Chaucer's honour. But these were unnecessary gestures. Chaucer had already created his own memorial. Because Chaucer was the first major English Verbal Gardener.

Before he came along English was in a bit of a state. William the Conqueror had confused things by speaking French and for three hundred years the country babbled along with several different tongues, with no king speaking English until Henry IV sat on the throne in 1399. Before then it was Chaucer who gave Old English the push it needed to rise back to the top, where, in various states, the English language has remained ever since. It's thanks to him that 375 million people now speak English! He was the first person in the history of English to use the terms 'tragedy', 'comedy' and even 'poetry' (although he spelt them all with 'ie' at the end rather than the modern trendie 'y'); this was a gardener with lofty aims.

Not content with naming these literary fields, Chaucer also harvested some pretty impressive word crops. Today's dictionaries cite him as the first user of such varied words as 'accident' and 'autumn', 'intellect' and 'ignorant', 'galaxy', 'famous', 'moral' and 'magic'. He created 'jeopardy' by joining the French words *jeu parti* ('a divided game') in *Troilus and Criseyde*, pilfered 'difficulty' from Latin and came up with 'zounds' as a jazzier* alternative to 'Christ's wounds'. He was on fire.

But, as Alex Games explains in *English Words and Their Curious Origins*, Chaucer didn't always succeed. 'Beblot', 'achatour' and 'acheck' are all words he attempted to introduce but which look entirely foreign today. Even these, however, are in the *Oxford English Dictionary*, meaning 'to blot all over', 'a purchaser of provisions' and 'to bring to a sudden stop' respectively. Even his dodgier, uglier words have survived, all because William Caxton made a machine that put them onto paper.

While on the subject of printing I should also herald Aldus Manutius the Elder, also known as Aldus Pius Manutius or Teobaldo Mannucci, an Italian humorist and printer championed by Lynne Truss in her punctuation triumph *Eats, Shoots and Leaves*. 'Who invented the italic typeface?' asks Lynne. 'Aldus Manutius!' she replies immediately. 'Who printed the first semicolon?' she asks, and before we get even the chance to answer – even though we might be able to guess this time – she shouts, 'Aldus Manutius!' again. And if she's right, that's a remarkable achievement, allowing people like me to do things like this: *these words are really important because they slope forwards*. As well as printing the world's first semicolon, he also helped develop the commas and full stops we expect at the end of our sentences today. There. And there. I could go on. This was also mightily impressive Verbal Gardening.

Back in England, the fantastically aptonymic Wynkyn de Worde took over from Caxton after his death and ensured his work continued at an even more rapid pace, opening up the first printing press on Fleet Street in 1500 and publishing over 700 titles in forty years. It was Wynkyn (it really is an excellent name – Wynkyn Horne; yes, that could work) who used Aldus's *italics* for the first time in printed English, and he that really pushed printing forwards. Fonts had been around for centuries (if you peer up to the top of Trajan's Column in Rome you can see the forerunner of what would become Times New Roman inscribed in AD 113), but the birth of printing meant a sudden explosion of typefaces. Thanks to Worde's advances, the likes of Claude Garamond and Giambattista Bodoni started designing letters, and were so successful that their surnames became words too.

The invention of printing therefore transformed the way words were passed on for ever. Men like Caxton picked up Middle English by the scruff of the neck and slapped it about until it became Modern English. That's not a bad achievement, ever so slightly more impressive than scrawling 'bollo' on the back of a toilet door in the Gordano Services. Since the twelfth century, but particularly throughout the first half of the fifteenth century, English was being transformed by what is enigmatically called the 'Great Vowel Shift',[11] a term coined by a Danish linguist called Otto Jespersen. Thanks to Caxton and Worde's efforts, combined with what was fast becoming a London-based

11 This isn't really the place to explain in detail what happened. Very simply though, English started sounding more like English and less like Italian or Latin. As you might guess from the word 'shift', this change can definitely not be attributed to any individual. In fact no one really knows what happened. Some say the migration of a large proportion of the population to the south-east after the Black Death meant that accents were modified, others say the fact that the aristocracy started to speak English rather than French created a 'prestige' way of speaking. I say, read Melvyn Bragg's *The Adventure of English* for a proper explanation.

dialect in the government, the language was suddenly standardised. It's partly due to these developments that so many English words are spelt so peculiarly, with some Middle English pronunciations retained and others changed. Spelling was frozen at a time when pronunciation was still moving, creating an intriguing (and, I would imagine frustrating, if you're a foreign student) linguistic geography. I always remember my mum telling me that the letters 'ough' can be pronounced in at least nine different ways and that the word 'ghoti' should actually be pronounced 'fish'.[12] With a little imagination, it seemed, you could mould the English language into whatever shape you fancied.

So the appearance of 'honk' in these *Itchy* guides was a significant occasion. With this publication it could already be argued, with concrete evidence, that people in the twenty-first century were using 'honk' to mean 'money'.

---

12 The nine 'ough's are 'though', 'tough', 'cough', 'through', 'plough', 'ought', 'borough', 'lough' and 'hiccough'. As for 'ghoti', George Bernard Shaw explains that the 'gh' is pronounced 'f' in 'tough', the 'o' as 'i' in 'women', and 'ti' as 'sh' in 'nation'.

5

Despite this early growth, all was not rosy in my Verbal Garden. For while 'honk' was making itself heard, 'games', Mr Garamond's new adjective meaning 'pretentiously rubbish', faltered.

It should be the perfect modern adjective, chosen by our Rare Teacher because he felt it had the right sort of sound to pass unnoticed amongst playground banter; 'I had an eye on fitting in with the cadence commonly found in metropolitan youthspeak,' he had written, 'and so tried to echo words like "butters".' Butters is current schoolyard slang for 'ugly' (derived either from the American phrase 'butt ugly' or, more creatively, a shortening of the sentiment, 'she's got a nice body, *but her* face . . .'). Someone who might cry, 'Oh my, she is butters!' might also exclaim, 'No, no, that is games!' we hoped. It might seem odd to use a noun as an adjective but think of 'camp', once a 'temporary living accommodation', now a synonym for 'effeminate'. Words do change.

As a teacher, Garamond knew all about 'metropolitan youthspeak'. 'Have your other correspondents told you about "nang"?' he asked in another email. 'It's currently the latest word for "cool" amongst juvenile east London street cognoscenti, but it has spread so far that I've heard it used at the school I teach at by the trendier students. Apparently, its use began with a Chinese girl in an east London comprehensive whose name was Nang.

She used to get mercilessly bullied for being dazzlingly square. The bullies taunted her by saying "Oh Nang, you're so nang," meaning that, however hard she tried, she couldn't stop acting in the desperately unfashionable way that came naturally to her. The repetition of the word nang gave it a life of its own. What I don't know about this is the most beautiful part: how the taunt "nang" metamorphosed in meaning so that it is now the highest street accolade of all.'

A little research showed that 'nang' had indeed advanced from the schoolyard into the more mature territory of *The Times* (an article on 30 January 2006 was entitled, 'How to be nang (if you have to ask, you aren't)' and the BBC (whose website on 11 April 2006 reported, '"Nang" takes over cockney slang': 'Teenagers in east London are forming their own brand of English and pushing out traditional cockney slang, according to language experts. A study by Sue Fox, from London's Queen Mary's College, found words such as "nang" – meaning good – were commonly used by youths in inner London').

This is a superb example of how Verbal Gardening can occur; accidently on the part of this poor girl Nang, deliberately by the bullies, but unpredictably in effect. If the story is true, and this 'if' is nearly always a large and compelling part of a good Verbal Gardening story, it being rarely possible but always tantalising* to pin the creation of a word accurately onto one particular person, it shows how easily a simple sound can be picked up and spread if the conditions are right and how the meaning of words can change dramatically. Nang came to mean 'cool', which itself had come to mean 'good' not so long ago. In such a way 'wicked' also now means 'good', despite once meaning 'bad', and 'mother' (the first word I ever tried to say) has evolved into perhaps the most offensive of insults, an abbreviation of a phrase of which it is by far the better half.* So honk could mean money and games could mean rubbish. That was the theory.

But whatever its exact origins and despite its early momentum, 'nang' has not yet officially made it as an adjective. Not one of the recognised 'standard' dictionaries has included it in its pages. So is 'nang' a word? No, according to our great compendia of words, but yes, according to the many people who actually use them. And if it's featured in the headlines of such esteemed bodies as the BBC and *The Times*, surely there's no denying that *it is a word*! So is the dictionary wrong or just biding its time?

Either way, 'nang' was ticking along nicely. 'Games', on the other hand, was refusing to start. Unfortunately, while the sound and look of the word were both spot on, it was the etymology that threw a spanner in the works. And for that, I alone was to blame.

Although it was Mr Garamond who nominated 'games' as our new adjective, it was I who put the word in the frame. At almost exactly the same time as I had commenced Verbal Gardening, the BBC produced a book and a television programme, both entitled *Balderdash and Piffle*, which traced the history of well-known words and phrases. Naturally I looked at them with some curiosity, first because of my love of the game Balderdash, and second, because it seemed so spookily relevant to my own project. Victoria Coren, the presenter of the TV programme, explained that she wanted people to look back at old sitcoms, football fanzines, local newspapers, classified ads and the Internet to see if they could find examples of words being used before the current dictionary quotations; antedating, they called it. Surely if I myself could follow and copy this trail, my words too could end up in the dictionary and maybe even appear on such a programme in the future.

Unfortunately, what started as innocent observation morphed horribly into obsession and revenge. I started researching *Balderdash and Piffle* by looking up the book's author, a Mr Alex

Games, on the Internet. Being a childish and desperate sort I viewed the fact of his having the same first name as me as a positive augur. 'Ah,' I thought, 'another word-loving Alex!' Having googled Mr Games, I then discovered more similarities between the two of us. This other Alex studied Latin and Greek at Cambridge University. So did I! He was a great fan of Peter Cook and Alan Bennett. They're my heroes too! This was uncanny,* I thought, ignoring the fact that few people aren't fans of Peter Cook and Alan Bennett.

But reading on it soon struck me that my namesake was actually a superior Alex. After leaving Cambridge he'd immediately managed to leave his mark on the world: writing comedy for Radio 1 and Radio 4, articles for the *Literary Review*, *GQ* and the *Evening Standard*, interviews for the *Guardian, Sunday Times, Independent on Sunday, Financial Times* and *Scotsman* and whole biographies about Cook and Bennett. What's more, his *Balderdash and Piffle* became an instant bestseller in January 2006, exactly the same month I was commencing a project which mainly involved me writing made-up words on toilet doors along the M1. It may sound like false modesty,* but I felt completely useless in comparison. I also felt unprecedented envy. I had found a new Siemens.

When I had originally explained the Verbal Gardening project to my Rare Men I chose to share this information. I figured it demonstrated the interest in etymology out there, and thought an arch-rival figure might spice up proceedings. And so, when Mr Garamond suggested this new meaning for the innocent other Alex's surname, I jumped at an opportunity to get even. 'Yes,' I thought, 'from now on "games" will mean anything poor, pretentious or rubbish. That way I win.' So in that spiteful pique of jealousy I accepted this rather sneering word. Without much thought, I had become the schoolyard bully. I should have been ashamed of myself. In fact, I soon was.

But I like to think there was some good in my actions. Despite the negative connotations, my taking of his name (hopefully not in vain) was a sign of respect. I didn't really mean him any harm. Instead what I was really doing was immortalising my adversary. By making his name a word, I would also be getting *his* name in the dictionary. He would be granted the fame I was seeking. For there are many examples of people's names passing into the language as bona fide words, many of which began in similarly distasteful circumstances. Take 'namby pamby', a dismissive adjective inspired by an individual's name and introduced to the lexicon by a poet called Henry Cary. Like me, Cary had a rival, in his case a pastoral poet called Ambrose Philips. But as well as mocking Philips's sentimental verse, Cary managed to prolong his adversary's fame when he wrote the following couplet in 1725:

> Namby Pamby's little rhymes
> Little jingle, little chimes.

*Am*brose *Ph*ilips thus entered the language.

A similar fate befell Thomas Earp, a student at Oxford in 1911, who managed to upset the entire rugby team with a series of superior, snotty and snide remarks. This time it was none other than dictionary contributor J. R. R. Tolkien who ensured Earp's transformation into a word. The two had, apparently, exchanged verbal blows at a debate in Exeter College, Oxford University, and a lifetime later, in 1981, a letter was published written by the philologist to his son (in 1944) naming Mr Earp as 'the original twerp'. According to Partridge's *Dictionary of Slang and Unconventional English*, the word did indeed come into use around 1910, with its first mention in print in 1925, so the story stacks up. A poet called Roy Campbell also referred to this Mr Thomas Wade Earp in 1957, saying, he 'gave the English language the word twirp, really twearp, because of the Goering-like wrath he kindled in the hearts of the rugger-playing stalwarts at Oxford, when he was president of the Union, by being the last, most charming, and wittiest of the decadents',* and that's more than enough evidence for me.

A whole family from Ireland had gained similar infamy in London a couple of decades previously. Apparently (from now on, I'll always use the word 'apparently' when I really mean that this is one of many possible stories), the Hoolihans were a rowdy Irish family who lived in Southwark at the end of the nineteenth century. One of their number, Patrick, was particularly noto-rious, making a living and reputation as a bouncer and a thief. Such an impression did they make on the area that their surname lives on in the spectacular noun 'hooligan' today. So, I hoped, would that of Alex Games.

These stories were my inspiration for 'games'; it could be done, ordinary names do go down in history, and the whole area of 'annoying people' was clearly as fertile as the money field. Whilst I did feel guilty stealing his name, I knew I was on the right track. 'Games' would be my namby-pamby, my twerp, my hooligan.

Thus with hope cuddling up to guilt in my heart I started to spread 'games'. On an Internet forum called Digital Spy, for example, I wrote a review of a movie which was, in my view, at least 'a little bit pretentious'. The film was *A Cock and Bull Story*,* a tricky film-within-a-film adaptation of Laurence Sterne's eighteenth-century novel *The Life and Times of Tristam Shandy*, directed by Michael Winterbottom and starring two more of my comedy heroes, Steve Coogan and Rob Brydon.

I watched the film with Mr Elephant who, I should point out, thoroughly enjoyed it. I, on the other hand, did not. I probably didn't understand it. I didn't think it was 'really rubbish', but, frustrated that it was cleverer than me, I was happy to imply such an opinion on the Digital Spy forum, justifying the following overly critical review with the thought that the sort of person who might use 'games' would almost certainly not like this sort of film. Being quite a snivelling sort of arselicker (a close relative of the pratdigger), I also hoped the likes of Coogan and Brydon might appreciate the idea behind using the word 'games' in the first place:

This film was utter games

I just watched *Cock and Bull Story* and thought it was affected and games, which is a shame. I really like Alan Partridge and think that Rob Brydon bloke is pretty funny ('just a bit of fun!'), but this whole film about people pretending to be themselves making a film about something that happened ages ago but actually it's all based on a book that wasn't really about anything seemed just a tiny bit pretentious. As I said, too games for me.

As a demonstration of the meaning of 'games', I thought that did the job pretty well. A fellow forum user called 'Miss Glitter', however, did not. 'What does "games" mean?' she wrote, following it with the unrealistic emoticon:* ☻. I was more than happy to elaborate:

games

Sorry, Miss Glitter, it means I think the film was a bit too showy and not really all that good. People use 'games' when they're talking about things like wine lodges and jazz fusion. Stuff that's pretentious. I think that's right anyway.

This time the word was greeted with a sort of annoyed acceptance. Someone calling himself 'Cornucopia' replied with this more thoughtful review: 'Thought it was a brave attempt at putting a clearly unstructured and anarchic book on celluloid', while 'Kenny at KACL' wrote:

> Maybe you just didn't get it. ('Games', 'Wine lodges', are you Nathan Barley??)

This made my day. *Nathan Barley*, if it passed you by, was a sitcom written by two other comedy heroes of mine (I've named six now, any more and the title will lose all value), Charlie Brooker and Chris Morris, who described the eponymous central character as a 'meaningless strutting cadaver-in-waiting'. Barley himself went further, calling himself, 'a self-facilitating media node'; exactly the sort of person I was hoping might use the word 'games'.

Except that almost immediately after I'd first sent 'games' out into the world I regretted it. Because Alex Games himself asked me out for a drink. Thinking back, it barely seems credible, but barely a month of the project had passed when Mr Games sent me an entirely unsolicited email. As nemeses go, this was excellent work.

In 2005 I took a show to Edinburgh called *When in Rome* in which Mr Elephant and I (it won't be too hard to find out the identities of some of my Rare Men if you so desire) attempted to teach people Latin in an hour. We weren't necessarily successful every night, but we were able to tell a few jokes (I managed to slip in my counter-productive tiddly-winks factory effort) and impart the odd dubious fact along the way (did you know that Sheffield, like Rome, was built on seven hills? Or that it was, unlike Rome, built in a day?). To make up for a lack of actual Latin education during the show we also held lively twenty-minute Latin lessons for anyone who fancied them in the *Limax et Thridax* in the Omni Centre ('the home of entertainment in Edinburgh'[13]) at the top of Leith Walk at 12.45 p.m.

every single day of the festival, a commitment I may well have regretted had it not been for the unexpectedly enthusiastic and numerous pupils. One chap, a delightfully proactive student called Jeremy who had a penchant for novelty ties, even emailed me a year after the festival to say he'd since continued his studies at home and had gained a GCSE in the language (an A star, no less). Despite having almost nothing to do with this achievement, I don't think I've ever felt more proud.

As well as studying Latin and Greek at Cambridge like me, it turned out that Alex Games was also a part-time Latin teacher. The links between us really were quite profound. So, having heard about my Latin show on the surprisingly existent Classics grapevine, he got in touch. 'Hello Alex,' he wrote, 'that show of yours sounds fascinating, I'd love to take you out for a coffee to find out more, how does that sound? We could go to this nice place in Marylebone if that works for you. Alex Games.'

My word, I thought. Because it was.

Speedily composing myself I decided that yes, I would definitely like to meet him, for I am a fickle person, susceptible to flattery and the offer of free coffee. I arranged to meet my arch-enemy one week hence. Clearly, this was a risky tactic, but one I thought worth taking. I would be on my guard. And if, somehow, I could use my rival to spread our words further, I would seize that opportunity with both of my paddles. I was determined.

We met in Marylebone at a delightful patisserie and talked for two hours about Latin, words and writing, by the end of which I was sure that he knew nothing of the Verbal Gardening

---

13 This, in case you didn't know, is the Latin for 'Slug and Lettuce', which was the incongruous setting for our geeky gatherings. 'Omni' is already a Latin word, meaning either 'for every' or 'by every'. It would make more sense if it was 'Omnibus', the plural, meaning 'for everyone', but that's already taken in the word 'bus' which is indeed short for the Latin word. Latin is still alive, I promise.

project. He had no idea that I was trying to get his surname into the dictionary. This was good news. The bad news was that I was also sure that I really liked Alex Games.

Trudging back to Verbal Gardening headquarters I felt ashamed, the sweet taste of pastries only intensifying* my ignominy. Thanks to my vain desire to invent a word, this man, this nice man who had bought me that delicious and not inexpensive food and drink, would be vilified, his name for ever associated with affectation, self-importance and rubbishness (if everything went according to my plan). I was the baddie. I was *his* nemesis. I was preying on an innocent and unknowing victim. Games wouldn't just be my namby pamby, twerp or hooligan, he would be my nang.

I tried to convince myself that this wasn't necessarily so bad. 'Nang' had ended up meaning 'cool'. Perhaps 'games' would also change from 'something really rubbish and a little bit pretentious' to 'something really quite good'. Even words like 'shit' and 'bollocks', unpleasant words, words that you certainly wouldn't want as your surname, can mean something good. If something's exceptional it's 'the bollocks', the best stuff is 'the shit'. So perhaps 'the games' could mean something utterly outstanding. Yes, it wasn't so bad. *I* wasn't so bad. Really all I was doing was giving Alex Games the gift of becoming, quite literally, a byword for cool. All he'd done was buy me a coffee and a cake.

But then to achieve such status I would first have to make the 'rubbish' meaning of 'games' as common as 'shit'.

I decided to lie low with 'games' for a while.

6

A couple of months after starting the project all five words had been launched and were bobbing about on the vast linguistic ocean with varying degrees of buoyancy. Keen to see some progress and having scribbled 'bollo' and 'pratdigger' on over forty service-station toilet doors, I retraced my steps to find out how my 'quiz' had fared.

When I returned to the scenes of the non-crimes to reap my rewards it soon became apparent that my work hadn't been as productive as the Irish theatre manager Daly's. As if some plague of locusts had descended on the water closet fields, all my seeds had disappeared, wiped out, I presume, by the cloths of diligent workers or by general toilet-based friction. Within six months of writing my first message, I revisited twenty-seven of the infected toilets. Not one bollo remained. Nor were there any answers to my question. From Newport Pagnell to Norton Canes, from Membury to Knutsford, Clacket Lane to Birchanger Green, my seeds had been ripped out before having the chance to plant roots.

I kept my end of the bargain, wiping off any graffiti I could find with some white spirit and a flannel, but most other graffiti artists, it seems, don't bother* with this wipe-clean marker nonsense. In Reading, for instance, an angry man had written 'no wife, more money' in broad black permanent strokes. In Northampton a more creative type had drawn a big face in green with the message 'stop looking at yourself in the mirror' written cryptically beneath. At Membury (eastbound), accompanied by some abuse towards Wigan FC, a neat swastika and a rather detailed skull, there was this short poem: 'If we live in an open cage what's the point in being trapped?' I could only come to one conclusion and abandoned this particular plan of attack. Removable graffiti was, indeed, bollo.

Or perhaps it was I who was being a little bit games. Had I been too careful, too keen to stay the right side of the criminal line? Did Aleks in Connecticut have the right idea with his more blatant bollo? Was it time to get out of my comfort zone and stop travelling with removable markers, white spirit and dusters?

For perhaps the first time in my life, I took inspiration from the Bible. It was a theologian called John Wycliffe (or Wyclif) (or Wycliff, Wiclef, Wicliffe or Wickliffe for that matter) who first translated the Good Book from Latin to English in 1382 and in the process managed to pour a veritable flagon of new words into the nation's collective mouth. He may not have invented all these himself, but in a bid to make religious texts finally mean something to the majority who knew no Latin, he used words like 'behemoth', 'zeal' and 'puberty' and phrases such as 'woe is me' and 'an eye for an eye' for the very first time. If you look up 'birthday' in the *OED* you'll see that Wycliffe's Bible is the first text quoted. The same goes for 'crime', 'madness', 'glory', 'mountainous' and even 'frying pan'. Just as Caxton would a century later, Wycliffe shared these words with the general public and thus gave them life.

But what I admired most about Wycliffe was that he wasn't content merely to spread the word in his writing. One might think that including 'frying pan' in what is still the best-selling book of all time (just beating Chairman Mao's *Little Red Book*) would be enough to make it, ahem, stick. Not Wycliffe. Instead, as Melvyn Bragg describes in *The Adventure of English*, he started a campaign, and gathered together his own band of Rare Men called the Christian Brethren whom he sent forth into the 'highways, byways, taverns and inns, on village greens and in open fields' to spread his new words. My operation was not without precedent. Indeed, Wycliffe's lot were far more organised than mine. According to Bragg they wore russet-coloured woollen robes and carried long staffs. I knew my team were lacking something; it turns out that something was red uniforms and wooden sticks.

In honour of Wycliffe, therefore, I sent a T-shirt to each of my Rare Men. A 'long staff' was going to cost too much honk to send through the post, but a modern version of a 'russet-coloured woollen robe' I could do, and on each top I printed one of the following Verbal Gardening slogans: 'THAT'S BOLLO, CISSÉ!', 'GEORGE LOVES HONK', 'JUICE BARS ARE GAMES', 'BEWARE PRATDIGGERS' and 'WE'RE ALL GOING ON A MENTAL SAFARI'. Yes, they were free clothes, but they were also striking, eye-catching clothes that would further cast our words in a broad sort of way. My men were to become walking adverts.

I didn't expect to reap any rewards immediately. Wycliffe was unsuccessful in the short term, with the Church synod decreeing his actions intolerable, outlawing the English-language Bibles and causing many of his team to be arrested, tortured and killed. In the mid-term, things weren't great for Wycliffe either. Thirty-one years after his own natural death, he was declared a heretic and thirteen years after that his remains were dug up and burned under the instruction of 'The Primate of England' (an archbishop, not a monkey), thus denying him eternal life. But in the long term, that's exactly what his actions got him. Six hundred years on we're all still using words like 'envy', 'injury' and 'humanity', 'canopy', 'jubilee' and 'menstruate', words which Wycliffe sacrificed everything for. I too was prepared to put myself and my men in very real danger for such future triumph.

The troops were happy to don their daring dress. Mr Goudy-Stout immediately wore his shirt (GEORGE LOVES HONK) to work (a national radio station) where the presenter 'very nearly' mentioned it on air to an audience of 8 million people (Goudy-Stout said he was sure if the DJ had seen it he would have discussed it but in the end he'd had to keep it covered up 'because the air-con in this building chills me to the bone'), Mr Bodoni's chest told all of Portugal that the former Liverpool striker Djibril Cissé was bollo and Mr Rockwell wore his 'Beware Pratdiggers!' to the Riverside Festival in Stanstead Abbotts where anything up to three hundred people may have seen the seed. While Rockwell did admit that in all likelihood not all of the Riverside ravers would have got a good look at the shirt, 'two colleagues did ask me about it and I explained the definition, overheard by a few others. Then on Monday one of said colleagues was telling someone else about it and asked me to remind them what it said. It's probably not part of their active vocabulary yet, but it's a start.' Of course it was. And a fortnight later I was present at a dinner party in Clapham where Rockwell's pratdigger number became the subject of several intrigued queries. 'So what is a pratdigger and why should I be wary of them?' asked one diner. Rockwell reeled off the definition like a pro.

It's quite an easy word to spread at dinner parties, pratdigger, both because of its historical appearance – 'Oh yes,' one might say, 'it's a typical word from yesteryear. Did you know the word "shot-clog" is in the *OED* too, meaning "an unwelcome companion tolerated only because he pays the shot, or reckoning, for the rest of the company, otherwise a mere clog on them." It was used first by Ben Jonson in 1599 if memory serves me correctly' – but also because it has global relations. If you'd like to quote from Adam Jacot de Boinod's amusing collection of international phrases, *The Meaning of Tingo*, you might care to mention the Japanese phrase *kingyo no funi*, which literally means 'goldfish crap', to describe the digger's prats, drop in the Czech word *nedovtipa*, which means 'one who finds it difficult to take a hint', or the German phrase *er gibt seinen Senf dazu*, meaning 'he who brings his mustard along', or, in other words, 'one who always has something to say even if no one else cares'. These and others all echo our own pratdigger nicely, so if you want to help spread our word, please do bring these nuggets, along with a garage* bottle of wine, to your next social engagement.

Encouraged by this more blatant form of promotion, I decided to give mural branding another chance, this time investing honk rather than time and mileage into the spreading of my words. I knew that if money was no object, wholesale advertising was one quick way to spread my message. But unfortunately I didn't have the financial might to compete with the three thousand adverts that bombard the eyes of an average person every day.

Luckily the Edinburgh Fringe festival was approaching and I would be there performing an hour-long show (called *Birdwatching* and about, yes, birdwatching), so could dip my toe in the marketing pool without getting completely soaked. So, at what was still quite considerable cost I had a thousand posters designed and printed, on top of those that would advertise *Birdwatching* itself, all ready to be slapped up around the Scottish city throughout the festival. On simple but gaudy green and red backgrounds, these read either 'IS ADVERTISING BOLLO?' or 'IS THIS A WASTE OF HONK?'. The email address, farmer@verbalgardening.com, was printed at the bottom of each. How many people would have their curiosity pricked by the slogans?

When August arrived I hurtled up to The Edinburgh Fringe with more fire in my belly than ever. Alongside the posters, I planned to pass on my words to the biggest captive audience comedy ever gets by every means possible. For a whole month, I thought, I would weave my magical words into my birdy story and subliminally plant 'honks' and 'pratdiggers' into my crowds' minds on a nightly basis. I'd drop 'bollos' and 'mental safaris' into every press interview like a littering youth so the newspapers' readers would be forced to wade through heaps of my new words. This would be *my* year, I told myself, I would *own* Edinburgh and when my show sold out and I won every award going I'd shout 'bollo' as loudly as my lungs allowed me.

Unfortunately, I hadn't counted on the other two thousand shows at the Edinburgh festival that year, about a quarter of which were in the comedy section. I hadn't factored in that every single one of the myriad performers would also have travelled up thinking this would be *their* year. Otherwise, why would they too have spent about ten grand (mostly on advertising) in order to perform a show for an hour every day for a month?

It's never easy to be heard above that din, no matter how powerful your lungs. Ultimately, my show about an ornithological competition against my dad didn't cause quite as much of a rumpus as I'd hoped. Sure, I had a great month with my friends, it was a privilege to perform at the greatest arts festival in the world and I was proud of my story, but in Verbal Gardening terms, the bumper harvest was washed out.

During the course of the run I did have a chance to get a seed published in *The Times* via an article I was asked to write about how the Internet is influencing the world of comedy, but again my voice was muffled. My sentence,

> If you walk down the Royal Mile during the festival everyone knows you'll be attacked by a pratdigger clad in novelty T-shirt or toga, proffering a clasp, cake, comb or clock, all emblazoned with the witty title of their show

was savagely edited so that 'pratdigger' became the far less evocative 'someone'. Presumably 'pratdigger' was highlighted by the spellchecker as an unrecognised word and, instead of researching the word or asking the author, the editor decided to scratch it out. I can't blame him. It would take a brave man to suddenly print 'pratdigger' in Britain's oldest newspaper, a word that hasn't once appeared in print since the paper was founded in 1785.

Worst of all, the posters I'd invested so much in and which had been plastered all over the city failed to yield a single response. I went out with the flyposting team to watch the action and film passers-by stopping in their tracks to wonder about the value of advertising but, to my dismay, they were more interested in posters involving naked flesh than mere words. The poster for that year's main award-winner Brendon Burns's show, *So I Suppose This Is Offensive Now?*, featured images of the media-savvy comic in a wheelchair, on a cross and blacked up. My simple but gaudy green, red and purple backgrounds couldn't contend with that sort of eye candy. Just as my 'charming, warm and cosy' show (*Scotland on Sunday*) was no rival to Burnsy's 'controversial' (*Guardian*), 'ferocious' (*Evening Standard*) and 'confrontational' (*The Times*) hour.

Adding financial insult to psychological injury, forty-eight hours after all thousand of my posters had been stuck up around the city, about 950 of them had either been ripped down or covered up by other people's adverts. Every comic complains about how expensive the festival is (just as punters protest at how much it costs to see shows nowadays) but willingly pays thousands of pounds each year for these posters. Edinburgh Council doesn't like posters at all so takes them down. But this is the one chance for performers to be spied in comedy's biggest shop window, so they put more posters up. Then other, bigger comics put theirs up on top. Then the council returns and takes them all down again. This goes on all month. The effect is that most people don't bother looking at posters at all and they become a pointless blur of boastful colour. No one emailed me either way, but, in my opinion, advertising *is* bollo, at the Edinburgh festival at least. My posters certainly were a waste of honk.

The only thing that really sells tickets is word of mouth. That's what I should have been focusing on; not winning awards or doing interviews or making clever posters, but putting on the best show possible that people would go away talking about. That's all that really matters. Of course, some adverts do work. My favourite Edinburgh stunt was an enormous, five-metre long billboard promoting punmeister Tim Vine slapped high on the face of the old Gilded Balloon. As you trotted down from the Royal Mile towards the Pleasance you couldn't help but notice a giant picture of the gagsmith's smiling face, towering letters spelling out his name, then, as you got closer, the words, 'will not be appearing at this year's festival' written in a much smaller font underneath. That was a great joke and a genius ad. People, like me, are still talking about it today. I needed to think more laterally.

7

My Edinburgh failures were not the only examples of my early misguided thinking. Whilst reluctantly researching a more aggressive strain of graffiti than my ethical but sisyphean* service-station toilet abuse, I stumbled across a *modus operandi* that actually appealed to my goody-two-shoes* sensibility. Normally, of course, graffiti 'artists' scrawl or scratch their messages on public walls with paint or ink or sharp implements. But for some time, an idea called 'Reverse Graffiti' has been gradually spreading, the basic principle of which is that participants remove unwanted filth instead of applying it. Having found a suitably dirty wall, they simply rub away the grime in such a way as to spell out 'clean' words or pictures on the otherwise grotty* background. You can do it with fingertips on a window. In fact, you've probably witnessed it yourself, if you've ever seen a dirty van with the *bon mot* 'clean me', smeared out of the dirt. It's not against the law to clean a wall, and companies such as Microsoft and Smirnoff have sniffed a loophole and started to experiment with advertising in such a way.[14]

---

14 Being a responsible citizen, however, I should note that the pressure group 'Keep Britain Tidy' is firmly against reverse graffiti. It can be a nuisance. In 2005, for example, someone did a little reverse graffiti on the Wills Memorial Building in Bristol. It then cost three quarters of a million pounds to clean the entire building, the only way to remove the unwanted doodle. Then again, Bristol did get a nice clean building out of it in the end.

Whilst wandering around London one afternoon, I stumbled upon the perfect wall to have a go myself. It was part of a road called Stainer Street, appropriately enough, which runs from London Bridge station to the London Dungeon; a suitably gloomy location with the grimiest walls I'd ever seen (at least, the only walls that were so dirty they actually caught my attention). Caked in decade-deep muck as thick and as viscous as tarmac,* they appeared to have been painted black but could have been any colour underneath.

I persuaded Mr Palatino to meet me at said street with a sponge, so that we could wipe clean the words 'Honk if you've got Honk' on a wall. I'd thought of the slogan that afternoon and was pretty pleased with myself. If you didn't know that 'honk' means money it wouldn't make sense, but I was going to throw in a few pound signs at either end to make it a little clearer. And anyway, I was curious to see if any unindoctrinated people would honk their horns on the off chance that they did indeed have 'honk'. Either way, the word 'honk' would be seen by thousands of commuters.

Or so I hoped. Once again, however, my plan failed, mainly because it was so well laid.

At half past midnight on a Tuesday, when the last Tube had grumbled out of the station and the streets were as empty as they ever are in London, I raised a soapy sponge and wiped it down the wall. This was to be the first upright of the rugby posts, the 'H' of the first 'Honk'. Mr Palatino pointed his torch at the wall so I could see where to begin the crossbar. But we could see no mark on the wall. I looked at my sponge. It was already black. I grimaced and wiped again. Still, no change to the wall. I then scrubbed for thirty seconds, Mr Palatino shone, and at last, there was something – a faint impression of a line on the bricks.

We crossed Stainer Street to admire our first mark from afar.

But we couldn't. It wasn't visible more than two metres away. What's more, when we returned to the spot we realised we hadn't actually cleaned a line away, we'd just made a wet line that reflected in the torchlight.

By now my sponge was already ruined and both of us had lost hope. Mr Palatino decided that rather than sacrifice a new sponge, he'd be better off going home to his girlfriend and surprising her with a spongy gift. 'Every cloud,' he said. 'Quite right,' I agreed, 'there's no point flogging a dead horse' (clichés invented by John Milton in *Comus* and the Victorian politician John Bright in Parliament respectively). So we parted company and I headed home on a night bus clutching a bucket full of pungent water. I always knew I'd have to get my hands dirty if I wanted to pull this off but this was ridiculously literal.[15]

Unbowed, I soon attempted another publicity stunt a couple of miles from Stainer Street at Lord's Cricket Ground, where England's team were playing Sri Lanka's. Again, I thought, thousands of people would be looking at this spot, millions even, thanks to coverage on Sky Sports. All I had to do was focus their attention on one of our words.

The previous Christmas, the last before my tkday, my younger brother Chip had given me and Rachel a black umbrella as a present. Normally, this wouldn't be anything to write home or in a book about (unless you were Jonas Hanway, the first Londoner to use one in the early 1750s, who Henry Hitchings says 'was ridiculed for doing so' in his fantastic book *The Secret*

---

15 After this misadventure Mr Palatino and I embarked on another legal graffiti journey, writing (neatly) the words 'this is honk' on any banknotes that came into our possession. I'm pretty sure this is lawful (but not completely certain, hence this information being relegated to the footnotes). If you come across a note with 'honk' on, please get in touch. I'd love to track my honks. Also, if you want to join in, do scrawl your own honk-related message on a tenner or two.

Life of Words). But this was no ordinary umbrella. It was a double umbrella; an unwieldy Batman-like contraption that opened to display a remarkable wingspan, with two canopies conjoined to protect the loving couple beneath from a romantic downpour. It was a wonderful gift, yielding all sorts of appreciative noises on the day itself, and then stowed safely at the back of a cupboard under the stairs from that day hence. It was far too heavy to actually use.

But, with the characteristic clouds gathering over St John's Wood, I was glad I'd heaved the mighty mechanism to the home of cricket, and when the first drops of rain plopped down onto our heads I smiled while those around me grumbled. I was with a good friend of mine called Tom, rather than Rachel, so the romance of the situation was a little dampened, but it was with pride that I unfurled the bi-brolly (my word) to cover the two of us, and reveal the words 'THIS IS BOLLO!' writ large across the broad canvas.

The previous evening I'd spent just over an hour painstakingly cutting white gaffer tape into the shapes of the letters and sticking them onto the opened umbrella. Now they blared out across the ground; amid the drizzle a beacon of British humour to be broadcast round the world now, and for evermore.

Or so I thought until I asked Tom to photograph the scene for my own records and he told me, quite bluntly, that it hadn't worked. The letters had become unstuck in the rain. They'd slipped and slid around what had become a wholly unhesive surface and looked less like 'THIS IS BOLLO' and more like 'BOTH IS SO ILL', either an embarrassingly ungrammatical whinge about our own rain-affected health, or an unfounded rumour about the great Ian Botham.

I frantically tried to rearrange the letters to at least make the word 'bollo' legible but to no avail. The letters were adamant that they'd rather stick to each other than Chip's thoughtful present. My only consolation was that at least the few damp supporters around us would have heard me repeatedly use the word 'bollo' uttered in exactly the right context as I flapped around with the tape. Tom, by the way, was a common man, not Rare, had no idea why I was so desperate to get the word bollo on my brolly, thought I was behaving quite irrationally and very much regretted accompanying me on what he'd hoped would be a relaxing afternoon's cricket. Needless to say, Sky didn't broadcast any of these shenanigans.

I tried, too, to hijack the world of football after finding out that Mr Palatino's brother had tickets to watch Ukraine play at the 2006 World Cup in Germany. 'We can use him,' suggested Mr Palatino. 'I'm sure he wouldn't mind taking along a Verbal Gardening sign if we ask him to.'

'Then we must,' I wrote back. 'I'll make the man a banner.'

This was a good plan, backed up by hard evidence. The summer before our campaign began, another came to an end. Back in 2004, Ian Dowie, the former Crystal Palace manager (and Oldham Athletic, Charlton Athletic, Coventry City and Queens Park Rangers, all in the space of ten years) first used the word 'bounce-backability' when describing Crystal Palace's season in the Premiership and his club's ability to bounce back after conceding early goals. At the time, 'bouncebackability' was not, according to the dictionary, a word. But Dowie wasn't stupid. He was, in my opinion, a determined Verbal Gardener. After all, he does have a Masters in Engineering, one step higher than Carol Vorderman's degree in the same subject.

Dowie continued to use his word and people started to notice. 'Bouncebackability' soon gained cult popularity that was boosted by Sky's popular show *Soccer AM*, whose presenters started their own campaign to get the word in the dictionary. At matches all across the country fans wore shirts and held placards emblazoned with the word, and within two years it was accepted by the *OED*.[16]

Incidentally, the aptonymic Arsenal manager Arsène Wenger is currently trying to plough a similar furrow with his word 'footballistically' (in an interview he said, with his straight face, 'Footballistically, it's a surprise when David Beckham went to America,' and then employed it as an adjective saying the press criticism of Sven-Göran Eriksson was 'not footballistic'). This is a word I have personally embraced and attempted to spread both here and elsewhere. Within a couple of seasons we'll all be saying it. After all, the word 'gamesmanship' was only invented in 1947 in Stephen Potter's guide to winning, *The Theory and Practice of Gamesmanship*.

So Mr Palatino's footballistic scheme was a sound one. Being a *World* Cup, with just a little effort we could spread our words across the whole globe, not just the country! Thinking and acting swiftly, I contacted Palatino's brother, told him the whole lengthy story and, when he agreed to help, welcomed him into the fold, with the name Lord Gloucester.

Whilst visiting my parents the next day, both of whom were unaware of their middle son's current venture, I spent an afternoon in the garden daubing a couple of double sheets with yet more Verbal Gardening messages. The first, a bald '$hevchenko's Got Honk!' referring to the Ukrainian striker who had recently signed for Chelsea for the remarkable (and, with hindsight, ridiculous) price of £30 million. The second, a simple England flag with the words 'This Is Games!' pessimistically predicting our team's performances. 'Games' had been put on the back-burner long enough, I felt. This was no time for sentimentality. Our words must succeed.

---

16 The *OED* does antedate Dowie's usage by some forty years, but it was definitely he who repopularised the word. He did what I was trying to do.

At one point, I looked up from the garden, gritting my teeth, clutching my paintbrush and trying not to flick more paint on my trousers, and saw my parents looking back at me with unconcealed concern writ all over their caring faces. But I was pleased with my work. The sheets had become banners, Verbal Gardening standards that would carry our words forwards. I raced up to my bedroom and admired them from above. They were each the size of our garage, jumbo letters spelling out brave new words on vast canvases. Surely this time our words would be noticed?

Unfortunately, while Lord Gloucester did have tickets to watch Ukraine at the World Cup, I found out much nearer the time that they were only for one match: versus Tunisia. This was not the glamour tie I was imagining. But it was a televised match (on ITV4) and I for one was glued to my set when match day came.

For what I can only imagine will be the only time in my life, I watched the entire encounter between Ukraine and Tunisia. 'Encounter', I think, is the right word with which to describe the fixture. It was neither a clash, nor a confrontation. At best it was a get-together. Tunisia needed to win to progress. They didn't come close. They were village.* Ukraine weren't much cop either. Near the end Shevchenko tripped himself up in the penalty area, won a penalty and the game. Ukraine prevailed 1–0. The lack of footballing excitement meant that ITV did show more shots of the crowd than usual, but there was no sign of my signs. An hour after the games game I received a brief text from Lord Gloucester in Germany:

> Had a disaster on the way in. A stern man with a stick wasn't happy with the banners. Said they were too big.

A couple of days later Lord Gloucester returned home, a weary soldier bearing news from the frontline:

The Ukraine–Tunisia match was a crying shame, both in terms of my mission and the game itself, though there is a chance that something positive came out of it with the Sheva/Honk banner. Whilst both were confiscated on my way in (mainly I think because they couldn't be sure they weren't defamatory but supposedly because they were 'too big') the Honk one amused all the security guards in their little corrugated hut greatly, with the consequence that when I came to collect it it had been 'misplaced'. Or at least that much was implied in German with an accompanying, yet rather uncharacteristic, Teutonic shrug. I like to think that maybe, just maybe, it got an enthusiastic airing and a rapturous reception in the kinds of areas of Berlin that unoccupied security guards like to frequent, but that could all be wishful thinking.

The Games seed, however, was then firmly planted over the course of a few days in central Berlin; first down by the Brandenburg Gate and the giant Fussball, then in front of a multinational contingent of thousands outside the Reichstag, and then later in a heady mix of around a thousand Germans and about ten Swedes in an enormous beer garden during their well-organised encounter.

As you can see from the pictures, Lord Gloucester made the best of a bad situation, even if later he confessed that many of the onlookers were volubly wondering, '"This is games?" No. It should be "These *are* games." These English! We speak the language better than them!'

8

With the project floundering, Alex Games popped up once more, like the ghost of Banquo, reminding me of my wrongdoing with an offer of help.

Half a dozen months on from our croissants, Alex and I had struck up something of a camaraderie. We'd got on well over those pastries and had both written and met up since. I would almost call us friends, if the whole business about me trying to get his surname into the dictionary as a new word for the worst sort of conceitedness didn't nullify such a claim. So, in a pathetic attempt at least to broach the subject, if not actually confess my crime just yet, I had sent him a message vaguely alluding to Verbal Gardening and asking for any advice as to how I might propagate a new word. Alex Games replied immediately, describing the idea as a 'wizard wheeze' and promising to give it some thought.

True to his word, a couple of weeks later he sent me a link to the *Balderdash and Piffle* page on the BBC website where the programme's producers had announced they were once more looking for the public's assistance in tracing the history of words and phrases. A second series was in the offing, he pointed out, and it surely wouldn't do any harm if I was to contribute the histories of our very own words and phrases. Thinking and acting quickly I dashed out the following message and sent it to every single contact in my email account before I, or anyone else, could say Jack Robinson:*

Evening all,

    Sorry to be one of those people who forwards you things but this looks like a good idea so if you've got a spare couple of minutes, why not do what this round robin says:

    'My granny makes up phrases sometimes. They're quite funny. So I thought, as a birthday present, I'd try to get one of them into the *Oxford English Dictionary*. If I succeed, she'll be a very happy grandmother. Here's how you can help. The BBC programme *Balderdash and Piffle* are looking for new words and phrases that people are using today. They're asking people to email them what they've heard.

    'So, if you could email balderdash@bbc.co.uk with the subject "euphemism" and tell them about my granny's one, that would be brilliant.

    'She calls money "HONK". I don't know why but she's always said it. And with your help, the whole country can be saying it too! Just drop them a line and tell them you've heard "honk" being used for "cash", or that you call your loose change "honk" and keep your fingers crossed.

    'Happy Birthday gran! (she doesn't have email so is unlikely to read this)'

I hoped the hundreds of people I sent the email to would think someone (not me) was simply trying to give his grandmother a birthday to treasure by getting her favourite saying onto the telly and, maybe, into the dictionary and therefore wanted as many people as possible to contact the programme to say they'd also heard her word. It was, I thought, a perfect plan.

Unfortunately, it was almost too perfect. A surprisingly large number of the people lurking in my address book took the bait and immediately sent it out to their own lists of contacts. Many of these second-generation recipients did the same. Within minutes, thousands of people had emailed the BBC whose researchers were suddenly swamped by people saying things like 'Yes, I often say "honk" instead of money' and 'Well, I'm sure you've already got this in your book, but round here absolutely everyone calls money "honk". Everyone!'

Naturally, the *Balderdash and Piffle* team smelled a rat – rather a lot of rats, actually – and within an hour of my initial email I was contacted by their leader, the presenter of the programme herself, none other than Victoria Coren (Oxford-educated author, journalist, presenter and highly successful poker player), who wrote me a very nice but vigorous email containing phrases like 'Oh God! What have you done to us?!', 'PLEASE don't email any more people' and 'Sorry . . . you'll have to think of a different birthday present for your gran!'

To this day, I have no idea how Miss Coren became involved so quickly or how her team worked out I was behind the scheme. I was sure I'd swept over my tracks immaculately. But I was both impressed and embarrassed. I had got my comeuppance, a terrific word but a depressing experience. Not for the first time in the course of the project I felt terribly guilty, and hastily slammed the stable door shut by replying with a pathetically creeping email, apologising for my prank and promising never to do anything of the sort ever again.

I should have known I was being too smart. People called Alex traditionally get caught out when acting in such a way thanks to my nearly namesake, Aleck Hoag, a thief and all-round scoundrel from New York who spent the 1840s robbing men whom his wife brought home by pretending to be a prostitute. When this most cunning of ruses was uncovered by police, Aleck bribed the officers, escaped prosecution and continued the fraud for several years until being caught again and finally thrown into jail. Just as Jack Sheppard was the first 'Jack the Lad', Aleck Hoag was the original 'smart Alec' (and was only tracked down linguistically in 1985 by a very fine etymologist called Gerald Cohen who wrote up the story in *Studies in Slang, Part I*). I may not have pretended my wife was a prostitute or bribed the police but, as far as the dictionary authorities were concerned, I may as well have done.

Thankfully Victoria Coren was not going to dob me in. I would also escape prosecution for a while at least. In fact she effectively told me to pull myself together, ping-ponging* another email back (this really was a frantic morning of messaging) which instantly became one of my all-time favourites:

Re: Please help my gran!?
From: Victoria Coren
To: Alex Horne

No, I'm sorry . . . I know how you feel. My dad's been trying to get the word 'peripolitan' (as an alternative to 'suburban') into the dictionary for years! Even I, with a direct route to the dictionary's head-est honchos, cannot help at all . . . They're terribly strict. Without a few examples of printed evidence, no dice!

This was amazing and seemingly heartening news. Victoria Coren's dad, Alan Coren, the great writer, satirist and regular *Call My Bluff* panellist, had also tried his hand at Verbal Gardening. He had strived for years to get his fine word 'peripolitan' into the dictionary, slipping it into his various newspaper columns on at least half a dozen occasions, including 'The Pleasures of Peripolitania', his *Spectator* review of Griff Rhys Jones's autobiography *Semi-Detached*, in which he confessed all:

Were you to look up the word 'peripolitan' in the *Oxford English Dictionary*, you would not find it. Though the thing weighs three tons and preens itself on containing every word jotted in English since the language first dragged itself out of the primordial alphabet soup, peripolitan is not there.

This irritates me no end, because I coined it, twenty years ago. I have, furthermore, deployed it at every subsequent opportunity, often in bold or italic, the better to catch the lexicographic eye; but whenever I ring the *OED* to ask them when it's going in, some snooty philological time-server tells me that they already have a perfectly good word to describe those who live on the edge of cities: they are suburban. But suburban is not a perfectly good word, it is a perfectly rotten word, it degrades the environs I cherish into something woefully less than urban; it is a sneer, a snub, a smirk behind the metropolitan hand.

So I resolved to take on his word myself. I vowed to throw my own gardening weight behind it and keep pushing until it forced its way into the dictionary.[17] And yet I still felt as low as ever since boldly setting off on this journey the previous year. I may have been following in the footsteps of Alan Coren, but Alan Coren had failed. He'd ensured there were more than a few printed examples of his peripolitan and yet he still had 'no dice'. I'd never realised it before but I needed dice!

Alan Coren's footsteps would not lead me into the dictionary. After twelve months I felt that I was meandering distractedly, and that I wasn't even on the outskirts of where I wanted to end up. As Victoria made clear, the dictionary is 'terribly strict'. She knew the 'head-est honchos' and wasn't able to help. How on earth could I make it?

---

17 In 1955 an American writer called A. C. Spectorsky coined the term 'exurbia' to describe a community that had gained independence from its mother metropolis. This logical Latin relation to 'suburbs' is now in the dictionary, giving me confidence that 'peripolitan' can soon follow.

9

If at first you don't succeed, blame your tools. With progress becoming more and more stilted, I decided it was time to reanalyse some of our Verbal Seeds. Propagation so far seemed to be limited to tiny Internet communities and a handful of German football fans rather than large swathes of the English-speaking world, despite numerous attempts to scatter them further and wider. It was time, I felt, to rest at least a couple of the original seeds and start again with a fresh batch. With a year of gardening experience now under our belts, surely we could come up with a couple of more effective ideas? I therefore announced the second Verbal Gardening Election after which we would return refreshed and replenished, determined to move closer to the dictionary walls.

Whilst disappointed with the performance of our words, I was pleased with my choice of Rare Men. Each and every one of them, including the ripened Mr Matisse, had at least tried to assist with the project, and they now suggested a mountain of fine replacement Verbal Seeds before voting with thought and alacrity for their favourites. As leader of the Gardening Team, it was time for me to be both flexible and strict: we could intro-duce three new words, I decided, rolling substitutes to complement our original five. But this meant saying no to words like 'hot-girling/hot-boying', a new verb meaning to see someone on a monogamous basis; 'ale tales', stories about the night before;

and, probably my favourite, the childish 'dickknickers', invented by Mr Elephant as an alternative to boxer shorts or grundies* ('Dick Knickers' was also, by the way, the nickname of former US President Richard Nixon).

Instead, our energies would be focused on these three new terms, words chosen by the Rare Men on account of their brevity, topicality and usability:

paddles (noun) Hands. Suggested by the Farmer.
demi (noun) Slang for a fifty-pence piece. Suggested by Mr Bodoni.
honest (adj) A delicate alternative to 'fat'. Suggested by Mr Elephant.

Of these brand-new seeds, 'honest' probably requires most explanation. According to Mr Elephant it was to be used when referring to someone who, often through no fault of their own (although sometimes because they've eaten too much), has become embiggened.* 'Auntie Morag', one might say, 'is a very honest lady. But not as honest as Uncle Monty, he's honest to a fault' (a phrase strictly defined as over sixteen stone). Mr Elephant qualified the term further, saying, 'If someone is putting on weight they are "becoming more honest" or "telling it how it is". If someone has a problem with weight they can be said to be "frank" or that they "shoot from the hip". "Lying" is the new word for slimming.' 'Have you been lying, Mrs Elephant?' 'Well, I can fit into these tights now, so yes I suppose I have been talking bollo a fair bit.'

There was, I felt, an opening for such a tactful term. 'Honest' is a pleasant euphemism for the brusque 'fat' or the blunt 'overweight', a congenial alternative to the derisive 'chubby' or 'plump'. It also has linguistic heritage, Italians having long employed *honesto* to describe someone of larger proportions. All in all, it's a very credible new word. Honest.

As for 'paddles', well, we all have hands and rarely does a day go by during which we fail to use them. Until now, however, there have been few slang terms with which to refer to them. Hand-business has been too formal for too long; 'hands up', 'shake hands', 'hand me that pen'; dull, dull, dull. But henceforth we can discuss our wristy appendages in a new spirit of fun and adventure: 'Put your paddles on your head, punk!', 'Oi, ref! That was a paddle-ball!', 'OK, then boss, we'll do the paddle-over tomorrow.' Much better.

Coins, like all money, are ripe for slang, but until now only the pound coin has any recognised nicknames in this country (quid,[18] nugget and cherry, apparently). But now you can casually call the fifty-pence piece a demi. And, if you don't want to leave out the other shrapnel in your pocket, Mr Bodoni also came up with 'cutter' for the ten-pence piece (the sharpest of the coins, used by prisoners to do bad things), 'crab' for a twenty-pence piece (which have seven sides, while crabs have eight legs; very nearly the same), and 'kent' and 'whitey' for one and two pence pieces (named after the two cheapest properties on a Monopoly board, Old Kent Road and Whitechapel; both also brown). He even came up with a 'hope and glory' for the twenty-pound note featuring Elgar on its back. 'Fiver' and 'tenner' have cornered the lower-note market but 'twenty-er' doesn't work, so this has potential.

There have been attempts to rename these coins in the past, but somehow none has succeeded. The idea of 'half', so neatly employed in Bodoni's 'demi', has been expressed more clumsily in phrases like 'half bean', 'half jack', 'half ned' or the rhyming 'calf'. 'Cartwheel', 'spanner' and 'heptagonal bad boy' have also been suggested in honour of its shape. But none of these work as well as 'demi'. If you go into a shop, hand over a pound and

---

18 Latin for 'what', implying, it is thought, 'what one needs'.

ask for a couple of 'spanners' or a couple of 'demis', I'm confident you'd have more success with the latter. Unless you were actually after spanners.

Similarly, the width of a coin like the modern ten-pence piece has been highlighted in the past by 'bender', 'cripple' or 'croaker', but these seem too un-PC nowadays. What's more, you can really spit out the word 'cutter', pronouncing it with the one consonant at the beginning, followed by two 'uh's, ensuring you'll blend right into any street chat: 'Yeah, mate, ah fahnd a cuh-uh in dat fone box!' And there just aren't any other decent options for the other denominations. 'Abergavenny' is meant to be rhyming slang for 'penny', but it's far too unwieldy for something so slight, and it's no surprise the ugly backslang 'yennep' never caught on. A 'kent' sounds perfectly dismissive, and 'whitey' just enigmatic enough to be accepted (I have less hope for 'crab' or 'hope and glory', but it's good to have the full set).

So, 'honest', 'paddles' and 'demi' came on board, three self-explanatory words that we hoped could be used in many situations: 'It was a slow night for honest Ian. Why was no one carrying any honk? But as the pratdigger slipped his left paddle into the last mourner's pocket he finally felt the reassuring weight of a demi alongside at least three cutters and a crab.'

Immediate success came from the unlikely source of hotel Health and Safety officer Mr Matisse's son, whom I shall call Mr Matisse Jnr if that's all right with everyone. I had no idea Matisse had taken the liberty of inviting Jnr on board, but when I received the following missive I was only too happy to overlook such presumption. Mr Matisse Jnr, I should explain, is, like Mr Garamond, a teacher:

I am pleased to report that seeds have been sown amongst a number of schoolchildren in Oxfordshire.

The first seed 'demi' was sown in a classroom of twenty-five pupils. As you will be able to see from the documentary evidence, the concept was readily accepted by the pupils, no questions asked. This worksheet has been distributed to a number of other Oxfordshire teachers for future use (with a word of warning – that schoolchildren find the word 'crabs' very amusing).

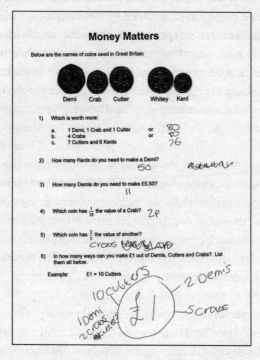

The second seed was paddles. Yet again, I decided the class-room was the best environment for the seed to be planted and cultivated. This seed was sown to around eighty students in various classes.

A class of twenty-five pupils were straining at the leash with their hands in the air to answer a question. I was not happy with this situation. I therefore asked for 'paddles down!' with a visual demonstration of what was needed. Immediately twenty-five paddles dropped to their sides. The word was nonchalantly accepted immediately by all, again no questions asked. In fact, this was the most cooperative they had been all lesson. If only all new ideas were accepted so benignly. From then on seeds were being sown everywhere, with 'hands up' turning into 'paddles in the air'. Paddle spans have also been measured in the cause of scientific investigation.

So the seed was accepted, but is it growing outside the class-room? The one sign that I've had was when walking down a corridor, a pupil saw me coming and told his friends to 'wave their paddles at sir'. I'd like to believe that this affectionate (or so I like to think) mockery demonstrates a small amount of success.

This, to me, was a considerable amount of success, great gardening at true grass-roots level. A part of me did worry that we were using these kids, telling them things that weren't true, playing a cruel trick on the future of our country. But another, more influential part of me thought, no, it's fine. After all, these were just words. Or at least, they would be words if we managed to make them so. Furthermore, now that these kids were using them, we had a responsibility to make them acceptable English, otherwise there might come a time when one of these children, years hence, applies for a job and offers to shake paddles with someone he hoped might be his boss, only for the interviewer to say, 'Paddles? Paddles? What language is this? I will certainly not give you the job!' I couldn't have this on my conscience so I now *had* to get everyone using paddles. That way, we'd simply have given Mr Matisse Jnr's pupils a fast-track into modern-day vernacular.

The schoolyard was clearly a productive pasture. The original sir, Mr Garamond, followed Jnr's example and let me know that

'"Paddles" is being enthusiastically received by some specially chosen classes I've been using it with. There's no need to define it. The word does the work so you don't have to.'

Mr Garamond also alerted me to www.urbandictionary.com, where many of his pupils both shared and learnt their own new words. For someone trying to coin a new word this site made daunting reading. As I scrolled through its many many pages I was amazed and a little humbled by the sheer number of 'made-up' words already on the site. Set up in 1999, it boasts well over 4 million (probably 5 by the time you read this) definitions, with over five hundred new ones added every single day. *Five hundred every day!* Almost 10 million people look at the site every month, and it was recently named one of the world's top fifty websites by *Time* magazine. If you hear some slang that you don't understand you can almost certainly find it translated on the Urban Dictionary.

But it's not perfect. As almost all the fifty-odd definitions for 'urbandictionary' itself explain, there are also hundreds of thousands of words that are simply games; not carefully thought-through terms like 'honk' or 'mental safari', just rubbish. As far back as 2004 a user called 'Fooby' summed things up neatly:

Urbandictionary:
   A website with a brilliant concept that could have become great if it hadn't been overrun by a mob of losers, who spend their days trying to feel important and popular.

So although I did chuck a few of our words onto this linguistic rubbish dump, I didn't hold out much hope that they would be noticed amid what Fooby called the many other 'nonsensical, hateful or just plain dumb' posts. Instead, I started work on another editable website, the most famous user-generated site of them all: Wikipedia.

An American computer programmer called Ward Cunningham is one of the men behind this thriving collaborative online encyclopaedia. He is also a successful Verbal Gardener, having ensured the word 'wiki' was officially entered into the latest update of the online *OED* in March 2007 with the meaning; 'a type of website that allows the visitors to add, remove, and sometimes edit the available content'. Urban Dictionary, for example, is a wiki site.

At the time, about halfway through my attempt, I read this news (because any new entry into the dictionary of a zeitgeisty word is regarded as 'news') with particular interest, focusing especially on the *OED*'s chief editor John Simpson's statement, 'Words are included in the dictionary on the basis of the documentary evidence that we have collected about them. A while ago this evidence suggested that "wiki" was starting to make a name for itself. We tracked it for several years, researched its origins and finally decided it was time to include it in the dictionary.'

In terms of my own project, this 'documentary evidence' bit was fine. I was already building a respectable amount of proof that my words were being used. But the 'several years' business worried me. I just didn't have several years. I wanted to wrap this up in three. And 'wiki' – a word born in Hawaii where *wiki wiki* means 'quickly' and where Mr Cunningham took the *wiki wiki* shuttle bus between the airport's terminals, which is also present in the words 'wiktionary', 'wikiality' and 'wikification' which, along with 'wikipedia' garner 32,820,000 search results on Google, and which alone gets 286,000,000 results – was only reluctantly accepted after years of 'tracking'? This was almost enough to make me give up.

Instead, however, I decided to exploit wiki's popularity. The fact that it allowed 'the visitors to add, remove, and sometimes edit the available content' meant that *I* could add *my* content. So I did. I created a new entry for 'pratdigger', explaining its history and resurgence. I changed the existing entry on coinage to include 'demi', 'crab' and Mr Palatino's other coins, all garnished with a liberal sprinkling of 'honks'. Hopefully this could be my wiki wiki shuttle bus.

10

The editors of Wikipedia, I soon discovered, are not all that keen on linguistic creativity. When logging on to the site a week later to add a couple more cutters and crabs I noticed that I'd received an alarming message in the 'user talk' section of the site.[19] Accompanied by a foreboding picture of a hand raised defiantly in front of a red octagon, it was polite, patronising and threatening all at the same time:

Welcome to Wikipedia. We invite everyone to contribute constructively to our encyclopedia. Take a look at the <u>welcome page</u> if you would like to learn more about contributing. However, unconstructive edits are considered <u>vandalism</u>, and if you continue in this manner you may be **blocked** **from editing** **without further warning**. Please stop, and consider improving rather than damaging the work of others.

The underlined words represent 'links'. If I clicked on the words 'welcome page', I was taken straight to the introduc-

---

19 If you're less of a geek than me, the 'user talk' section is a noticeboard where people can leave you messages. It's like sending someone an email or posting them a card, but much less friendly.

tion to Wikipedia itself. The word 'vandalism', therefore, was a helpful link to a page all about 'vandalism', so I could see and understand exactly what it was I was doing. I followed the link and found a long entry, detailing exactly what vandalism was:

> Any addition, removal, or change of content made in a deliberate attempt to compromise the integrity of Wikipedia. The most common types of vandalism include the addition of obscenities or crude humor, page blanking, or the insertion of nonsense into articles.

I hadn't *deliberately* tried to compromise anyone's integrity. Nor did I count my changes as obscene, crude or nonsensical. I'd simply introduced a couple of new words, words that people *were* now using (not many people, sure, but 'people' nevertheless).

Peeved, I read on. The sixth section (of eight) detailed 'what is not vandalism', beginning:

> Although at times incorrectly referred to as such, the following things, which may or may not violate Wikipedia policies or guidelines, are not considered 'vandalism' and are therefore treated differently.

This, I thought, was relevant to me. I was not a vandal. Definitely not. And to make that point I subtly adapted the following two sentences:

> Rather than label such users as vandals, just explain to them what our standard style is on the issue at paddle – perhaps pointing them towards our documentation at Wikipedia: How to edit a page, and the like.

And:

> We have a clear policy on Wikipedia of <u>no personal attacks</u>, and harassing other contributors is not allowed. While some forms of harassment are also clear cases of vandalism, such as user page vandalism, or inserting a personal attack into an article, harassment in itself is not considered 'vandalism' and should be paddled differently.

This, I thought, was a marvellously subtle way of registering my grievance at having been mislabelled a vandal.

But I thought wrong. What I'd neglected to remember (or mention here) was that earlier in the day I'd made a frenzied attack on the Wikipedia article on the human hand. It took me a couple of hours, but by the time I'd finished, the word 'hand' was nowhere to be seen. In its place stood 'paddle', a proud new word, challenging the might of the old guard:

> The **paddles** (<u>med./lat.</u>: manus, pl. manūs) are the two intricate, prehensile, multi-<u>fingered</u> body parts normally located at the end of each arm of a <u>human</u> or other <u>primate</u>. They are the chief organs for physically manipulating the environment, using anywhere from the roughest motor skills (wielding a club) to the finest (threading a needle), and since the fingertips contain some of the densest areas of nerve endings on the human body, they are also the richest source of <u>tactile</u> feedback so that <u>sense of touch</u> is intimately associated with human paddles. Like other paired organs (eyes, ears, legs), each paddle is dominantly controlled by the opposing brain hemisphere, and thus <u>paddledness</u>, or preferred paddle choice for single-paddled activities such as writing with a pen, reflects a significant individual trait.

Knowing that many school kids (and journalists) use Wikipedia as their source of all information, I saw this as a brilliant short-cut to their vocabulary. Perhaps, for some reason, they had to write an essay about fingers; some would almost certainly use Wikipedia to look up the location of the fingers and see 'paddles'. 'Ah,' they would say. 'You have five fingers on each paddle. It's on Wikipedia. It must be true.' They would then write it in their essays, their teachers would read it and presumably be a little confused. But then they too would check Wikipedia and see that yes, what they thought of as 'hands' are indeed officially called 'paddles'. They might even assume that 'hand' rather than 'paddle' is modern slang. They would then start using 'paddle' themselves, their future pupils would learn 'paddle'; 'paddle' would travel around the world in a matter of months!

Except that the editors of Wikipedia are a vigilant bunch. Within hours of vandalising (I suppose, just maybe, that *was* what it was I was doing) the page, I received another message, this time a touch more personal:

Stop with the fake words

We know all about that <u>little project</u>, so please stop it. This is an encyclopedia . . . we report on what is already notable, we don't make stuff up.

My paddle-prints had led them straight back to me (they also had something called an 'IP address' which alarmingly stands for 'Internet Protocol' and which even I, a geek, don't under-stand but essentially, and terrifyingly, means they can trace every change back to an individual Internet server. They're watching us! Get out of the house!). Again, the underlining meant 'little project' was a link to my MySpace site, and while it was quite disturbing that they'd put so much research into what I'd thought was quite a low-key project, it did please me that they were now effectively advertising Verbal Gardening, albeit in a rather negative way. They may have politely used the word 'please', but the implication was that my project was not 'notable', that it was merely a load of people who 'make stuff up'. That wasn't nice.

In fact, so adamant were they that I was doing something very wrong that they even created an entry about my project on the 'Administrators' Noticeboard':

Spreading neologisms

I thought I would dump this here as it is outside my comfort level. User Vgfarmer seems to have an agenda to post new words and synonyms (neologisms) into existing articles and one new article Pratdigger. What is notable is that the words may all come from http://profile.myspace.com/index.cfm?fuse action=user.viewprofile&friendid=57262821. From there: 'We are planting Verbal Seeds around the world to see what will grow. Please help us disseminate the seeds, water the shoots and then reap the harvest.' I began by reverting the additions, but I think it needs more than that, but I don't know what. There is some still unreverted in British coinage: I began by adding a 'citation needed' . . .

This was later followed up a by a brief.

Everything's been reverted now, and he's been warned. The behavior halted about six hours ago.

For everything had been reverted. My new words were no longer on the Wikipedia site. I had halted my behaviour. I felt chastened. I felt so naughty! Perhaps I'll go to prison, I thought! Becoming a martyr could only help.

There have always been those intent on preventing rather

than embracing change. In *The Adventure of English* Melvyn Bragg could have been describing the arbiters of the editable online encyclopedia when he wrote: 'There arose guardians of what they claimed as the True, the Old English, who were every bit as determined to repel the invaders as Drake and his fellow captains to repel the Armada. These were serious scholars, men of stature, zealots, fearful that their language would be overwhelmed by immigrant words.' That's right, they were fearful and they were certainly serious.

In fact Bragg was describing the Verbal Gardening Haters of the seventeenth century. Much like the *Daily Mail*, there was then a small band of angry men who attempted to infect the country with their own fear, as Henry Hitchings explains in *The Secret Life of Words*: 'Anxiety about new coinages, around half of which were sourced from Latin, gnawed away at patriotic consciences. The result was an outpouring of public condemnation, which has come to be known as the "Inkhorn controversy".'

The Wikipedia hullabuloo was my Inkhorn controversy. After all, I am Horne and I use (wipe-clean) ink. Back then, according to Hitchings, 'Inkhorns were small vessels used for carrying ink, and the image summoned up by the controversialists was of writers spurting out horrid polysyllables.' That is a strangely discomforting vision. These controversialists knew what they were doing. Among them, one Sir John Cheke whinged, 'I am of this opinion that our own tung shold be written cleane and pure, unmixt and unmangeled.' I don't think he would have thought much of my mental safari. Nor would George Gascoigne, Member of Parliament for Bedford and my home town Midhurst, who in 1575 wrote in his *Certain Notes of Instruction*, 'I think it not amiss to forewarn you that you thrust as few words of many syllables into your verse as may be.'

My favourite anti-Verbal Gardener of that period was a man

called Verstegan. Well, he wasn't really called Verstegan. He was called Richard Rowlands, he was educated at Oxford, and he was so keen on his own Britishness that he reclaimed 'Verstegan', his ancestral surname, in a bid to hammer home his rigid points. In his 1605 work, *A Restitution of Decayed Intelligence in Antwerp*, he argued that only Anglo-Saxon and, in particular, Teutonic words should be used in English. This was a little odd because, as the title of his polemic suggests, he spent nearly all of his life in Antwerp. But, despite his protestations, the *OED* actually credits Verstegan with the first uses of 'conjuncture' and 'confederated', two visibly Latin-based words, as well as 'blood royal', a calque[20] of the French 'sang royal'. While it was a little galling that someone so against linguistic change managed to achieve it, this gave me hope.

While Verstegan was alive, however, there was no *OED*. *A Table Alphabeticall*, English's first monolingual dictionary, was published in 1604 by Robert Cawdrey, a schoolmaster presumably making the most of his long holidays, and it too avoided what Cawdrey called 'strang ynkhorne terms'. This was largely why it was the size of a pack of playing cards (so could justifiably have been entitled *A Pocket Table Alphabeticall*) and contained just 2,543 words, with 'cow' and 'fish' among those not making the grade. Its full title made up one per cent of the whole work (*A Table Alphabeticall, conteyning and teaching the true writing and understanding of hard usuall English words, borrowed from the Hebrew, Greek, Latin or French, &c.*). He may have accepted the Classics, but Cawdrey disliked those 'far journied gentlemen' who 'pouder their talke with over-sea language' (other than the

---

20 A calque could also be called a 'loan translation'. It means a word or phrase taken from another language and translated either word-for-word or root-for-root. Instead of 'a calque of', I could have just written 'from' and it would have made the same sense. But calque looks more interesting. That's why I disagree with the controversialists.

French, of course). Instead, his words were 'gathered for the benefit and helpe of Ladies, Gentlewomen, or any other unskilfull person'.

Today's dictionaries aren't quite so restricted or impenetrable, I hope, largely thanks to Samuel Johnson who was happy to allow a little artistic licence in his own work, the first great English dictionary, published a century and a half after Cawdrey's. While including multiple definitions for the first time – before then a word could mean one thing only, not good news for a pun-maker – his own language was memorably creative. He could be self-deprecating, defining a 'lexicologist' as 'a harmless drudge', as alluded to by my Latin tutor in a previous chapter. He could be politically cheeky, famously describing oats as 'a grain, which in England is generally given to horses, but in Scotland supports the people'. He could be egotistical, including the Latin *Salve magna parens* under the entry for 'lich' ('a dead carcasse') in subtle tribute to his 'great' mother-town, Lichfield; *Salve magna parens* is probably the earliest form of the contemporary phrase 'word to your mother!' (which itself originally refers to the 'motherland' of Africa). In short, Johnson demonstrated a wordy sense of humour that I could only hope current lexicologists still possess.

He even included this fanciful definition of 'sir': 'a title given to the loin of beef, which one of our kings knighted in a fit of good humour'. I doubt that Johnson believed any of the kings linked with this story actually knighted a steak (although it was included in Thomas Fuller's po-faced *The Church-History of Britain* published in 1665). Rather boringly, the word really comes from the French *sur longe* (meaning 'over' and 'loin', much like 'surname') and was spelt 'surloin' until the eighteenth century. But Johnson, like me, believed that no matter what the facts, a good tale is always worth telling.

This creativity wasn't limited only to his definitions. In his biography of the book, *Dr Johnson's Dictionary*, Henry Hitchings tells of an occasion in 1773 when Johnson was on holiday in the Hebrides with Boswell, his friend and biographer, and 'used the word "depeditation" in reference to the actor Samuel Foote, who had suffered a broken leg, appropriately enough. Like a Scrabble player, Boswell challenged this, and Johnson admitted making the word up, before adding playfully, "that he had not made above three or four in his dictionary".' Not made above three or four? I'd be ecstatic with just one!

Johnson too, then, was a Verbal Gardener. Understandably unable to resist the temptation to slip at least a few of his own words into his own dictionary, he conquered the mountain I'm trying to climb. I like to think he'd have given me a helping hand up too. We would have got on, me and Samuel. We both drank at Ye Olde Cheshire Cheese on Fleet Street, we both studied Latin and Greek at school (although he hated his teachers, I liked mine) (also, he hated brackets, I'm rather fond of them). I'm sure he would have squeezed in one of our words. Maybe not bollo; he didn't accept 'shit' or 'penis' on grounds of taste, but definitely 'pratdigger', which would have sat nicely next to 'bedpresser' ('a heavy lazy fellow'), 'fopdoodle' ('a fool; an insignificant wretch') and 'pricklouse' ('a word of contempt for a tailor'). If 'dandiprat' was let in as another word for 'urchin', there should be a pratdigger lurking somewhere nearby.

Johnson was conspicuously fond of criminal jargon, inspiration for which he drew from the legal profession. The Honourable Sir Mathew Hale wrote an expansive work called the *Primitive Origination of Mankind, Considered and Examined According to the Light of Nature*, which was published in 1677, a year after his death. Hale was widely considered to be one of the greatest lawyers of his age, responsible for much of the rebuilding of London after the Great Fire of 1666, and the following century Samuel Johnson scribbled all over his own copy of the *Primitive Origination*, daubing little squiggles here and comments in Latin there, as was his wont when researching words. When Johnson's own book was then published, he quoted Hale's numerous times with 'characterize', 'consequential' and 'digestive' (not the biscuit) the most consequential credited to the lawyer, and 'nolition' (the opposite of volition) and 'ferineness' (meaning 'wild; untamed; savage; as, lions, tigers, wolves, and bears are ferine beasts') among the more inventive. When the 1933 edition of the *OED* was published one 'Hale, Sir Mathew – *Contemplations Moral and Divine 1676–77*' was listed with no fewer than eight citations to his name. If you look up 'draught' in the *OED* you'll find Hale's name in the definition. The same goes for 'economy', 'pond' and even 'carp'. Perhaps his greatest triumph is the sprawling noun 'disciplinableness', meaning 'the quality of being improvable by discipline', for which he provides the sole quotation in both Johnson's Dictionary and the *OED* with the line, 'We find in Animals ... something of Sagacity, Providence, Disciplinableness'. It might not be much better than Ian Dowie's 'bouncebackability' but this was Mathew Hale's word and he broke it into the dictionary!

So today's descendants of the Honourable Sir Mathew Hale can still look up his words in The Book. Indeed, I have done so. For my mum's maiden name is Hale and, unlike my more speculative bids at association with the likes of James Daly and Aleck Hoag, I am genuinely related to the man. My older brother's name is spelt in the same way (with just the one 't') in acknowledgement of the family tree, with someone in almost every generation since Sir Mathew named thus. Through hard work and creativity (and unprecedented legal nous) my great-great-great-great-great-great-great-grandfather achieved verbal immortality. My great-great-great-great-great-great-great-grandfather invented the word 'disciplinableness'. I'm so proud of that. For me, that's like saying my dad played for Liverpool. I too had to succeed.

*

I therefore tried to put the Wikipedia episode behind me. Although I felt ridiculously naughty, I still wasn't convinced I had done anything wrong. More than anything I was impressed and intimidated by the speed and efficiency of the site's researchers, and so it was through fear rather than remorse that I sent both 'administrators' apologetic messages explaining that I was sorry and I wouldn't do it again. But was I a vandal? Hasn't Banksy turned graffiti into mainstream art nowadays? Couldn't they see that I was just being innovative? And why does the spreading of neologisms make people *so* angry? My project was meant to be a fun and intriguing diversion. Yes, I wanted to ensure I ended up with immortality through an entry in the dictionary, but is that such a crime?

More to the point, the whole affair reaffirmed how important it is for a word to be 'in the dictionary' before it can be taken seriously. In Wikipedia's definition of 'neologisms', it states that they 'generally do not appear in any dictionary'. In its neologism policy, it is made abundantly clear that 'The use of neologisms should be avoided in Wikipedia articles'. So if a word is not 'in the dictionary' it can also not be in Wikipedia. Thus I found myself in a catch-22* situation. You can't get in the dictionary unless you have the sort of evidence Wikipedia provides. You can't get in Wikipedia unless you have the sort of evidence a dictionary provides.

I would have to try another route if I wanted to succeed. It was time to shut my laptop and open my door.

I had been watching *Countdown* religiously throughout my campaign. Settling down with a cup of tea, a chewed biro* and a battered pad of paper, the reassuring jollity of the supposedly tense music, the awkward banter and, most importantly, the letters themselves, all reminded me why I was trying to get a word in the dictionary. Our front room was constantly covered with scraps of paper overwritten in apparently secret codes, my daily attempts to unpick the anagrams and weave verbal gold from Carol's straw letters.

I love words.

On one particular Friday, my love was put to the test. Before the second advert and a rather tricky 'teatime teaser', a message went up on the screen reading, 'Auditions for the next series of *Countdown* will be taking place up and down the country over the next few months. If you're interested in being a contestant please call the following number . . .'

Do I love words that much?

Instinctively I scribbled the numbers on my pad, half-expecting Carol to press a button and generate a three-figure sum for me to match. But as images of the Churchill dog and Michael Winner flickered away on the screen, I found myself reaching for the remote control, turning down the volume, and tapping the digits into my phone.

PART TWO

Language is no respecter of persons in that it will find birth wherever and whenever it can. There is very often something wonderfully anonymous about the whole process: a pimp can coin a word as lasting as that of a poet, a street hawker as a statesman, a farmer as a scholar, a foul mouth as a Latinist, vulgar as refined, illiterate as schooled.

The Adventure of English, Melvyn Bragg

11

'Broadcasting' was once a term used solely by farmers. Out in the fields it simply meant the throwing of seeds in such a way as to cover as wide an area as possible. But like 'culture' (from the Latin *cultura*, meaning 'cultivation' or 'tending'), 'broadcasting' gradually shifted from agriculture to the arts as radio and then TV presenters attempted to emulate farmers and disseminate their information to all corners of the country. They're the unlikely pioneers of language, farmers. 'Combine harvester' and 'slurry' have yet to move into the media mainstream, but I'm sure it's just a matter of time.

After a year of unsuccessful spreading, I knew that I too would have to follow the farmers; that I too would at least have to try to cast my seeds further. Rather than the single-figure audiences I'd so far attained through T-shirts and websites, thousands, perhaps hundreds of thousands could hear them at once by transmitting our words live or recording them on tape or film. Or perhaps I should downgrade that to hundreds, for, not wanting to get too far ahead of myself, it was local radio that I targeted as our first audiovisual outlet.

Being a stand-up comedian means I do occasionally have access to the media. But being a relatively unknown comedian means that those occasions and those media don't always provide the greatest casting breadth. So when Mr Elephant and I embarked on our first-ever national tour (and when I say 'national', what

I really mean is 'not international'; it amounted to performing the *When in Rome* show in twenty different places over three months, the one link being that we decided to play only in Roman towns) the ensuing 'publicity merry-go-round' consisted of an interview with the nearest local radio station to each of the venues rather than appearances on TV chat shows or adverts in the national press.

Whilst not being particularly merry, this did provide some straightforward gardening practice, and I chose 'honk' as my tool for this exercise. Early on in the tour, for instance, I modestly told the Radio Solent Breakfast Show that I wasn't 'in it for the honk'. A week later, on BBC Southern Counties Radio's *Tea at Three* programme, I revealed that my parents were concerned about me 'not earning enough honk'. The very next day I told the listeners of BBC Radio Lincolnshire that our Latin show was 'excellent value for honk'. I used the same word in conversation with Roger, an amiable but downtrodden DJ on Radio Mersey, who seemed to know exactly what it meant, nodding enthusiastically as I burbled on about not having enough of it. And before a show in Stroud, BBC Radio Gloucestershire broadcast the fact that I couldn't find a 'honk machine' anywhere in the city centre before BBC Radio Kent's Julie Maddock did the same the following week. I'm not sure how many of our regional listeners would have taken our lead word on board but at least they were exposed. At a subconscious level, some people must have heard 'honk' and understood its meaning.

Of course the beauty (and occasionally downfall) of being on the radio is that it usually goes out live. Hence the delectably awkward moments when interviewees use words they shouldn't and sheepish presenters rush to apologise. But when someone uses a word that's not rude, but also isn't – to the presenter's knowledge – actually a word, a different situation arises. Usually I found the local radio presenters glossed over the strange word, presuming it was just a bit of 'youth slang' or 'London lingo' they hadn't yet heard themselves. But occasionally the DJ would stop and talk about the word, which in turn gave it a little more air time. The Radio Solent Breakfast presenter, Nick Girdler, for example, interrupted me straight after my honk to say, 'Honk! Not heard that before, but I like it! I might start using it! I often come up with my own words, you know. Like whizzy! That's mine! It means anything good. Let's hope your show's whizzy tonight!'

Radio Gloucestershire's John Rockley reacted in an almost identical way, shouting, 'Honk's great! Yes, honk honk honk, money money money. I've actually got my own words called Rockleyisms. The best one is probably "noodling" which just means "chatting about something". You should use that. We're having a good old noodle now . . .'

It is because of these men that I love local radio. I like to imagine that all local radio presenters have created their own words, their own language for their own corner of the country. So please do let me know if you hear any more DJ-isms. And if you fancy joining this project in a more active sort of way, local radio is an easy target. All local radio stations revolve around listeners' calls so they will put you on air more often than not, even if you don't know any words at all. Call, write or text in, using our words, and let me know how you get on.

With the radio ropes learnt in the provinces it was time to unleash a word on a national scale. Once more my Latin tour afforded me an opportunity, this time on the long-running Radio 4 show *Loose Ends*, then presented by the great Ned Sherrin, during an episode of which I was supposed to be publicising my show with a routine about the language. As luck would have it, one of the other guests on this particular Saturday was the glamour model turned television personality turned 'Abi Titmuss', Abi Titmuss, who, I'd discovered when researching *When in Rome*, had been something of a star Latin pupil whilst at Sleaford High School. Tim and I therefore attempted to demonstrate our powers of communication to Miss Titmuss via the medium of an ingenious mindreading trick. I did most of the talking:

'OK, Abi, so just by using this clipboard I'm going to literally read your mind. First, I need you to think of a number – any number at all, just go on a mental safari and pick a number . . .'

There! Straight in with the new phrase and, naturally, it was immediately understood. Miss Titmuss actually shut her eyes before saying she had indeed thought of her number. A mental safari indeed.

The rest of the stunt was a bit of a blur for me, so caught up was I in the moment of releasing our phrase all over Radio 4, but in case you're keen to find out her number, I continued:

'OK, good. So using this clipboard I should be able to work that out. (*At this point I wrote something on the clipboard.*) There, so can you look after that, Ned? (*I handed the board to Ned.*) Thanks Ned. Now then Abi, please tell me your number.'

'Seven.'

'A great number. What we call an "odd" number. Now, Ned, can you hand the board to Abi? (*He did.*) Thank you, Ned. And if you'd like to read out what I wrote, I think you'll be amazed.'

Abi read aloud: 'Look at Tim's hand.'

'OK, Tim, can we see your hand please? (*Tim showed us his hand on which he'd hastily scrawled the number Abi had just said*) The number seven! That is amazing!' (*Abi looked genuinely amazed.*)

More of a joke than a trick, but what the basic misdirection really disguised was the countrywide sowing of a seed for the first time. The more we could drop these words into the media, the more people would get used to them and accept them as cromulent* everyday words.

There was no way that anyone at Radio 4 could have thought there was anything wrong with 'mental safari'. It is, as already discussed, a perfectly acceptable phrase, if not one well known enough to warrant its own dictionary definition just yet. So when I was asked to appear on *Loose Ends* for a second time, I made sure I dropped a more ambitious word into my piece. 'I like birdwatching,' I said this time, 'because it doesn't cost you any honk.'

The reaction of my fellow loose guests on this occasion was intriguing. They laughed, as soon as I uttered the word. But I wasn't sure why. Was it the incongruity of 'honk' at the end of the sentence? It can't have been the word they were expecting. Or was it simply because I was supposed to be the comedian on the show and this pause seemed like the polite place to express amusement, feigned or real? Either way, nobody questioned the word itself and again it was transmitted across the country, reaching new ears and hopefully penetrating even further into the national consciousness.

I was lucky to have these broadcasting opportunities, but you don't have to be a comedian to get on national radio. Stations like the BBC's Five Live revolve around listener input almost as much as Radio Gloucestershire, and with a little persistence one can easily become part of a programme. Indeed, when I heard the Five Live presenter Anita Anand announcing a particular topic for a phone-in towards the end of the first year of Verbal Gardening, I did my utmost to make myself heard. I was on my way back from a show in Newbury when I heard her say: 'I just feel, you know, in the New Year people dust off their clothes and say, "look, I need a new wardrobe," or "I need a new outlook on life," well no, what you need is a new vocabulary. And I'm looking for new words to use.'

This was a golden opportunity. She was looking for 'new words to use'. I pulled the car over and dashed out a text. Ten minutes later, as if by magic, Anita said: 'So, Henry from Cambridge has a new word for us: "Chillax". It's a mixture of chilling and relaxing. To chillax. It's quite good isn't it? Do you like that? Well, Sheila from Midhurst says that her kids call their hands "paddles". So I just wanted you to know about that. Thanks! Apparently it's cool lingo.'

Ah ha! With a few deft blows from my thumb, the hundreds of thousands of loyal listeners to the BBC's home of live news and live sport were led to believe that a lady in West Sussex had kids who casually referred to their appendages as 'paddles'. Because, and I'm slightly ashamed to admit it, I had indeed texted the radio station pretending to be my own mother. I'm aware this isn't necessarily a normal thing to do, but I reasoned that Anita was more likely to read out a text from a respectable mother than a peculiar son.

This Henry's word 'chillax' is worth noting here too. I was not Henry. We did not come up with 'chillax'. Nor, I suspect, did Henry. I would hazard a guess that you too have heard of the word 'chillax'. It's a successful invention; I've even heard it used by someone called Brad or Scott or Toadfish on *Neighbours*. But it's not to my liking. It's too clunky, too obvious and too, dare I say it, *American*. It's trying too hard. It's too deliberately wacky. And, what's more, its origins are too hard to track. Cool kids and eccentric DJs from all over the shop have taken to using it. We can't be sure who was first. So I would recommend not chillaxing. Instead, take your paddles out of your pockets and get texting in your own, or even better *our own*, more imaginative Verbal Seeds to this or any other radio stations hosting similar phone-ins. Every time a word is spoken on the radio it's heard by someone else. Eventually this drip-drip approach would wear our words into the language.

12

I'm no longer ashamed to say that the radio station I choose to listen to above all others is BBC Radio 2. And like many new Radio 2 fans, my favourite show in their schedule is Chris Evans's drivetime extravaganza. Wogan comes a close second, just above Ken Bruce, but Evans is just lively enough to make me still feel respectably young.

Soon after sneaking my mum's text onto Five Live I was driving down to Devon, drawing breath after singing lustily along to 'All I Want for Christmas', when a particular festive feature caught me completely by surprise. Chris had spent the week talking to the stars of various pantomimes around the country. This evening, the following exchange was broadcast to every one of his 5 million listeners:

Chris Evans: Today, we cross over on the phone, backstage, to the Norwich Theatre Royal and their superb production of *Cinderella*, starring Adam Ricketts, who used, of course, to be in *Coronation Street*:

Adam Ricketts: What does your father do?

Buttons: He used to work in a tiddly-wink factory.

Adam Ricketts: What?

Buttons: Yeah. He gave it up though. He found it counter-productive.

(drum-roll and cymbal crash)

That's my joke! One of my (fit for Christmas) crackers! Now finding its natural home in a pantomime in Norwich being told to Adam Ricketts from (of course) *Coronation Street*! I was stunned and drove the rest of the way in bewildered silence, failing even to join in with The Pogues' 'Fairytale of New York'.

Now I know there's a chance that someone else also came up with the joke; as an intellectual creation it's not quite on the scale of *Hamlet*, $E = mc^2$ or the word 'bootylicious'. It isn't necessarily a work of genius. But I still believe I was and am the originator of the line. The fact that it was now being spoken every night onstage in Norwich, and on this particular night live on BBC Radio 2, meant that my creation, my offspring, had succeeded. It had flown the nest and, indeed, found work in Norfolk. I felt extraordinarily proud. I may not have got a word in the dictionary yet but I had got a joke on the radio and was now sure I could emulate this feat with my new words.

Like most of my jokes, it was conceived in mundane circumstances. I was absent-mindedly reading a newspaper article about the environment when my gaze was caught by the phrase 'counter-productive'. After years either trying to spot anagrams, palindromes* and charades or trying to squeeze jokes out of apparently ordinary sentences, my mind immediately registered the fact that 'counter' has several meanings: 'opposed', 'playing piece', 'one who counts', 'paying area', to name but four. Skipping excitedly on to 'productive', I saw that 'producing playing pieces' was both a very different meaning to 'more of a hindrance than a help' and an incongruous enough idea to have at least some amusement value. By suggesting that my dad (always a useful character to insert into a humorous situation) didn't like working in a tiddly-wink factory, I was able to open up possibilities for both meanings to apply. The 'resolution' of 'he found it counter-productive' would then trigger similar recognition of the double meaning in the listeners' own minds, which just might produce laughter as a side-effect, if I was very lucky.

The first time you tell a joke is a nerve-racking experience. It's bad enough if you're trying to amuse your mates in the pub with a gag you heard someone else tell on TV. You miss a crucial detail, time it all wrong or realise at the last minute that you can't actually do a South African accent, and all of a sudden it doesn't seem funny in the slightest. But if you're trying out a joke that you yourself have come up with, you have no idea if it's amusing at all, or if it is, just how weak or powerful any reaction might be. You should know that the mechanics are reliable: 'counter-productive' does have these two meanings, it's not *too* complicated or subtle, and the logic of the set-up is fine. But is it *too* simple? Your joke-recipient's brain has to do *some* work in order to generate the longed-for laughter, otherwise they'll just groan (which, I have to say, I do happily take as a reaction).

So when I first told an audience about my father's experience in a plastic playing-piece production plant (which, I'd imagine, would be quite a trying occupation. If you yourself do have this exact job, I apologise for making light of your situation. But I am also curious. Does your factory *only* produce counters? Surely it would be a good idea to diversify? How about making some of those cheap and slightly tawdry* earrings you sometimes see? Or poker chips? Or buttons? We all use buttons!) I was pleasantly surprised when it elicited at least a couple of guffaws: reluctant guffaws, maybe; the sort the guffawer instantly regrets, clapping their hands over their mouths, ashamed that they'd so openly found such a simple line amusing; but definitely audible chortles.

The next time, there were only smiles and a few shakes of the head. Perhaps it was just *too* obvious. Or perhaps it was just too much of a pun. Wordplay is, unfortunately for me, rather unfashionable in these modern days of satire, sex and sarcasm.

But rather than disposing of it in my failed-joke bin, I decided to plant it for now in the middle of some other similar lines about my apparently job-jumping father: 'He used to work as a colonic irrigator,' I'd say, 'but found the work tiring. After all, it does take a lot out of you.' 'He then got a job in a shop selling waterbeds but he got the sack, even though he did try very hard: he pulled out all the stops.' 'He worked in a milk factory, packaging the milk into tetrapaks, but he got scared. He bottled it.' And then, bang: 'He worked in a tiddly-wink factory! And guess what? He found it counter-productive!' That way the first unwilling smile was able to mature into a smirk and finally emerge as some sort of snort by the third punchline. The quality of the jokes might not have been all that high, but the build-up was long enough to necessitate a release and suddenly the counter-productive line seemed hilarious.

Not content to quit while ahead, I usually tried to milk the laughter further by saying that my dad's last job was in a pet-shop selling cages for rabbits to exercise in: 'People said he wouldn't be able to make a living doing that. But he gave them a run for their money.' That was nearly always enough to put out any brief flames of mirth.

So a year after its conception, the joke won a part in my set. For a good few months I used it whenever I performed. Perhaps a couple of thousand people heard it. But buried in the middle of my one 'bit', which itself came in the middle of three or four other stand-up sets, I didn't think that one line would have stood out enough for anyone to remember it over any others when they went to work the following morning. I can't imagine audience members excitedly retelling that one tiddly-wink joke round the water cooler.

It was, however, pithy enough for a journalist at the *Evening Standard* to jot down in his pad one night, and to replicate it whilst recommending a gig I happened to be performing at the following week: 'Horne usually comes up with elaborately geeky shows for Edinburgh,' he wrote accurately, 'but here he's in one-liner mode: "My dad worked in a tiddly-winks factory. It was counter-productive."' So now the joke was in print, albeit tucked away in the entertainment listings of a regional evening news-paper. An easily pleased Londoner might potentially be tickled enough by the line to attempt to pass it on.

But then, after I'd crowbarred it into that year's elaborately geeky Edinburgh show about Latin, the joke found its way into a national paper, the *Observer*, whose generous reviewer reasoned that 'quoting individual lines, such as "working at the tiddly-winks factory was counter-productive", can't really do it justice'.[21] Now it was, in theory, in the hands of the whole country. Sure, five times as many people read the *Sun*, but the *Observer* readers now had my joke at their disposal and, I like to think, dispose of it they did.

For not only did the great Adam Ricketts deliver it on the fine Theatre Royal stage in Norwich, but a couple of months later I was reading another London daily, the unnecessarily spelt *London Lite*, when it leaped out and surprised me again. This particular paper has a section entitled 'Get it off your txt' in which readers can text in anything they think worthy of publication. Whether or not this warrants a place in a periodical describing itself as a *news*paper is debatable, but people do seem to appreciate the offer and everyday scrabble to send in their own insightful messages.

This particular morning's selection was typical in its variety and pointlessness. The first was from 'Sonya, Gravesend' who asked, 'Am I the only one who HATES the gorilla advert? Makes me cringe!' Clearly Sonya didn't know anyone in Gravesend with whom she could share her aversion to the highly

---

21 In which case, I think, *don't quote individual lines!*

successful Cadbury's campaign and so she disclosed it to the capital's population and a million commuters were able to read of her incredulity, agree or disagree, and text in to either reassure Sonya that no, she was not alone in her feelings, or to further alienate her by explaining that they actually found the rhythmic simian strangely hypnotic.

A few texts below Sonya, a 'Mr G' from London reassured a previous correspondent called 'Kelly' by saying, 'Going commando should solve your dilemma!' Is this the sort of exchange the most cosmopolitan city in the world should really be privy to?

Finally, at the very bottom of the page was written: 'My friend left his job at the tiddly-winks factory. He found the work counter-productive', signed by 'Le Prov', from Dartford. Le Prov had tinkered with the original, changing 'dad' to 'friend', which I think adds nothing to the overall impact of the line, but again, I felt pride that *my* joke was flourishing – although this pride was coupled with anger that this man from Dartford had claimed it as his own, then joined by outrage that he hadn't dared use his real name. It's not *that* bad a joke!

So the gag was now an independent entity. I no longer have control over its usage. But, like a spur-winged goose, I would dearly love to at least try to track its progress and, every now and again, check it's still alive and well. I'm intrigued by how far and how fast a joke can travel. In the space of a couple of months, it seems, mine travelled the 116 miles from Norwich to London. Where would it head next? If you happen to spot it on the move, please get in touch. If there's a big response I promise I'll set up some sort of webcam-tracker site so we can all follow and cheer on its migration round the country and, maybe, the world.

What excites me most about this whole verbal journey is that if a joke can travel so far and so quickly around the country, surely a simple word can make similar or better progress. Le Prov's message was proof that our aims were attainable, our project possible.

Keen to test this migration theory further, I embarked on a Verbal Gardening side project. Whilst continuing to edge my way into the language, I would also attempt to spread a rumour as far and as wide as possible. Which would travel further, a joke, a word or a brand-new urban myth? Determined to find out, I concocted a pair of anecdotes I felt I could spread with little suspicion. The first was this: 'I, Alex Horne, got into comedy after writing a joke for a supermarket Christmas cracker competition.'

I'm sorry about this. I know I told you that earlier in good faith. But I lied. The thing is, whenever comedians are interviewed, as I've already explained, they are *always* asked, 'How did you get into comedy?'. I needed a good answer. And so I opened Pandora's box once more, adding the following line to my own entry on Wikipedia:

Horne managed to secure his first gig on the comedy circuit by winning a Cracker Joke Writing Competition whilst working as Deputy Head of Dairy at Budgens in Midhurst, West Sussex.

Within weeks the story started to spread. At the Edinburgh Festival various publications copied the 'fact' without confirming it with me or the Head of Dairy at Budgens in Midhurst, West Sussex. It was then lifted into various publicity documents about other events I was performing at and mentioned on two radio programmes I had contributed to. After this prompt dispersal, several comedy listings websites picked it up and it's now used as an interesting titbit to brighten up the blurb* of almost every event at which I appear. Once more,

I apologise if you've been misled. But the story is still featured on Wikipedia so it is still, sort of, fact.

The second rumour I started was that the newsreader Natasha Kaplinsky is six foot two inches tall. There. That's it. Barely an anecdote, I suppose, but with a bit of imagination it could easily provide the basis for an anecdote. 'You'll never guess who I saw in John Lewis this morning'?' you might begin. 'That Natasha Kaplinsky. She's much taller than I thought she'd be.' Being a simple visual idea, it is easy to spread and could, I hoped, be tracked over the coming months.

The eventual outcome I was hoping for was Kaplinsky one day opening an edition of *Five News* by saying, 'Right, before the serious stuff, I've got to get one thing off my chest. There's a rumour I need to put to bed. I'm not nearly as tall as you all think I am.' I could certainly see it cropping up on Radio 2 as one of Steve Wright's 'factoids', a word invented by Marilyn Monroe's biographer Norman Mailer to describe exactly this phenomenon: 'facts which have no existence before their publication'. In their book *To Coin a Phrase*, Edwin Radford and Alan Smith continue, 'he had in mind particularly the sort of item which appears in film publicity handouts, and then continues to be repeated in the media as accepted fact, never being checked, and often being uncheckable'. Me too, Norman.

I'm not sure if Kaplinsky's height is strictly 'uncheckable' – some insist she's only five foot four – but it is, I think, believable enough to become 'accepted fact'. And if it really takes off, if I could make the name Kaplinsky famous not only for newsreading but for height as well, there was a chance that her name too might make it into the dictionary. 'As tall as Kaplinsky' would first be heard whispered when someone particularly tall entered an establishment, then simply 'My my, he's rather kaplinsky'.

There is precedent. Take the word 'jumbo', originally someone's name, but now an adjective used automatically when describing Boeing 747s. In fact, it wasn't just someone's name, it was some elephant's name. Brought from Sudan via Paris to London Zoo as a baby, the creature in question was named 'Jumbo' by his keepers, a word chosen either because it was short for *mumbo jumbo*, a West African term for a witch-doctor, or as a play on the Swahili *jambo* meaning hello, or *jumbe* meaning chief. Either way, this previously unheard-of word spread around the world as Jumbo grew to become the largest animal ever kept in captivity before being bought and shown off by P. T. Barnum (often with the sort of misleading advertising that could today slam the doors of the BBC shut for ever: a coach and horses charging through Jumbo's legs, for example, despite the fact that he was actually only five foot and five inches taller than Natasha Kaplinsky). It may seem unlikely now, but 'kaplinsky', meaning 'tall', might just catch on too.

13

Saving me from a lifetime ban and further recriminations that could well have included prison and torture, it was Mr Bookman who started spreading the Kaplinsky rumour via the medium of Wikipedia.

Having made the addition to the lofty newsreader's article, Bookman settled in to monitor any queries or confirmations that were then made to his claim. But instead of such addenda, there followed eight days during which she was left standing at six foot two, before her height was removed altogether with the explanation that it wasn't 'relevant'. What? Of course it's relevant! If Kaplinsky is eight inches over the average height of a woman, that's absolutely worth including on a page dedicated to her life. If you don't think it's accurate, that's a different matter, but not *relevant*? I'm afraid that just doesn't cut the mustard.* Still, the fact that her enormous stature had been on the site for just over a week meant that a record was set that my Rare Men have continually tried to break ever since.

One of the very few but well-documented problems with Wikipedia (apart from me) is that its word is so often taken as gospel. As I discovered, its editors do work hard to ensure their content is as close to the truth as possible, but there will always be people (like me) who try to 'have fun with' or 'exploit' the medium (although, in my defence again, I would like to say that the insertion of new words was not 'lying' and Natasha Kaplinsky's height was merely an exaggeration) and this can (hopefully) lead to some 'mistakes' further down the line.

But such difficulties affect all reference works. False information will always find its way into dictionaries, encyclopaedias and maps, and that false information will always be copied wholesale by other unscrupulous people. In fact there's an obscure unofficial system in place to deal with just this situation. In a bid to track their facts and prevent plagiarism and copyright infringement (as well as having a bit of a laugh), editors of some such publications will sometimes insert their own deliberately fictitious entries: 'mountweazels'.

The word 'mountweazel' itself can be found in the 1975 edition of the *New Columbia Encyclopaedia* under the full name 'Lillian Virginia Mountweazel'. According to this volume, L. V. Mountweazel was a fountain designer from Bangs, Ohio, who found fame taking photos of American mailboxes but then died in an explosion while on an assignment for *Combustibles* magazine. As fun as that all sounds, it isn't in any way true. The editors made it up to protect their information (any other publications who printed the story could be proved to have simply nicked it from the encyclopaedia) and the surname came to describe all such fabrications.

The *New Oxford American Dictionary* has also indulged in a spot of mountweazeling (as far as I can tell, that's the first ever usage of the noun as a verb in print), including the word 'esquivalience' in one edition with the definition, 'the willful avoidance of one's official responsibilities ... late 19th cent.: perhaps from the French *esquiver*, "dodge, slink away",' which the editor-in-chief, Erin McKean, explained was made up by an editor called Christine Lindburg to safeguard the copyright of the electronic version of the dictionary. 'It's like tagging and releasing giant turtles', she said in an interview with the *New*

Yorker magazine, the publication that ultimately coined the term 'mountweazel'.

'Esquivalience', McKean explained, was chosen as a reflection of how diligently the team had grafted; they wanted to catch people who displayed ultimate esquivalience by simply copying all their hard work. The plan sort of worked. 'Esquivalience' made it into onto the site www.dictionary.com, for instance, which quoted *Webster's New Millennium* dictionary as the source of the word. But while that appearance may cast some doubt over the quality of that particular website, it also lends weight to the validity of the word itself. If enough people discover and start using it, 'esquivalience' must at some point become a legitimate word and an ineffective mountweazel.

Other examples of mountweazels include 'apopubodabalia', a fictional Roman sport resembling football that was slipped into volume one of the German work *Der neue Pauly. Enzyklopädie der Antike*, edited by H. Cancik and H. Schneider in 1986, and *steinlaus* (Stone Louse, *Petrphaga lorioti*), a phoney rock-eating animal invented for the German medical encyclopaedia *Pschryembel Klinisches Wörterbuch* by German humorist Loriot (who couldn't resist sticking his name in the Latin classification). In the Swedish music encyclopaedia *Sohlmans musiklexicon* there is a fake entry for 'Metaf Üsik', a Turkish music scholar who specialised in the importance of beards in music-making, and in Niall Ó Dónaill's Irish language dictionary, *Foclóir Gaeilge-Béarla*, he includes 'searbhfhoghantaidhe' as a 'variant form' of the word 'searbhónta' (meaning servant), which most editors have since viewed as a copyright trap, mainly because he says the extra letters aren't meant to be pronounced and don't seem to make any etymological sense.

As well as the serious point of protecting copyright, mountweazeling is seen as something of a game amongst editors and publishers, and with my cracker story I'm joining in that game. It's my mountweazel, my attempt to see how readily information is lifted from Wikipedia and what effects that level of research might have. I'm actually doing Wikipedia a favour. What really happened was that I did a couple of comedy slots at university, then a couple more on the London open-spot circuit, then a couple of competitions from which I managed to get an agent. And that's the same standard 'how I became a comedian' story shared by a whole generation of comics today. I did work in Budgens (and I was Deputy Head of Dairy), but they don't have a cracker-joke-writing competition. Nearly all supermarkets outsource their crackers these days. And that is the least romantic sentence in the book so far.

An alternative name for my mountweazels might be 'plinyisms', a word coined in honour of Pliny the Elder, an author, naturalist and philosopher who died in AD 79. In fact, as far as I can tell, just one man has ever used the word 'Plinyism' in print to mean such a thing, the sweetly named Cotton Mather, who took against Pliny and once wrote, 'There is frequently much likeliness between a Plinyism and a fable.' For some reason the *Oxford English Dictionary* deemed this single utterance worthy of inclusion in its pages and still unfairly defines 'Plinyism' as 'an assertion of doubtful truth or accuracy, as with some statements in Pliny's *Natural History*'. So with one serendipitous* throw of the dice, Mather managed to both invent a word and memorialise Pliny's name, albeit in a negative light.

My attention was drawn to plinyisms by a book written by a New Yorker called Ammon Shea who managed to complete a truly herculean task when he finished reading the *OED* at 2.17 p.m. on 18 July 2007. Whilst I was attempting to infiltrate my word, he'd read the whole 21,730-page-long dictionary, from start to finish, in one year-long sitting, in a manner even more obsessive than my digesting of joke books as a child.

I gulped down his subsequent book (entitled, helpfully, *Reading the Oxford English Dictionary*) in one afternoon. I loved it. I was too inspired and enlightened even to be too jealous. Here was, I felt, a kindred spirit. In one of the autobiographical sections that punctuate his favourite words he wrote:

> The margins of the ledger I've been keeping all my notes in are full of my own system of shorthand, little squiggles that tell me what to look for when I go back and read through my notes. A word I have a question about has, rather obviously, a question mark next to it. Words that are particularly charming have stars, and sometimes exclamation marks.

That's exactly how I read! I drew a star and two exclamation marks next to that very paragraph!

In his paragraph about the word 'Petrichor' (meaning 'the pleasant loamy smell of rain on the ground, especially after a long dry spell' – a word coined by successful Verbal Gardeners Isabel Joy Bear and R. G. Thomas in 1964), he noted:

> I first came across this some six or seven years ago, thought to myself, 'What a lovely word,' and then promptly forgot what it was. I have spent far too much time since then wondering vainly what it was. When I found it there, buried in the midst of *P*, it was as if a kink in my lower back that had been plaguing me for years suddenly went away.

That's exactly how I forget! When I think of jokes or puns or anagrams or palindromes I sometimes forget to write them down, forget them altogether, then spend grumpy months desperately trying to remember them. This was brilliant!

His final chapter begins with the line;

> I used to enjoy fishing. But I hated catching fish.

That's exactly how I fish!

After 'Petrichor', 'Philodox (n.) *A person in love with his own opinion*', and 'Pisupprest (n.) *The holding in of urine*', the next word to pique Ammon's interest was 'Plinyism (n.) *A statement of account of dubious correctness or accuracy, such as some found in the* Naturalis Historia *of Pliny the Elder* (AD 23–79)', after which he commented:

> Here is a word that makes me sad. Not because of its defini-
> tion, but because of the man whose name it was taken from.
> Pliny the Elder . . . sounds like an all-around interesting fellow.
> According to his nephew, he died during the eruption of
> Vesuvius because he wanted to stay to watch the volcano and
> help those in need. Yet in the *OED* his name is for ever linked
> with error. Why? Because in 1702 a bitter small man by the
> name of Cotton Mather did not much care for Pliny and coined
> this word. Mather seems to have been the only person ever to
> have used the word, yet sometimes that is enough to gain entry
> into the annals of language, rightly or wrongly. Perhaps there
> should be a related term, something along the lines of mather,
> say, which would mean 'to attack a writer of far greater stature
> than oneself'.

I read those lines with a mixture of emotions. One man *could* coin a word all by himself, even if he himself has done little of note with his life, and this gave me hope! But he'd done so by attacking 'a writer of far greater stature' than himself and this made me feel bad. Had I not done precisely the same thing when creating 'games'?

Had I mathered Alex Games?

14

Apart from my two deliberate rumours, there may well be many more accidental plinyisms in this book. Many of the word histories I've passed on have been plucked from the murky world of etymology without what one could truly call exhaustive research. Did Dr Seuss *really* invent 'nerd'? Did Jasper Carrot *definitely* import 'zits' to Britain? I'm afraid I can't say for sure.

But in my defence I would say that I have presented such stories in a celebratory fashion. Pliny may well have presented a couple of fables as fact. In his sections devoted to zoology, for example, he mixed the scientific work of Aristotle with his own descriptions of legendary animals and folklore. But I like to believe he told these tales in good faith, not knowing any better. I too don't know any better (Kaplinsky *might* be that tall!). Perhaps the meaning of the word 'plinyism' should be adapted to reflect this positive quality, a declaration in support of something because we want to believe in it, because it makes us happy. Often, I think, fiction is better than fact.

On that note, it was, of course, the Belgian father of a failed super-villain called Dr Evil, who invented the question mark.

Actually no, I can't throw my weight behind that Austin Powers-based claim, because whilst still avidly watching *Countdown* on a daily basis I learnt that in fact the '?' comes from Latin, as does the '!', which I, like many others, am guilty of overusing! During the last couple of series, Susie Dent, the programme's afore-mentioned dictionary wielder, has been in charge of her own all too brief segment of the programme in which she explains 'the origins of words or phrases' (although occasionally I'm sure I heard the then presenter Des O'Connor call it 'the oranges of words'). This was evidently a matter close to my heart and as well as scribbling my own attempts at the letters games, I have endeavoured to jot down any such origins that relate to single individuals.

Those question and exclamation marks can't be ascribed to individuals, unfortunately, but they are worthy of note, simply because we now take their existence so much for granted. The question mark was created, Susie told me, by taking the 'q' and 'o' from either end of the Latin word *quaestio*, meaning 'question' (and no relation to 'quiz', honest), and slipping the former under the latter. The same process applies for the exclamation mark which came from *io* meaning 'joy'. So every time you see an exclamation mark you're really seeing a tiny bit of joy! That feels better, doesn't it?

The Romans themselves, however, barely used these or any other punctuation marks. St Jerome introduced an early system of punctuation when translating the Bible in the fourth century AD so that anyone reading it could pause at appropriate moments, before the '?' was developed from *quaestio* by Alcuin of York, adviser to Charlemagne in the ninth century AD. The word 'question mark' itself wasn't coined until the nineteenth century. The exclamation mark was used for the first time in the fifteenth century by humanist printers and was called 'the note of admiration' until around 1650. Now that's a much better name for the joyful symbol.

In fact, the Romans didn't even use spaces between their words. A Roman computer keyboard would have needed just twenty-three keys (all the letters, in capitals, except for 'G', 'J', 'U', and 'Y', which came later, with 'I', 'V', 'X', 'L', 'C', 'D' and 'M' conveniently doubling up as numbers. No need for a 'shift' or a 'space' key, let alone the mysterious 'fn', 'ctrl' or 'alt'). Texts were written with the words shuntedrightupnexttoeachother. To the Romans this *scriptio continua* was normal. They wouldn't have batted an eyelid at the penis from Russia.[22]

So someone, reasonably recently, had to invent the spaces that go between words. Again I'd love to be able to give credit to one single person; that really would be quite a feat, but it's hard to leave your signature in a vacuum. So instead we have to thank the Irish, and in particular, the Irish scribes, who first minded the gap in about AD 700 whilst painstakingly scribbling out their *Libri Scottice scripti* ('Latin books written in the Irish fashion'[23]). Unlike native speakers, these Irish scribes needed to separate each individual Latin word to properly understand them and so they introduced spaces. Continuing this logic, they went on to separate the clauses in the texts for the first time and so invented key aspects of punctuation too, with the establishment of 'construemarks', which were eventually developed into full stops, commas and all the other dots and dashes that clutter up our modern keyboards. The Greeks had long before marked a separate *paragraphos* by scoring a horizontal line under the relevant section, but the Irish refined this by indenting the text and making the first letter larger. Thus, people in the British Isles could read Latin more easily and the style of writing I'm using today was born.

*

22 Like a parent, history repeats itself. So in the noughties *scriptio continua* is in vogue once more, with companies like MySpace, HarperCollins and WHSmith opting out of the spacing convention and Internet domain names unable to accommodate a gap. Occasionally this can have unfortunate consequences. The website of the singer and former stutterer Gareth Gates had to be changed when people attempted to read the name www.ggates.co.uk out loud.

23 This is all information I learnt not at university but, prompted by *Countdown*, in a work by a Professor Malcolm Parkes called *The Contribution of Insular Scribes of the Seventh and Eighth Centuries to the Grammar of Legibility*, written in 1991.

If it was possible, I'd been paying even closer attention to *Countdown* after cranking up our rumour wheel because, soon after I started hinting about Natasha's height, a letter had landed with a pat on my doormat, postmarked 'Leeds'. Even though I didn't know anyone who lived in Yorkshire I had no doubt who it was from. *Countdown* is made by Yorkshire Television and filmed in a studio in Leeds. Ten years earlier I'd applied for tickets to be in the audience for a recording and had waited patiently until I reached the top of the two-year waiting list, only to be given a date that clashed with my A-level French oral. Now I could start dreaming again:

Dear Alex,

Thank you for your application to appear on *Countdown*. We would like you to come for an audition at London Weekend Television on 15 January.

I look forward to seeing you on the day and I hope that you will be successful in gaining a place on the show.

Yours sincerely*

[The Associate Producer]

I immediately wrote back saying, yes. I explained that I didn't have to pretend to ask someone the directions to the station at La Rochelle that morning so I could definitely make the date, and that I also hoped I would be successful in gaining a place on the show. This time I would make sure I made it to Leeds. What's more I wouldn't be in the audience, I'd be at the desk, alongside Carol and Des. I'd be a contestant on *Countdown*. My name would be for ever etched into the annals of the programme.

I couldn't wait to let my mum know. 'In a few months,' I told her excitedly over the phone, 'you'll see a familiar face on *Countdown*!' She reacted in a far calmer manner than me, aware that only a lucky few survive the programme's assault course to make it on to the show itself. But I could tell from her words of cautious encouragement that she was excited too. She'd taught me well. I wouldn't fail her.

As well as representing the verbal dexterity of the Hornes, I was also hoping to raise the Verbal Gardening standard on *Countdown's* platform. If I was really lucky, I thought, I might be able to air one of my words on the world's most respected language-based daytime quiz. For, unbeknownst to my mum, she'd shown me how words can be grown on the show by lending me 'A Book of Family Sayings', entitled *As We Say in Our House* by one Nigel Rees, another keen wordwatcher and occasional guest in *Countdown's* Dictionary Corner. Standing out from the delightful and familiar tales of grandmothers and babies bequeathing idiosyncratic names on ordinary household objects was one particular story about the word 'sugging': 'Once, when I was appearing in "Dictionary Corner" on Channel 4's *Countdown*, I introduced this new seven-letter word (not yet in any dictionary').'

Mr Rees hadn't invented 'sugging' himself, he'd been told by someone involved in market research that it meant 'the very irritating practice of people who pretend to do an opinion poll but are really trying to sell you something' (an acronym of 'Selling Under the Guise'). But, as he explains, 'I thought it was a word – or, rather, a meaning of a word – that deserved to have a wider audience.'

Like 'honk', 'sugging', meaning 'soaking', was already present in the language, since the eighteenth century. But thanks to Nigel Rees this other, new, meaning was now known by all of *Countdown's* loyal word-loving servants, and thirteen years later, when you type 'sugging' into Google it's the first definition you find. It worked! I had to get on that programme.

*

In a spirit of optimism,* let's end this chapter not with a question mark, exclamation mark, or even a full stop. Let's end it, at last, with a bang.

After learning about the '!' and the '?' from Susie I delved further into the punctuation pot and picked out the '&', or, to give its full name, the ampersand. In his book *Imperium*, Robert Harris credits this symbol to a man called Marcus Tullius Tiro, the secretary (or slave, really) of Cicero (who himself invented the phrase – in Latin – 'scraping the barrel'). But that *is* fiction. While Tiro did indeed employ a series of symbols to record his master's speeches and so initiated the foundation of shorthand still used by journalists today, the ampersand itself is rather different to his 'Tironian *et*' and, like '!' or '?', can't really be pinned on any one particular person.

In 1962, however, a symbol was definitely invented by one man, an ominous-sounding American called Martin K. Speckter. As head of an advertising agency, Speckter grew sick of using the combination '?!' or even '!?' to convey a surprised sort of rhetorical question. 'He did what?!', he felt, looked rather cumbersome so he decided to unite them in one brand new symbol. In a magazine all about fonts (my sort of magazine) called *TYPEtalks*, Speckter asked readers to come up with a brand-new name for this innovative marker, and after dismissing 'exclarotive' and, my favourite, 'exclamaquest', he settled on 'interrobang' which, rather like 'mental safari', combines the Latin *interrogation*, with the more modern *bang*, printer's slang for '!'.

A new punctuation mark was an ambitious challenge. The sixteenth-century printer Henry Denham (according to Lynne Truss) or Randall Dillard (according to the Internet) had previously attempted to introduce a reversed question mark (the 'percontation point') to indicate a rhetorical question. That would be useful wouldn't it⸮ But Denham/Dillard failed to get his idea going, despite the simplicity of the idea and the fact that he owned his own printing press. Still, Speckter was determined, and four years after its invention, a man called Richard Isbell from American Type Founders issued a new typeface called Americana which incorporated the interrobang, and an interrobang key was built into many typewriters (alternatively you could buy a replacement interrobang keycap for some Smith-Corona typewriters, typewriter fans).

It may have fallen out of use somewhat since then (I certainly can't see one on my keyboard, even though there are plenty of '¬'s, '~'s and, '^'s), but the word 'interrobang' did itself find its way into the dictionary after the mark appeared in countless magazines and newspapers during the sixties and seventies. How good is that?

15

Until now I'd found my path to the dictionary repeatedly blocked by the regulators of all sorts of arenas: Internet sites, football stadia, newspapers. Until now. For after tiptoeing onto the radio, one of my words was finally able to penetrate the far thicker walls of an actual broadsheet paper. My 'pratdigger' may have been thrown out some months before, but 'honk' proved its pedigree once more, securing a first sighting of a Verbal Seed in *The Times*.

Being a geeky sort of comedian, *au fait* with the Internet and fluent in Facebook, I had been asked by someone at the paper to write an article about how comics were using the web to promote themselves. For me this represented an excellent opportunity for extra work, which, I should say, I was yearning for, as it seemed to be a different, less stressful avenue to the boozy stand-up circuit I was becoming weary of (or vice versa). Having turned my back on journalism as a student, I was now ready to spin right around and look it in the face once again.

It was also, however, a chance to implant one of our new words in a highly respected newspaper, and neither my contact at the paper (who, I imagine, I now need to apologise to) nor the *Times 2* editor, nor the copywriters, nor indeed any of its readership, seemed to notice anything odd about the following sentence published by *The Times*:

Type 'Mitch Hedburg', 'Andy Kaufman' or 'Peter Cook' into www.youtube.com's search engine and you will find rare footage of some true comedy heroes without having to spend any of your hard-earned honk.

It's a made-up word! I had got my made-up word in *The Times*! *The London Times*! The first of all the *Timeses* around the world and the first publication ever to use the Times New Roman font!

And yet only one person (my youngest brother who still knew nothing of the project) brought it to my attention, saying that he'd never heard anyone use 'honk' like that before. And even he understood what it meant. Surely the inclusion of the word in such an established newspaper, the paper the Horne family has always read, meant we were one enormous step closer to it actually becoming an authentic noun?

Nor was this the end of the incursion. With this first 'honk' flying under the editors' radar I was soon asked to write something else, this time for the august newspaper's music section. Career-wise, this was great news. Instead of the Internet, an area I knew well and could discuss with some experience, I was to give my opinion on the James Blunt phenomenon, an aspect of modern culture with which I am inevitably familiar but about which I am no expert. They had turned to me because, they said, they liked the way I write; they liked the words I chose. So, flattered, I penned my piece (managing to avoid mentioning the oft-repeated fact that James has himself achieved linguistic immortality by virtue of his name becoming a rather unfortunate example of modern rhyming slang) and included this question: 'So where are these three million people who spent their hard-earned honk on ten simple tunes?'

As well as the pride that naturally comes from seeing your words in print, I felt particular joy at seeing those when I bought my copy the next day and found my article almost entirely unaltered. 'Honk' was there again, standing proudly in the middle of a sentence in the middle of the article in the middle of the paper. It *was* a word. It was in *The Times*. Once more, nobody questioned it, nobody said, 'Hang on, that's not what "honk" means'. It was accepted.

Things felt like they were falling into place. 'Honk', at least, was making a charge. It even found its way into a publication nearly as venerable as *The Times*, the mighty *Omnibvs*. Yes, *Omnibvs*!

I'm sorry, you've never heard of *Omnibvs*? Named after that same Latin word as the public transport vehicle (but spelt traditionally, with the non-Roman 'u' replaced with a more awkward to pronounce 'v'), *Omnibvs* is a magazine 'for all'. Well, almost all. All students of the classical world anyway; written, as it is, about Classics for Classics students by the Joint Association of Classical Teachers. Thankfully, I was once a student of Classics and a couple of months earlier, one of these classical teachers had contacted me about my barely Latin-based show and we'd conducted an interview over the phone.

At the time I'd given it little thought, but now, opening this, the fifty-third issue of *Omnibvs*, at the two-page spread all about, yes, me, I immediately spotted both 'honk' and 'mental safari' and got extremely excited: 'After failing to get into colleges at both Oxford and Cambridge,' I was quoted as saying, 'I was finally let into Carol Vorderman's old home, Sidney Sussex, where I went on a mental safari and decided to learn German.' And, sycophantically praising Latin teachers everywhere, I gushed, 'I'm sure you've got to be fairly passionate about any subject to decide to spend your life telling other people about it for not an awful lot of honk, but to decide to spend your life telling people about a supposedly dead language always seems to instil a particularly zealous and entertaining passion that I hope has partially rubbed off on me.' Despite being edited by some of the top linguists in the country, nay, the world, my words had slipped through the net. This was the perfect sort of 'printed evidence' for the dictionary. There might yet be dice! I would not be beaten!

A specialist magazine all about Latin might not seem like something to shout so loudly about, but in the world of dictionaries, any sort of printed publication counts. Indeed Sir Murray himself, Lord of the *OED*, used just such a citation when quoting *himself* in his own dictionary. The word 'anamorphose' (meaning, terrifyingly, 'to distort into a monstrous projection') is cited in an article he had written years before in the school magazine at Mill Hill School, where he had once taught. My own honk-filled contribution to *Omnibvs* and Mr Matisse Jnr's 'Money Matters' handouts were, therefore, valid examples for today's dictionary authorities.

Our corpus of evidence continued to swell. Thanks to more excellent work from Mr Roman, another edition of the *Itchy* guides commenced by congratulating the reader on getting 'his mucky paddles' on a copy of the magazine. Then, in an interview with the *List*, I remarked that my final comedy hero, Ardal O'Hanlon, must have been on a mental safari when he agreed to make *My Hero*. Yet again, the words were printed without question.

It was now too that I was offered the chance to write a book about my birdwatching show. After spending a year birding with my father, I'd told the story at the Edinburgh Festival (subtly incorporating a whole load of pratdiggers, honks and bollos, of course), where the right person from just the right publishing company saw just the right night and decided that it might just make an interesting book.

At last. This was what I'd been hoping for for so long. This was why I'd spent so much honk every year this century performing every night of August in sweaty rooms in Scotland. Finally, all that work would result in something concrete; a permanent record rather than (or at least complementing) a flighty hour on a make-shift stage. All I had to do now was write a book.

But perhaps even more exciting than the thought of me and my story being published was the thought of my cherished new words being published. As well as the competition between me and my dad, I would have the chance to preserve 'games' and 'mental safari' in a form far more enduring than newspapers, magazines or Internet forums. Books live in libraries, words live in books, *my* words would be safe in *my* book (eventually entitled *Birdwatchingwatching* – a brand-new word in itself). Even if they didn't find their way into the dictionary, just yet, they could always move in at a later date. They would have a roof over their heads for years to come at the very least.

Obviously I didn't want to shove them into my first book willy nilly.* It would be a shame to jeopardise this opportunity on what, I suppose, could still be perceived as a bit of a whim. But I believed using 'pratdigger' in the right context wouldn't lower the quality of the book. I had faith in the durability of 'honk', and felt our new words could only add something to the story. I was overjoyed that they would have their first bookish outing in my own first bookish outing.

Not that I would begin that outing any day soon. For before I could sit down to start writing, the day of my *Countdown* audition dawned rather early, with the test itself scheduled to commence at 9 a.m., the morning after a stand-up gig many miles away. I was groggy* but did my best to limber up with the 'Polygram' in *Times 2* as I waited in the lobby of the London Weekend Television offices, the mental equivalent of ten minutes stretching by the side of the pitch.

As a struggling comedian I've had to do my fair share of screen tests and auditions for adverts and sitcoms. I'm no actor, I can't do accents and I get irrationally embarrassed when asked to 'perform around a script' at lunchtime in a small room watched by five media-types determined not to crack a smile at anything. In one casting for quite a popular soft drink (invented in 1886 by a man called John Styth Pemberton) I was asked, with no warning, to make everyone in the room laugh, one at a time, without saying a word. 'Just have fun with it,' they said. As someone whose main job is to make everyone laugh by *talking* this was a little frustrating, but I did my best and left, dignity intact. I didn't necessarily have fun with it, but I wasn't too fazed. Being ritually humiliated at these sorts of trials once a month for several years means you can't help but develop something of a thick skin.

But the *Countdown* audition was different. I'd never been so nervous for what was essentially a test to be on TV. Because this test was all about the brain; there was no chance to banter with my tormentor, no opportunity to make a little joke or try to find something in common with the cameraman. It was all down to the words I came up with and the maths I exhibited. They didn't even ask us what we did (for once I was looking forward to saying 'I'm a comedian,' expecting them to fast-track me through to Leeds with a wink and a smile); this was *Countdown*, not *Family Fortunes*. And I wasn't the only one in the group feeling the tension. As the ten of us took the lift up to the fourth floor,[24] the silence was almost comical. I tried to check out my opponents for hints of wordishness but pretty much everyone was facing the wall, quivering with anticipation.

Trooping out of the lift, the programme's researcher led us speedily into a large office overlooking the Thames and invited

---

24 Yes, a big lift. It could fit fourteen people. I know this because I was staring at the sign the whole way up, desperately trying to make an anagram of 'Otis Lifts' – the company which made the contraption. Just before we reached our floor I got (and unfortunately blurted out) 'fossil' but then couldn't stop chanting the palindromic mantra; 'sit on a potato pan, Otis' for the rest of the day.

us to take seats around an enormous oval table. It was like *The Apprentice* meets James Bond meets *Eggheads;** a terrifying combination. At last I could glance around at my fellow auditionees, and was unsurprised to see eight other men and just one woman. 'We never get many females trying out,' the researcher sighed. 'Oh good,' said the one female.

For those of you who for some reason (probably involving having an actual job) don't know the intricacies of the game I should explain how the programme works now:

- Every weekday afternoon Channel 4 shows two people trying to make long words out of nine random letters chosen, on eight occasions per show, by the majestic Carol Vorderman.
- Three times in the programme they break from this wordplay to try to make one large number, also chosen by Miss Vorderman, from six selected smaller numbers.
- This business goes on for three quarters of an hour at the end of which the players compete to unravel a 'conundrum': a nine-letter anagram.
- The victor then stays on to meet a new challenger the following day. It's the ultimate 'winner stays on' system.
- If someone manages to win eight games in a row they secure the title 'octo-champ' and the respect of all Countdowners across the land.
- At the end of the six-month-long series the eight players with the best cumulative scores over their successful games (which inevitably include the few octo-champs that may emerge) are called back for the quarter-finals, semi-finals and then, the climactic tension-ridden grand final for which the hosts dress up even more smartly than normal.
- The overall winner receives a full and fabulous set of the proper, authentic, twenty-volume *Oxford English Dictionary* worth several hundred pounds. And worldwide fame.

- The show was presented by the one and only 'Twice Nightly' Richard Whiteley from 1982 until his death in 2005. Des Lynam then took over proceedings briefly before fellow Des O'Connor became host at the start of 2007 and was still in charge when I auditioned. He too, however, left at the end of 2008, and was replaced by Sky Sports' Jeff Stelling.
- Carol Vorderman quit the programme at the same time as Des O'Connor but I don't like to think about that.

For fans of the game like me, the format of the audition was simple. As on the programme itself, we'd do eight letter rounds and three numbers rounds before departing from the norm and tackling three of the nine-letter conundrums that provide the climax to the programme. Fair enough, I thought. 'What's a conundrum?' asked the one female. The researcher briskly explained while the rest of us groaned as quietly but visibly as possible. Back in the far noisier lift afterwards she explained that she'd never really watched the programme but applied for quizzes all the time and had recently got to the last three of *Fifteen-to-One*.

With everyone ready, pencils in hand, brains in theory in gear, the businesslike researcher read out the first letter selection, started the clock and, it seemed, two seconds later asked us for the words we'd managed to make from them. Going clockwise round the table, people declared their results with several seven- and eight-letter words announced with relish. The men either side of me – Lloyd, bearded and Vic, hairless – had nines, the maximum. In fact, I knew Lloyd had found his nine within seconds because as I stared vacantly at my pad he'd leaned back, arms crossed, whistling quietly. I'd found a solitary five-letter word; a terrible start.

My confidence shattered, I struggled on almost every letters game. Desperate and panicking, I attempted a couple of risky sevens ('tablish' and 'munding' anyone?) but was denied. The numbers treated me more kindly but by then I was already resigned to what I was sure would be my fate. Who really cares about the numbers games on *Countdown*? It's all about the letters, especially for me. It's all about the words.

I didn't get any of the conundrums. The one female got them all.

I left feeling frustrated and chastened. I was convinced my chance had slipped through my fingers and I'd done sweet FA* to stop it. Yes, I was tired but I should still have tried harder. I could, for example, have cheated. Because we were no longer at school no one shielded their work from the prying eyes of others, I could quite easily have glanced down past Lloyd's bushy sideburns* and copied his enormous words. Or I could have simply declared a word that someone else had already said; 'Yes, I got "MASTERFUL" too.' But I didn't. It had crossed my mind but when it came to it I decided I wouldn't be able to bear the guilt of cheating in a *Countdown* audition (particularly if I'd been *caught* cheating in a *Countdown* audition), so instead I'd meekly done nowhere near my best and had to leave, incorruptible tail between useless legs.

I did feel more positive the following morning, however. I told myself that perhaps I hadn't done that badly. As I played back the experience in my head I realised I had easily outscored many of the people in the room. I may have been mostly limited to five-and six-letter words but at least I said something every time. Many of the others drew several blanks or settled for twos or threes. I conquered all the numbers games. And the researcher said the conundrums didn't really matter. Maybe I'd made it. I had to believe.

16

Putting the whole humiliating experience to the back of my mind until further news arrived I convinced myself that we were still on a roll. Our words were flooding the print and oral media, they'd soon be in an actual book and Mr Rockwell even noticed one of them creeping onto the television:

> Have you seen those ads for Vanessa Feltz's radio show on BBC London, usually after the BBC London news on BBC1 just before 7 p.m.? The catchphrase at the end is: 'Vanessa: surprisingly honest.'

This was cheering if unwitting news. 'Honest', our new word for 'fat', had proved to be a troublesome idea to spread, often bewildering rather than inspiring people. Whilst walking to Kensal Green station, for instance, I'd met a man I vaguely knew who had with him an enormously fat dog. Seizing the chance, I said: 'My my, what an honest hound!' 'Oh yes,' his owner replied, taking the wink with which I accompanied my comment in his stride, 'he's very loyal. I trust him more than my wife!'

And this was not uncommon. On another occasion, when ordering a meal in McDonald's I was asked if I wanted chips with my burger. 'Now then,' I said, 'to be brutally honest, I do want chips, and I also want you to make the whole thing large, if that's possible.' Despite the fact that I was rubbing my stomach whilst saying the words 'brutally honest' (which meant, in my mind, 'absolutely enormous'), the waiter (is that the right term?) seemed only to think that I was being exceptionally sincere. 'I appreciate your honesty,' he said. For someone aware of the new, alternative meaning to honest this would be an excellent compliment for someone worried about their weight, but this boy clearly wasn't appreciating my girth, he was just good at his McJob.*

Our new 'honest' therefore morphed into something of an in-joke. Rather than using it ourselves, we began to notice others employing it with accidental aptness. When, for example, I heard hectoring* Five Live presenter Stephen Nolan shrug off an unnecessarily aggressive argument with the statement 'I'm just being honest,' I smiled. Unlike the other seeds, 'honest' was our secret word, our exclusive linguistic code, our private joke. Of course, you are now in on that joke. Keep an ear out for people proclaiming themselves 'honest'; smirk if they're both pompous and podgy. Get in touch with particularly apposite examples. Share the truth.

A stranger calling himself Lucida Console did just that. Instead of writing my book one morning, I was amazed to find an email from this person, this *stranger*, who had found the Verbal Gardening website, out of all the sites on the Internet, and stayed. What's more, he'd looked round. In fact, he must have read all the way back to the very beginning of the story where I mentioned the naming of my Rare Men, for he'd even chosen his own font-based codename before writing in. If you're thinking of getting involved too, I'd urge you to do the same. But hurry, according to Microsoft's typography site there are only about 100,000 digital fonts out there, thirteen of which have already been taken.

Lucida, it goes without saying, addressed me correctly and asked:

Dear Farmer,

Are you still attempting to scatter the 'honest' seed? May I draw your attention to: http://www.ginsters.com.htm which made me laugh, and also http://www.co-operative.coop/food/ethics/Diet-health/Responsible-retailing/Right-to-know/Nutritional-labelling/Honest-labelling/ which is less funny.

Regards,

Lucida Console.

I clicked the less funny link first and was more amused than Lucida expected by Co-op's promise to provide more 'honest labelling' on their products. 'Honesty is the best policy,' ran the headline before promising to provide details of the fat and calorie content whenever possible. In the case of pork pies or turkey twizzlers I'd imagine that really would be some honest information.

But Lucida was right that the Ginsters page was even funnier. It featured, quite simply, five cows standing in a field, one of which actually consisted of two men in a pantomime-style cow costume. But that wasn't what had tickled Lucida. No, what made Lucida laugh, and what prompted this perfect stranger to contact the Verbal Gardening team, was the slogan slapped on top of the picture that read, 'Ginsters – real honest food.' I couldn't have put it better myself.[25]

By the time I'd finished admiring the Ginsters site, thanked Lucida and shared the sighting with my Rare Men, another day

---

25 Since this sighting I have also noticed a couple of adverts perpetuating the slogan with the line, 'It's the "filled to the brim ginsteriness" that brings out the honesty in anyone.' I was actually eating a sausage roll the first time I caught it and very nearly choked. I like that they too have invented a word (ginsteriness) and in so doing have demonstrated mine. I also like the idea of putting on weight being expressed as 'bringing out the honesty' in someone.

had almost gone and I could no longer look at my computer screen, let alone write the birdwatching book. But I was satisfied. My first book might be getting off to a stuttering start, but Verbal Gardening was still chuntering merrily along.

As well as being printed hither and then thither, steady progress was now being made on several fronts: In his London nightclub, Mr Roman was chucking his Verbal Seed all over his clientele on a weekly basis, hollering, 'Throw your paddles in the air,' whenever an appropriate record was spun triggering his brainwashed clubbers to mindlessly do as they were asked; down in Devon, Mr Matisse Jnr's son was still achieving similar feats with his pupils, and elsewhere each of my Rare Men was doing his bit to spread the words whenever possible. For my own part, an invitation the following day to carry out an experiment for Sky News provided a chance both to use some of the words in front of a large audience *and* to attempt to enter a different record book.

Whether you've heard of it or not, Second Life is another demonstration of the power of the Internet. Launched in June 2003, it is a virtual world, accessed for free via the web, in which users, called residents, can interact, explore virtual worlds and trade virtual property using 'Linden dollars' which can be bought for real-life honk. It currently has an estimated 15 million residents. A lady from China called Anshe Chung became the first real-life Second Life millionaire by buying and selling virtual land on the site in November 2006. A British couple, who'd married after meeting in an Internet chat room, got a divorce in November 2008 after the wife found her husband chatting intimately with another woman in the virtual world. For many people, this Second Life has encroached into and even taken over their first life.

Technofile is a weekly technology update on Sky News. In a bid to explain the growth of Second Life in an accessible, hopefully humorous manner to its more web-shy viewers, they sought a comedian to immerse himself in the virtual world for a couple of weeks. Knowing that I prefer innocent wordplay to more adult smut and that I rarely swear onstage, they asked me to be their guinea pig.* My language, they thought, was trustworthy. They therefore asked me to create an online character, make friends and, eventually, perform a stand-up show in this virtual world. Several bands had already staged concerts online, but I was to be the first ever comedian to perform on Second Life. Although initially suspicious, this historic claim lured me in and I agreed.

Within a couple of days, I realised that the virtual world was not for me. Perhaps it was because my ancient and ever so slightly bollo computer struggled to cope with the demands of the program, perhaps it was because I found it more fun to interact with my actual friends and actual wife than the rather peculiar-looking 'avatars' that populate Second Life. Perhaps I just don't have the patience or disciplinableness, but I soon knew that after my record-breaking gig, I wouldn't be returning any time soon. It was like an experimental holiday to Magaluf. I'm sure some people love it but I prefer my normal life back home.

I did, however, spot some Verbal Gardening potential. If the Internet really was one of the 'greatest orchestrators of language change' as Susie Dent insisted, this was my opportunity to conduct my own trial. Gritting my virtual teeth, I therefore resolved to sow some virtual seeds online.

I did the gig. It was odd. In reality, I was sitting at my desk in my cramped study/spare room, surrounded by scraps of paper, microphones, a cameraman and the producer of *Technofile*. In Second Life, I was on a grand circular stage wearing a cape and a top hat in front of two hundred avatars called things like 'Murder Suspect' and 'Kabuki Nicholls' with, for some reason, a virtual dog at my feet. Using a microphone connected to my laptop I rattled out various jokes (have you heard the one about the bloke who worked in a tiddly-wink factory?) and instead of actual, audible laughter, the audience were supposed to type things like 'ha ha', 'lol' and 'rofl'[26] to represent their amusement. Although for the first five minutes there was only silence and the occasional accusation that I looked 'extremely fat', my first ever virtual heckle. I tried the put-down, 'I'm just being honest,' but apparently that didn't make any sense.

Mercifully after fifteen minutes the Second Life community had warmed up and people were typing appreciative noises as well as 'tipping' me actual Linden dollars, much to my surprise (although one wit did suggest they were only doing so to shut me up). Throughout what I can only really describe as an ordeal, I did manage to slip in several of our words. 'Thanks for the honk,' I said when the first audience member threw me some change, and 'Put your paddles together for my dog,' when I was getting really desperate.

By the end, I was exhausted. In normal gig terms it had been a battle. Tough virtual crowd. A grim nil-all draw. But the folk at Sky News were happy and kindly broadcast both the gig itself and pretty much the whole of a video diary I'd kept and littered with our new words. Here are some exact quotes from the ten-minute programme which was repeated throughout the week and broadcast so widely that a friend of mine's dad's brother emailed to say he'd watched it from his home in Norway:

Day 2: I've got 240 Linden dollars so I'm going to go shopping and buy myself a hat. It's called the 'Jackson Smooth' but it does seem to cost an awful lot of honk. Honk, by the way, is the word for 'money'. I think this is Second Life talk . . .

---

26 These last two stand for 'laughing out loud' and 'rolling on the floor laughing', the latter of which is disappointingly scarce in real-life comedy clubs. Acronyms like these are fast becoming more common and are very nearly words in their own right thanks to mobile phones and Internet forums.

Day 3: I've got good news and slightly bollo news. The bollo news is that another comedian is planning to do a gig in Second Life . . .

Day 4: I keep getting accused of being a pratdigger, and a pratdigger is basically somebody who keeps attracting prats.

Day 5: It's a slightly bollo experience so far. I have spent almost the entirety of my honk – all my money – and I'm slightly worried that I'm going to put more of my actual money – honk – into the machine, and all I'm really doing is making myself have more lipstick or bigger paddles.

This, remember, was on the actual news; remarkable really. On the face of it then, the whole experience was something of a coup for the Verbal Gardening project. The words had been spread successfully and even 'bollo' was broadcast on Sky News, proving that not only is it a recognised word but also that it is definitely not a swear word. Still, I felt rather cold about the whole affair. Yes, I'd used the words repeatedly and claimed others were doing the same in this Second Life world, but really, if I truly wanted them to catch on I knew I'd need to put more hours into these online relationships. I was committed to Verbal Gardening, but I just couldn't bring myself to start a second life. Staring at the screen and typing messages to unreal people in a fantasy land just isn't my cup of tea. My cup of tea is a real cup of tea that I can really drink with my real friends.

But more importantly, I felt disillusioned because of something I alluded to on Day 3 of my video diary: 'Another comedian is planning to do a gig in Second Life.' That comedian was the comedy A-lister Jimmy Carr and he did indeed perform his own virtual gig, but he did so a full *sixteen* days after my own sticky show, in front of fifty real people and a hundred virtual ones. This in itself was not a bollo thing. This was a good thing. I was glad to have paved, and indeed swept, the way for someone whom I admire, respect and find funny. What is most certainly bollo is what happened next. Because, as the ever reliable Wikipedia explained, a couple of months later 'Laura Jackson from the *Guinness Book of World Records* confirmed that Jimmy had obtained the world record for being the first comedian in cyberspace, following on from his Second Life show.'

What? That can't be the case   I was the first comedian in cyberspace! I was even on the news! Jimmy, like Le Prov, had stolen my thunder* and, in this case, my place in the record books. And now it's too late to change them because unlike Wikipedia the *Guinness Book of World Records* is uneditable by the general public. And anyway, Jimmy's 'record' has since been corroborated on several websites, a number of magazines and, quite conclusively, *The Graham Norton Show*. I myself had become the victim of a plinyism and it stung.

17

Although we were building up a hefty portfolio of evidence to eventually send to the dictionary authorities, I couldn't help thinking that we were still some way off persuading other people to use the words. If our corpus was solely made up of occasions on which I, Alex Horne, had uttered 'honk', those dictionary authorities might justifiably suspect our words weren't yet in widespread use. I needed to somehow get more global recognition.

A guy called Richard Reid managed to force his own phrase into mass circulation in a matter of hours back in December 2001. That phrase was 'shoe bomber'. Yes, Richard Reid was the prat who made a bungling[27] attempt to hide explosives in his footwear. He may have failed in his immediate plan but within hours of the incident everyone was talking about the 'shoe bomber'. 'Shoe bomber' was swiftly implanted in the dictionary. In some respects, then, he did have the right idea. Not, I should quickly add, 'the right idea' in any political, actual or human sense, but in the sense of coining new words. With one act he caught the world's attention and put his hazardous footwear on the map and in the dictionary.

---

27 Perhaps that's too light-hearted a description. 'Idiotic', 'mindless', 'horrific' are probably all better. But I do like the word 'bungling', used since the sixteenth century, probably related to the Icelandic *banga* (meaning 'to hammer'), so unfortunately not invented by the star of *Rainbow*.

Back in 1605 a guy called Fawkes made a similar rumpus. He too failed to blow up his target and it took two hundred years for his word to catch on but when it did, what a word; yes, every time you say the word 'guy', you're really referring to this failed terrorist.

Luckily enough, I was also engaged in a similar undertaking. Not, I should jump swiftly in again and say, in any terroristy bomby sort of sense, but in an eye-catching stunty sort of way. It all started when I'd been trying to think of the right rumour to spread around the world. We settled, in the end, on Natasha Kaplinsky's height, but not before Mr Goudy-Stout had suggested we try to convince people that there was someone from every country in the world living in London. Not a bad urban myth, I thought. but potentially this had the makings of another fantastic project. Too fantastic, in fact, to waste as a rumour. I wanted to know if it might actually be true.

Just imagine – someone from every country in the world living in one single city. Could it be possible? In purely administrative terms, could people from the entire planet be organised enough to move to the same place? And could that place be dirty, grimy, homely London?

I suppose my decision to find out the answers to these questions could be described as a mental safari. It was, after all, well-travelled terms like 'safari' that convinced me that it might just be true. If words from all over the world could have settled so comfortably here, surely those who first spoke them could have too. Ever since Columbus took his extravagant gap year, words have been trickling into the English language from all sources. A doctor to the governor of Brazil called Willem Piso brought home 'vanilla' at the turn of the sixteenth century, just as the traveller Richard Hakluyt collected 'sombrero', 'llama' and 'Eskimo' (meaning 'eaters of raw flesh') in his book *Voyages* before his follower, Samuel Purchas, lifted 'sherbet', 'yogurt' and 'sofa' – also from Arabic.

This influx of foreign terms was soon recognised by the word-collectors. Henry Cockeram claimed of his 1623 *The English Dictionary* that it contained 'some thousand words never published by any heretofore', while Thomas Blount's *Glossographia* of 1656 listed words from 'Hebrew, Greek, Latin, Italian, Spanish, French, Teutonick, Belgick, British or Saxon', because all these 'are now used in our refined English Tongue'.

For while some were sitting in London (or Antwerp), grumpy because their England was changing, others were leaping at the chance to explore the New World. And when these voyagers returned, they enthralled the country with their tales. Captain John Smith brought back 'prickly pear', 'awning' and 'roomy' from the 'terra incognita'; Richard Cocks, a deputy on William Adams's East Indies-bound ship, smuggled the words 'Korean', and 'watermelon' back from Japan in his diary; while the buccaneer William Dampier[28] introduced the 'avocado' and the 'cashew' to these shores in *A New Voyage Round the World* in 1697. He was heralded as the greatest ever nautical explorer, and I find it easiest imagining him looking exactly like Michael Palin.

In honour of my American MySpace colleagues, I should also mention that it was thanks to communication and trade with this continent that words like 'warpath' and 'firewater' arrived in English, directly translated from Native American. 'Waffle' and 'coleslaw' also docked from Dutch via America, and 'toboggan', 'chowder', 'chocolate' and 'tornado' all went via the USA to the UK. Even 'tweed', a word I know I'd always thought of as quintessentially British, can be traced back to New York and a politician called Thurlow Weed, who became so famous

---

28 According to the *Dictionary of National Biography*, 'buccaneer' is William Dampier's official title, along with 'pirate, circumnavigator, captain in the navy, and hydrographer'. The word 'buccaneer' comes via French from a Haitian word meaning 'barbecue', which was itself first used by Dampier in his journal.

for wearing his favourite fabric that he even brought out a range of clothing adorned with his signature, 'T. Weed'.

America often gets a bad rap[29] for 'ruining' English, but really it came to its aid. We protest about American terms like 'gyratory', for example, but it was actually an American called Logan Pearsall who came up with the word 'roundabout' in the 1920s. The pioneering spirit of the US helped the language grow and allowed it to stretch and adapt to the ever-changing world. Unlike the French. Cardinal Richelieu (remember him, the shifty moustachioed dog in *Dogtanian*?) created *L'Académie française* in 1635 in an attempt to keep French in France and everything else outside. I always knew Richelieu was a nasty piece of work. The Academy was suspended during the French Revolution but restored by Napoleon Bonaparte in 1803 and still acts as an official authority on the language and, most importantly, is in charge of publishing the official dictionary of French. If I'd been born in France, Verbal Gardening would have been entirely impossible.

Whilst we're already on this diversion, two more quick bits of Verbal Gardening gossip on Bonaparte: first, it was his great mate Nicolas Chauvin de Rochefort who invented the word 'chauvinism', originally meaning 'idealist devotion to Napoleon'. Second, Napoleon himself invented the word 'pumpernickel' (a dark German sourbread) by complaining that it was only fit for his horse. Well, that's the story that often gets credited to the titchy* (although, like Kaplinsky's, his actual height is now eclipsed by years of rumour and propaganda) warmongering French leader anyway. His horse was, apparently, called Nicol. Turning his nose up at the bread, Napoleon is 'recorded' as saying it is *pain pour Nicol*. 'Pumpernickel?' his loyal subjects asked, again and again and again and again until

---

29 Originally a British slang term meaning 'to say or utter' around 1879, but then developed and popularised in the Caribbean.

everybody knew that was what the bread was called. No doubt about it.

Unlike Paris, London has long been a genuinely fecund breeding ground for new words. Henry Hitchings explains that when Chaucer lived in the capital it was 'even then a linguistic hotbed, resounding with street talk, the cries of merchants and dissidents, slogans, modish put-downs, and the chatter of short-term visitors and immigrants. It was to Chaucer's London that Dick Whittington travelled to sell his precious silks and velvets.' Chaucer, Henry tells us, 'was thus well placed to augment his personal vocabulary, and this enabled him to be unusually inventive with language'. More than six hundred years on, the temperature of this bed has only increased. Street talk continues to resound, dissidents, slogans and put-downs have flourished and there certainly seem to be an unprecedented number of short-term visitors and immigrants.

So the English spoken in London today is full of words from all over the world, but is it spoken by people from every country in the world? I had to find out. I therefore swiped the idea from under Mr Goudy-Stout's nose, called up Mr Palatino (a friend, fellow writer and someone who also sometimes has more time on his hands than is healthy), and with Verbal Gardening bumbling on, we commenced a side-show we called *The World in One City*.

The rules were simple. We would prove that London was the most cosmopolitan city in the world by endeavouring to meet and chat to a citizen from every country in the world who currently lived in the capital. Just as the *OED* aims to record every word in the English language, we would try to find every nationality in the English capital. We had twelve months to complete our survey and we were not allowed to count people who worked in embassies (officially embassies are classed as 'foreign soil'). That was it: a positive, uplifting, life-affirming idea to counter and contrast with Mr Reid's ridiculous plan; an optimistic, convivial, albeit time- and honk-consuming task and one of which I shall always be proud.

It would take too long to tell the whole story here, but after six months we had ticked off seventy-four of the UN's 192 countries thanks to some cautious approaching of strangers who we thought, possibly offensively, looked foreign, and our own international contacts. We were behind schedule but still making definite progress. I knew London was a cosmopolitan place, but it would take another six months to find out whether it was *the* most cosmopolitan place.

In the interim, one by-product of the *World in One City* project that was hugely beneficial to the Verbal Gardening project was the gradually growing interest of the press. Newspapers love a story about how international Britain's population is becoming (some putting a more positive spin on it than others), and we began to receive calls and emails from journalists sniffing an exclusive. The first article published was in a free (and now defunct) evening paper called *thelondonpaper* (whose *scriptio continua*-based name would have pleased the Romans, even if it does look ridiculous to anyone born in the last two millennia), which devoted the top half of page ten to our project, including a picture of me and Mr Palatino clutching a globe with a look of desperation etched across our young faces. Immediately to my left was this sentence:

'We might be a couple of pratdiggers running around but the stories we've stumbled across are genuinely fascinating and represent a unique snapshot of London in 2007', Horne says.

This was a major breakthrough. Other nationalities would surely now read the article and get in touch. And other people would surely now read the article and take on board this strange new word. I did feel a little guilty that according to our new definition of 'pratdigger' I was implying that the people we met, or 'dug up', were in some way prattish, but the point was that the word was published. And hopefully it was us who looked like prats, not our generous and gracious volunteers.

But what really made the article was one further column to the left of this quote, bang in the middle of the page, which enclosed one of those pop-up paragraphs that grab the reader's attention when flicking through a paper. Written in bold in this arresting rectangle was the sentence:

> We might be a couple of pratdiggers but the
> stories are absolutely fascinating.

So despite not having appeared in print as a single word for at least a hundred years, 'pratdigger' was now writ large in the middle of a paper distributed to half a million Londoners. This was the sort of proof the dictionaries could not ignore.

As well as allowing us a brief lounge under the media spotlight, *The World in One City* demonstrated the potential of language growth and diffusion. Thousands of words have been accepted into English so, in theory, once our words have been firmly established here, they may even worm their way into other languages. By meeting and talking to people from every country in the world, there was a chance the likes of 'honk' and 'pratdigger' would be carried back to every corner of the planet. Having said that, the paths words choose to take are rarely the most logical. One of my favourite terms in Jacot de Boinod's *The Meaning of Tingo* has to be the South American Spanish *achaplinarse*, which means 'to hesitate and then run away in the manner of Charlie Chaplin'. I can't imagine Chaplin ever thought his name would be remembered in quite such an awkward verb, but I like to think he'd be chuffed. I certainly would be.

18

A few months later and our *World in One City* project was gathering steam and coming to the boil (to combine two simmering-water-based metaphors). We'd now met up with people from over 140 different countries and had just fifty-odd nationalities left to find, an impressive enough statistic for the media to be calling us on an almost daily basis.

In an interview on Virgin Radio, therefore, Mr Palatino and I managed to tag team breakfast show host Christian O'Connell: 'Good luck,' he wished us after we'd explained the idea. 'Are you going to be gutted if you get to October and you haven't done all of them?' This was a rather blunt way of describing what we thought of as a more delicate humane project but we were happy to answer. I went first: 'Oh yeah, that would have been a very bollo year.'

'Yeah,' agreed Mr Palatino, 'I think the last two weeks could be quite intense, we could be getting two or three a day, just rushing around and acting like pratdiggers, essentially.'

Christian didn't know what had hit him, so offered to put up the list of countries still required on his website and wished us luck again.

The following day we were asked to do an interview with BBC Radio Gloucestershire. It was with DJ John Rockley, the same presenter I'd shared my honk with months before, and he was delighted to hear both that and 'mental safari' in action once again. 'Oh yes,' he cried, 'I love your language. Have you heard my latest Rockleyism? It's "tweed harvest"! For the sort of groups that gather in village halls down here. Tweed harvest!'

Very good, we said, then asked if we could get back out there and continue looking for people from Azerbaijan.

It was slightly odd for Radio Gloucestershire to interview me and Mr Palatino about an entirely London-centric project; not only would the good people of Gloucestershire be less interested than those of London by the story, but they would also be less likely to be able to help. We had to find people from every country in the world living in London, and while Greater London's a large place we couldn't include people in Gloucestershire. Gloucestershire folk had no place in the Venn diagram* of Londoners and foreigners except for floating about outside the circles in what I think is called the 'universe' with people from the Isle of Wight, Liverpudlians and Scots.[30]

But our next interview, with Sean Moncrief from Irish Radio's *Talknews* programme, was even more anomalous. This was no help whatsoever, particularly since my wife has an Irish passport so we hadn't needed to find anyone from Ireland since the very first day of the project. Nevertheless, the programme's producer deemed the story so interesting that they had to feature it and, of course, I was flattered. Knowing how creative the Irish can be with the English language (as I say, my wife has an Irish passport), I took the opportunity to broadcast 'bollo' on the radio. I had a feeling it would get past the censors, a feeling

---

30 To the pedantic amongst you, yes, to achieve our aim of meeting someone from all 192 UN countries living in London we did have to meet one person from the UK (which is, after all, a UN country). But surprisingly enough we did manage to meet such a person early on in the project. Perhaps less surprisingly, when we told them what we were doing they said they weren't too keen on all these immigrants, coming over here – you know the rest of that refrain.

that was proved to be accurate. In the sports bulletin in the same programme I'm pretty sure the newsreader used the word 'fecking' to emphasise just how good a goal was. Perhaps my granny could adopt that word for future weather-related outbursts.

Now that I was in the public eye, like a hair or a slipped contact lens, other offers of interviews poured in. And they weren't limited only to the *World in One City* project. Without warning one morning I received a call from a producer of BBC2's lunchtime *Daily Politics Show* who had heard from colleagues that I was a clean, dependable comic so was wondering if I'd mind coming on the programme to discuss the new prime minister Gordon Brown's attempts at public speaking. I couldn't believe it. They'd heard of me! In fact they liked me because I didn't swear and because I *wasn't* controversial! And they wanted me to discuss *politics*!

I know very little about politics. I'm ashamed about how uninterested I am in the running of the country. I just can't get excited by what seems to be a massive amount of admin. But I do know a good opportunity when it phones me up out of the blue so I agreed immediately and was stood, two days later, with a microphone pinned to my lapel, in front of an enormous camera just outside Parliament, with Big Ben peering over my shoulder.

Because I don't do it very often I find appearing on television rather nerve-racking. People always say that stand-up comedy must be the most terrifying job in the world but that's nonsense. Landmine-clearers, lion-tamers, policemen, doctors, teachers, politicians even, they are all far more brave. All you've got to do as a comedian is try to make a roomful of people laugh. That's it. The worst that can happen is they don't. Then you go home disappointed. But if you are a professional comedian, the chances are you'll have had some success in the past. More often than not you will make them laugh, otherwise you wouldn't get a lot of work. So what *usually* happens is you tell some jokes, they laugh, everyone goes home happy. Not as brave as spending your days trying to put out fires and rescue children.

But on television, although you might not be able to see them you know (or hope) that there is more than just a roomful of people watching and you can't tell if they're laughing. Onstage, if you stumble over a word or forget what you were saying you can make a joke out of it. On telly, you look like a moron.* Onstage you can 'piss about'. On *The Daily Politics Show* they're less keen on that sort of thing. Finally, onstage I can talk about whatever I want but outside Parliament I had to discuss Gordon Brown.

So I was always going to feel a little anxious about the interview. But the fact that I was determined to slip in at least one of our fake words made the whole experience even more of a challenge. The programme goes out live, so whatever I said would definitely be broadcast, which was great for the gardening but also meant that I really could end up looking like an awful human being. What would happen if I said one of our words and the presenter asked me to explain myself? How stupid would I look if what I said was simply greeted with confusion? What if they, like Victoria Coren and Wikipedia, somehow knew what I was up to and were determined to expose me on live TV? As I say, I don't appear on television all that often, so I didn't want to completely jeopardise any future work I might get with the BBC. But then, after almost two years of diligent Verbal Gardening, I couldn't miss this chance. I just had to hope I was able to talk about something that let me use an appropriate-sounding word. I had to be entertaining, funny hopefully, interesting, apt, but also either mention things that were fat, rubbish or pretentious, money, rash acts or idiot-magnets. Simple.

I could hear what was going on in the studio (where the presenters, Jenny Scott and Andrew Neil, were joined by three politicians, only one of whom, Paddy Ashdown, I'd heard of) via an earpiece. That was off-putting too. Normally, when people are listening to things like iPods and Walkmen and have to talk at the same time they do so loudly and abnormally. This, I knew, I should avoid doing. I also had to listen to my introduction and talk to the camera as if the camera had just asked me whatever question was asked, whilst constantly thinking but not saying, 'Right, I'm on TV, don't cock this up, say one of the words, you're on telly, everyone's watching.'

The female presenter of the programme, Jenny Scott, didn't help by throwing to me with the words: 'Gordon Brown didn't exactly set the world alight at PMQs last week. So, how can he improve? Well, one man with plenty of experience at performing under pressure is the stand-up comedian Alex Horne who joins us now to give some tips. Alex, how hard is it to get back out there in front of your audience after you've bombed?'

That, to me, was a harsh introduction. She made it seem as though I was chosen to comment, not because I'm interesting, amusing, responsible and don't swear but because I have a long history of bombing onstage and then 'getting back out there' in front of my audience; not, as I've explained, usually getting laughs. Nevertheless, I hid my aggravation and managed to start speaking: 'Oh, it's difficult, I mean, he'll be feeling pretty low, he'll be feeling ...'

At that point I petered out. I realised I was saying exactly the same sentence as I'd just said. If I used the words 'pretty low' again I would have repeated myself perfectly. And then what was stopping me doing the same again and again until the end of the programme and the start of *Working Lunch*? Taking a deep breath, I relaunched: 'I mean, I've been in similar situations and you do feel ... like a pratdigger.'

There! I'd related my own experiences to the Prime Minister's *and* managed to slip in one of our words. If you took our meaning of 'someone who attracts prats' it doesn't really make sense, but the word was out there. I was so relieved I managed to follow it with the tiniest of jokes: 'But he's done the right thing; he's got back on the horse. He probably would have been tempted to phone in sick, but that's not a good long-term solution for a prime minister.'

Phone in sick! What a funny idea for the Prime Minister to phone in sick! Andrew Neil even chuckled audibly. I'd done well.

And so did Gordon Brown. I'm not sure if he'd been listening to my introduction in the same way as I'd been following Jenny's but after our build-up he came out and did his stuff (not using any made-up words as far as I could tell) and unlike his first Prime Minister's Questions outing, he spoke commandingly.

Satisfied with how I'd performed first time round, the producers turned to me for more in-depth analysis after Brown had finished: 'Well let's see if our expert, the comedian Alex Horne, agreed with that,' said Jenny. I'd never been called an expert before. I blushed. 'So Alex,' she continued regardless, 'do you think he did a better job this time?'

'I do, yeah, I think he held his own.' Yes, I said 'yeah'; a bit colloquial, quite urban, pretty cool. Well done me. 'Performance-wise', (is that a phrase?) 'there were no tears or tantrums and if I had someone like David Cameron heckling me I think I would lose it. I'd go on a mental safari and just break down. So I thought he did well.'

In the space of twenty minutes, two of our Verbal Seeds had gone out on BBC2 in a historic programme analysing the first and second speeches of the UK's fifty-second prime minister. And even though Jenny followed my use of pratdigger with the quip: 'no tears, no tantrums, and not many jokes either. He must have taken your advice' (does she not know that I was the inventor of *the* tiddly-wink factory joke?), I felt enormously pleased with myself. I skipped back over Parliament Square – then realised I was still wearing my microphone so skipped back, gave it to the sound man, and then walked back to the Tube again, not skipping this time, but still in a more cheery fashion than usual.

The very next day another letter arrived from Leeds:

> Dear Alex,
>
> Thank you for attending the recent *Countdown* auditions in London.
>
> I am sorry to inform you that you were unsuccessful in gaining a place on the show.
>
> I would like to say how much we enjoyed meeting you and wish you all the best for the future.
>
> Once again, thank you for taking the time and trouble to attend, I hope you continue to watch and enjoy *Countdown*.
>
> [The Associate Producer]

I *had* done as badly as I'd feared and after the confirmation I didn't leave the house for two days. For the three months before I'd been telling everyone I encountered that I had this audition coming up. I was convinced I'd breeze through, that I'd get on telly, that I'd say my words in the *Countdown* studio. Now I had to admit that I'd failed. 'What did you do wrong?' I was asked repeatedly over the following weeks by people who presumed it'd be easy. I had no reply.

I couldn't face telling my mum. Instead I resolved to try again. By return of mail I asked for another audition. You can apply three times to be on the programme,[31] I was quite prepared to blow all my chances in one glorious shoot-out.

---

31 I should point out that this rule has since changed, so you can now apply any number of times. If you thrice fail, try, try again. Unless you're absolutely positive you've had enough humiliation for one lifetime.

To my surprise, it was just a fortnight before a third letter from Leeds invited me to my second audition in London – in just six weeks' time. I was amazed another opportunity had arisen so soon but, the letter said, the producers were still looking for contestants for the forthcoming series and I had another chance. Determined not to make the same mistakes again, I cleared my diary for a full forty-eight hours before the allotted audition day, downloaded hundreds of conundrums from the Internet, slept and practised hard. With just two lives remaining I needed to nail it this time. There was no way, I thought, I could handle the pressure of a final *Countdown* chance.

Apart from an appearance on television's best programme, I felt there was still something lacking from the project. Our new words were doing fine, but they were almost too subtle. They weren't making a splash. So instead of simply substituting new verbal ideas that looked a bit like old verbal ideas I decided we needed to be bolder. It was late in the day, with just a year until my thirtieth birthday, but I informed the Rare Men that we needed to come up with a brand-new word: a word, unlike the previous seeds, that really hadn't been seen before; a new combination of letters, nothing too wacky or ugly, but something that we could truly say was ours. I asked them to think, yet again, of a concept – not one of those clever terms that you get in the *Guardian* to describe an amusing social phenomenon, but something more fundamental that we could all recognise and understand and on which we could bestow the perfect moniker.

We needed a word that described a phenomenon, like wiki, that hadn't been named before. This would be the ultimate Verbal Seed, a seed we could throw our colossal collective weight behind and spread with confidence and abandon. A truly original word whose progress we could track as it sped its way from person to person, town to town, country to country.

We needed to come up with a new 'chav'; our very own 'booty-licious'.

The Rare Men dutifully stepped up to the mark once again, suggesting a plethora of imaginative ideas for this hitherto unlabelled concept. 'How about a word for something that is done for money rather than art or love?' proposed Mr Goudy-Stout, 'or the one song you like from an album, which is why you bought the album or people you nod to in the street but who you never have a conversation with or scooter drivers who are shit at driving?'

These were excellent suggestions, recognisable but unnamed things that would benefit from their own tags. But after much soul-searching I realised the word I wanted us to spread (and at this point I admit I was ignoring the democratic aspect of the project and behaving like the egotistical megalomaniac behind the ultimately vainglorious self-important narcissistic project we all feared I might be) had been under my nose the whole time.

19

I started this project because I was worried about the passing of time and wanted to ensure I left my mark somewhere along the way. The trigger was my ten thousandth day on earth and *that* was exactly the concept we would name. That was the idea we would solidify in a word and share with the world.

As you might just remember, this landmark does have a name: tkday. But that is *our* name. We invented 'tkday', a word we felt was ripe for the job. How well did it do with you? Did it snag your eyes as they moved across that early page? Or did you accept it as a word you just hadn't heard of? I suspect 'tkday' did strike you as a bit odd. It is a strange-looking little word. But a lot of thought went into its creation.

I was convinced the subject itself was a good one. For a start, we love birthdays. Our ruling queen, the Queen, loves them so much she has two. Indeed we love any reason to celebrate a day: Christmas, Easter, St Patrick's Day, both the Queen's birthdays, Friday, Saturday, Sunday, even thirsty Thursday, Bank Holiday Mondays and, particularly, New Year's Eve, even though it merely represents the passing of more time. There was definitely room for one more special occasion. I remember learning at school that the French celebrate another birthday on the day in which a Saint with the same name as themselves has their 'Saint's Day'. If that happened in this country, we'd all change our names to 'Wednesday'. We love special days; they give us something to look forward to. 'Wednesday Horne' would have a fun-filled life.

For too long now we've been chained to the Gregorian system (well, since 1752 in England, 170 years after Pope Gregory XIII decreed Aloysius Lilius's system of leap years was definitely the best idea and the rest of Europe took heed), a predictable plodding arrangement that sees Christmas landing coldly in the middle of winter every single year. By focusing more on this decimal idea of counting days in the thousands, we could celebrate mini-tkdays ('kdays', to be precise) at different times of the year every thousand days. It would be exciting! As well as Christmas every December, we'd celebrate Jesus' tkdays with his next one, when he'll be 760,000 days old, landing on 16 January 2027; two Christmases in one month = double Christmas![32]

We shouldn't shun the idea of a 'tkday' simply because it's an unusual measurement. People were suspicious of the metric system, but 'kilometres' and 'litres' are now well established in the language, if not on road signs or in pubs just yet. In Allan Metcalf's *Predicting New Words* he includes a cheering story about a nine-year-old Verbal Gardener, 'the youngest successful word coiner on record', who succeeded spectacularly with a novel number. In 1939 a mathematician at Columbia University called Edward Kasner wrote a book with his colleague James R. Newman called *Mathematics and the Imagination*. Neither of these men was nine years old but as they themselves wrote, 'Words of wisdom are spoken by children as least as often by scientists.'* They continued:

> The name 'googol' was invented by a child (Dr. Kasner's nine-year-old nephew) who was asked to think up a name for

---

32 For those of you who are worried about the lingering effects of *scriptio continua*, the 'Gregorian system' is definitely not a system whereby one decides to name a child 'Greg' or 'Ian'.

a very big number, namely, 1 with a hundred zeros after it. He was very certain that this number was not infinite, and therefore equally certain that it had to have a name. At the same time that he suggested 'googol' he gave a name for a still larger number: 'Googolplex'. A googolplex is much larger than a googol, but is still finite, as the inventor of the name was quick to point out. It was suggested that a googolplex should be 1, followed by writing zeros until you get tired.[33]

The child, unnamed in that book, was called Milton Sirotta (or Siroter, depending on whose account of the story you trust) and today his 'googol' is not only in the dictionary, it's also the first word many of us type when using the Internet, with Google inspired by Milton's term and the most popular search engine on earth.

Nor was Milton's achievement unprecedented. In the sixteenth century the mathematician Robert Recorde, a fellow of All Souls College, Oxford University, coined the word 'zenzizenzizenzic' to describe a very large figure (a number to the power of eight, or, in Recorde's own words, 'the square of squares squared' from *zenzic*, a German word from the Italian *censo*, meaning 'squared'). As ludicrous (and as close to French headbutt challenger Zinédine Zidane) as it looks, this word did indeed make it into the online version of the *OED*, which lists it as a 'historical curiosity'. Surely 'tkday' could be granted entry on similar grounds?

Even more impressive (if that's possible) is the fact that in the same 'Recorde book' as he invented the Z-word (which contains

---

33 Though charming, this wasn't a mathematical enough definition for the professors, who went on to pin a 'googolplex' down as 'a specific finite number, with so many zeros after the 1 that the number is a googol'. This is a ridiculous figure: 'There would not be enough room to write it, if you went to the farthest star, touring all the nebulae and putting down zeros every inch of the way,' so I for one am glad there's a reasonably lengthed word for it.

more 'z's than any other in the dictionary), the mathematician introduced the '='. Yes, in his *Whetstone of Witte*, written in 1557, he was the very first person to use the 'equals sign' with the following sentence:

> I will sette as I doe often in woorke use, a pair of paralleles, or Gemowe [twin] lines of one lengthe, thus: ==========, bicause noe 2 thynges, can be moare equalle.

It may not look exactly the same as the neat '=' we use today, but there's no denying the lineage. And I like the fact that his 'pair of paralleles' were about an inch long. Why not That could only have made maths more satisfying: 5 x 5 ==========25. That's better. And, in case you're wondering, while the originators of '+', '-' and 'x' are frustratingly anonymous, we do know that the division sign (÷) was first used in an algebra book from 1659 called *Teutshe algebra* by Johann Rahn (who also designed '∴', the symbol for 'therefore'). Back in the sixteenth century and more literary circles, the Dutch humanist Desiderius Erasmus (whom I include in this mathematical paragraph in honour of the palindrome, 'sums are not set as a test on Erasmus') coined the name 'lunulae' (meaning 'moon-like' in Latin), a term still used today to describe round brackets (six of which I've used in this sentence alone).

So despite appearances and precedents, 'tkday' could become as standard as 'google' or the equals sign. Just because it doesn't 'fit in' with the way the earth spins round the sun shouldn't matter. We're humans! We can do what we want! And lots of humans do do what they want! A *pal* is a Hindi measure of time equal to twenty-four seconds. Why measure twenty-four seconds? Because it's a laugh! A *ghari* is twenty-four minutes! They're having fun with it! The *OED* includes 'sesquihoral', an adjective meaning 'lasting an hour and a half'. Yes! The Chinese word *xun* means either a ten-day period in a month or a decade in someone's life. The Indian word *lakh* means 100,000, while 'crore' means 10,000,000 and a *crorepati* is someone with 10,000,000 rupees (hence *Slumdog Crorepati*, the name of Danny Boyle's film in India). That's the spirit! Counting to ten is fun. Why do you think we've got ten fingers on our paddles? It's so we can count the kdays till our tkday! That's the sort of speech I was preparing to give when the tkday celebrations started taking over the entire country.

At first glance it might appear an ugly, cumbersome word. It's certainly unlike normal English, with no vowel separating the hard T and K. The only other example I've found of those two letters standing side by side at the front of a word is in Jonathon Green's book of slang where he tells us that meat killed in an abbatoir is called 'teekay' or 'TK meat' in butchers' slang (who knew there was butchers' slang?). HK, according to Green, is the term for meat that's been killed at home (the T of TK presumably stands for 'trade'). On balance, I'd say I'd rather have a TK burger than one which vaguely implies the death of a pet.

But there are plenty of examples of words which look similarly spiky and unusual prospering, especially in recent times. The 'word' 'Y2K', for example, sprung up during the nineties as a modern alternative to 'the year two thousand', particularly with reference to the mythical millennium bug. Y2K does now appear in several dictionaries and would, I'm sure, be more widespread, if only there had been a global catastrophe when the millennium ticked over.

In *Predicting New Words*, Metcalf goes on to examine the reasons why some words fail and some succeed. 'Y2K', in his opinion, is now only moderately well known not because of its looks, but because the year itself has passed by. He also spends a lot of time discussing the word 'sputnik', another word with a slight resemblance to our 'tkday'. 'Sputnik' was the Russian word for the first satellite sent into orbit in 1957 meaning, literally, 'something that is travelling with a traveller'. At the time, as Metcalf explains, the word made quite a splash: 'Upon hearing the news and the name *sputnik*, Clarence L. Barnhart, editor-in-chief of the *Thorndike-Barnhart Comprehensive Desk Dictionary*, pulled the page where *sputnik* would appear, consigned a lesser word to oblivion, and inserted a three-line definition of *sputnik* in its place. Only then would he allow the new printing of the *Thorndike-Barnhart* to proceed.' Fifty years on, however, and the real meaning of the word is hardly known. 'Perhaps', Metcalf argues, 'it looked too strange.'

Strangeness in a word, however, should not be dismissed as a flaw. An odd-looking word can soar to remarkable, even record-breaking heights, simply because it looks so odd. After all, the most universally understood term in the whole of the English language is the bizarre two-letter word, 'OK'. We all say 'OK' all the time. We don't think about it. It constantly seems to be on the tip of our tongue, the first sounds to pop out when we are asked anything at all. It has become an adult 'mama', despite the facts that it doesn't resemble other English words (except, now, 'tkday') and that we still don't really know where it came from.

The birth of 'OK' is perhaps the ultimate Verbal Gardening story because, while it almost certainly did sprout from just one person, its branches, stems and roots are now so gnarled and intertwined it's impossible to work out for sure who that one person is. There are many, many theories. Allan Metcalf insists that he knows the truth; that 'OK' definitely represents a deliberate misspelling of the phrase 'all correct' as 'orl korrect'. In the late 1830s, he tells us, there was a 'craze for humorous abbreviations' in America with 'OW' also used to mean 'all right.' Not hilarious, but humorous. The following is an extract from the *Boston Morning Post*, 23 March 1839: '. . . perhaps if he should return to Boston, via Providence, he of the Journal, and his train-band, would have the "contribution box", et ceteras, o.k. – all correct – and cause the corks to fly, like sparks, upward.' Despite making no sense whatsoever, this is, in Metcalf's opinion, the first-ever published OK.

According to Metcalf, this obscure jokey abbreviation survived and flourished mainly because it was picked up by a candidate in the following year's presidential election. Martin Van Buren, born in Kinderhook, New York, was given the nickname 'Kinderhook Cabbage Planter' by his witty rivals, the Whigs. His own Democrats combined this with the fashionable 'OK' to spin the name to their advantage with the slogan, 'Old Kinderhook, OK?' And that was that; a not very good joke made up by someone *whose identity is still unknown* was made enormously popular by a politician.

But this ungainly anecdote is far from being the only explanation. Others suggest 'OK' is a simple version of the Scottish 'och aye' or the Finnish *oikea* meaning 'correct'. Some maintain it represents the Haitian city 'Aux Cayes', famous for its rum, or the dock in New Orleans where workers would take cotton *au quai*. The Germans swear that Baron von Steuben signed documents '*Ober Kommando*' when he fought with the US Army in the War of Independence; confectionery fans contend rather that it grew from biscuits made for the army in the Civil War by Orrin Kendall & Sons, who stamped 'OK' on their products in their factory in Chicago.[34] It might be from Greek (*ola kala*), Wolof or other West African languages (*o ke* or *waw kay*) or even

---

34 There is another folk etymology from the Civil War linking the word 'hooker' to a general called Joseph Hooker, whose undisciplined men were famous for frequenting the redlight district. While the general and his naughty men did exist, the word, like the profession, is much older, probably and predictably coming from the verb 'to hook'.

Choctaw Indian (*okeh*). It could be a reversal of the boxing KO. Or it might be a mixture of all of these things.

But I like to think it *was* one man who invented it, one man who lent his own initials to create the most famous expression in the world. So I'm going to give my backing to a humble railway freight agent called Obediah Kelly who is said to have written his initials on any documents he checked. Working on the trains, we are asked to believe, these letters were then dispatched out in every direction, taking the meaning of 'fine' along with them, in much the same way as my 'I am the bollo!' messages were being sent hither and thither on Tubes and trains in the UK. It's no more likely than any of the other hypotheses, but it's the one I want to believe and that makes it as good as fact in my mind.

I try to reflect a little of that fogginess in the etymology of 'tkday'. It looks like it's probably from 10K, short for ten kilo (the Greek prefix for a thousand). But the letters *could* be the initials of one of our finest Rare Men, the ever creative Mr Elephant, who actually celebrated his own thirtieth birthday on the same day we launched 'tkday'. Despite being an elder statesman (decades younger than our Health and Safety watchdog Mr Matisse but older than everyone else), Mr Elephant is the sort of person who has always been bad at adult things like bank statements, driving or not getting locked out of your own house on your birthday and waking up the next morning on someone else's sofa with red wine on your T-shirt and said sofa, so a coming-of-age moment might just have been named in his honour.

I need to believe that individuals can successfully coin words. Encouragingly, the second-most universally understood word or phrase in English was unquestionably the work of one man, although his actual name has been rather forgotten in the process. For it was that man, John Styth Pemberton, who sloshed together a load of cocoa nuts, caffeine, coca leaves and various other secret ingredients in a bath-tub in his backyard in 1886 and thus invented Coca-Cola. He may only have sold his concoction for the modest price of $283.39, but the immortality of the name is priceless. It's the world's only successful product with two names, 'Coke' and 'Cola', something Mr Roman was aiming to emulate with 'honk' and 'hoot'.

A century after its creation, the Coca-Cola company brought out its own new drink, OK Soda, harnessing, in theory, the two most powerful brands in history (if we can call OK a brand, which we can: it's a brand). The deep and meaningless slogan for OK Soda went, 'The true nature of OK-ness is elusive. OK-ness embraces mistakes and contradictions. It is optimistic, yet ironic.' Unfortunately that doesn't really make sense and people were too confused to buy the drink. But it does show how unusual-looking words can be used. 'OK-ness' is in the *Oxford English Dictionary*, defined more sensibly as, 'The fact or quality of being OK' and used as early as 1935. If 'OK-ness' is in, 'tkday' could surely follow.

After all, like those madcap abbreviators from the 1830s, we modern folk love sharp shortnings and kool spelling. Tkday fits right into modern vernacular. We watch endless TV with our TV dinners and try to buy KY jelly from TK Maxx. In fact, it's this letter 'K' that is currently so fashionable. *K-9* is one of the best films ever to come out of Hollywood* (I know I'm in the minority here), everybody likes Peter Kay, Jay Kay from Jamiroquai and J. K. from Rowling (that's 'everybody' in the loosest sense – i.e. 'some people') and the breakfast cereal Special K has almost made us forget about the KKK. A simple 'K' transforms the mundane 'today' into an exciting 'tkday', which itself fits neatly into the contemporary trend of text-speak or txtonyms. 'Tkday' is already a snappy abbreviation that can sit happily beside 'lol's and emoticons, blogs and podcasts. It's book. Which is predictive-texting slang for cool.[35] Which is a synonym of wicked. Which now means good.

Tkday is all these things. Have I convinced you yet?

---

35 If you try to type 'cool' in a text message with predictive texting switched on the word 'book' may be suggested first. Ingenious kids have therefore started using it as a new word for 'cool'. This process has been named 'synokia' by an Oxford-educated physicist called Chris Simpson in the English Project's book *Kitchen Table Lingo*. Other examples that may yet become synonymous are 'awake' and 'cycle', 'shot' and 'pint', 'woohoo' and 'zonino'.

20

With a year and two weeks until our self-appointed closing date, I proudly announced the birth of our final word:

Tkday (noun). A person's 10,000th day on earth, traditionally celebrated with a tkday party (the traditions of which are still to be ironed out). It represents the time in someone's life when they actually are an adult (rather than sixteen, eighteen or twenty-one years – which are arbitrary and wrong). It's about this time in life that you should probably know how to change a tyre/fuse/partner, not feel too awkward when you meet other adults and have vague but nagging thoughts about starting a pension.

Unfortunately my attempt to spread news of its arrival on my preferred radio station was unsuccessful. Five million people listen to Chris Evans's show, which means that only a tiny percentage of those who try to get more actively involved can succeed. The one time I did actually penetrate his protective layer of researchers and producers with a message sent to the studio, my joint favourite DJ (alongside Radio Gloucestershire's John Rockley) read out something crucially different to the text I'd sent in.

In a typically fervent feature called 'Office News', Chris read a number of texts from office workers, including:

Chris! We celebrated office boy Chip's birthday today! He's 10,000 days old and we had a cake. He's about 27 and a third by the way.

That's my brother Chip! But it's not my word! Whether it was by a member of his staff or a part of Chris's own brain, the 'tk' was edited out and 'birth' put in place. Such a slight difference but so crucial. Hence the continued success of Chinese Whispers on the dinner party circuit. He did pause after the text before saying, 'Oh I see, so it's a special birthday,' but he never said the word 'tkday'. I was furious. I even turned Radio 2 off. For a bit.

This was not the start I was hoping for. Nor did things get any better very quickly. Our high-concept digital birthday proved incredibly hard to bring up in conversation (after all, mine had passed almost two years previously). I therefore endeavoured to find the people for whom it was most relevant; twenty-seven-year-olds. But not just any old twenty-seven-year-olds, celebrity twenty-seven-year-olds, famous people who had their tkdays coming up in the next few months.

It was, though, a rather chastening list to draw up. Logically these people were all younger than me. But while I could cope with comparing myself to Darius Danesh or Kerry Katona, maybe even Paris Hilton or Jamelia, the rest were just too successful for my liking: England captain John Terry, tennis star Lleyton Hewitt, Beyoncé's colleague Kelly Rowland, these were all people of the same vintage. Elijah Wood, Christina Aguilera, Justin Timberlake, Vanessa Carlton – they'd all managed to achieve so much that their names seemed destined to be remembered in the future, even if they didn't get a word in the dictionary. It wasn't fair. If any of these people wanted to get their word in the dictionary they'd just have to tell their adoring public and the work would be done for them. I'm sure even Kanzi the Bonobo (born on the same day as footballistic badboy Alan Smith) could coin a phrase if he so wished. And he's a bonobo.[36]

Nevertheless, I knuckled down and got on with the task at hand, sending each and every one of these stars a home-made tkday card via their agents and spreading news of their impending landmark through their respective fansites. It was time-consuming and, on the surface, unrewarding. No one sent me a thank-you card. Not even Vanessa Carlton.

But I like to think that in some small way my afternoon spent cutting out letters, sticking on sparkly sprinkle dust and sending mysterious tkday cards around the world will have made a difference. Presuming the agents didn't shred them on the spot, each of these people would now have known the tkday concept. And celebrities, as we all know, rule the world. If Christina Aguilera celebrated her tkday, we'd all know about it.

With almost exactly a year until our self-appointed closing date, my second *Countdown* audition loomed into view.

While I was boning up* for the test, the series shown on TV had been nearing its end and the quality of competitors in the final eight was daunting. A quietly assured young man (well, probably the same age as me) from Northern Ireland called David looked the hot favourite, finding 'diamines', 'ovates', 'nortena', and 'tzarina' in a single episode. I'd never heard of these words before; nor, to everyone's surprise, had Susie Dent. But there they were, in her dictionary, so he definitely wasn't making them up.

Without Susie's reassuring presence in the Dictionary Corner of my screen, the small amount of confidence I still possessed may

---

36 A bonobo, as well as being a brilliant word, is an ape. Kanzi, as well as being in his late twenties, has featured on the cover of both *Newsweek* and *Time* magazine because of his ability to communicate.

well have crumbled to nothing. For as well as humbly admitting she didn't in fact know every single word in the language, her daily monologues on the origins of other, slightly more common words were consistently fascinating and gainfully distracting, especially when they involved individual Verbal Gardening stories.

It was thanks to *Countdown*, for instance, that I discovered that American President Theodore Roosevelt was a Verbal Gardener. During a hunting trip in Mississippi in November 1902, an American Black Bear was cornered by dogs, beaten and tied to a willow tree by his men, then offered to the hitherto unsuccessful President as an easy target. Admirably, Roosevelt refused to shoot the sitting bear but ordered it to be killed by others in an act of mercy. As soon as this scene was captured in a cartoon in the *Washington Post* days later, toys were created with the name 'Teddy's Bear' and, Bob's your uncle,* just eighty years later, my little brother Chip named his bear Ted.

Yes, I thought, names can become words. Games could become a word!

The jockey James Foreman Sloane had similarly circuitous success. You've almost certainly never heard his name before, but I'm sure you'll have used (or at least heard of) a phrase that came into existence thanks only to him. Before accidentally turning his hand to matters linguistic he pioneered the 'monkey riding' position jockeys still ape today. He was, however, a rather difficult man and, after being struck from the jockey club on account of his arrogance, he died alone and in poverty. 'Todhunter' was his rather splendid (other) middle name and on his death the *Washington Post* wrote, 'everything of Tod's is gone'. The phrase 'on one's tod', however, was born.

One must make sacrifices, I thought, if one is to succeed!

A Duke of Saxony, Susie explained one afternoon, triggered the entrance of 'turncoat' to the language sometime around

1557 with an ingenious reversible coat. Normally blue (the colour of the Saxons), he would turn the white (the colour of the French) inside out whenever strolling around land bordering France and that, apparently, was enough to fool his enemies and for the word 'turncoat' to be born.

In the nineteenth century, Arthur Wellesley, the first Duke of Wellington, wore rubber boots before anyone else (*and* had the synonymous beef dish named after him); James Brudenell, seventh Earl of Cardigan, modelled a knitted jumper that opened at the front during the Crimean War; and over in a slightly camper field, Jules Léotard was brave enough not only to perform daring deeds on the flying trapeze, but to do so wearing the first ever skin-tight one-piece garment covering his torso and midriff but leaving his lovely legs free and unsheathed. Unfortunately it wasn't until sixteen years after his early death that people starting using his surname to describe this economic article of clothing, so he wouldn't have known his name has lived on in such a dignified fashion.[37]

Clothing can work, I thought! The bollo brolly may have failed but the Verbal Gardening T-shirts might just make the difference!

There seemed to be limitless tales of words and phrases created by everyday people. 'That old chestnut' was originally an innocent line in a play called *Broken Sword* written by William Diamond in 1816. One character had a tendency to say the same joke over and over with very subtle changes – like Le Prov's reworking of my counter-productive gag; another char-

---

37 Readers might be familiar with today's 'unitard', also a skin-tight one-piece garment, but differing from the traditional leotard thanks to its long legs. They're a bit like a leotard and tights combo. Freddie Mercury, wrestlers and superheroes have all tended to wear them. They're a good example of how a word can be so accepted that speakers adapt it according to the traditional rules of their language even though those rules shouldn't really apply (the thing about the original 'tard' is not actually its' 'leo'-ness).

acter, Pablo, finally cracked and said, 'A chestnut. I have heard you tell the joke twenty times and I'm sure it was a chestnut!' The actor playing Pablo at the time found himself at a dinner party, away from the theatre, hosted by a pratdigger. One of the more prattish guests started telling a well-known corny* joke, and Pablo gave 'that old chestnut' its first airing outside of the play. Again, that one moment was enough. The conditions were right, the phrase was memorable and, like my Rare Men, the protagonists worked in the world of communication. They planted the seed (well, a nut), it grew and conkered all (that's the sort of joke of which Richard Whiteley would have been proud).

That's me! I thought. If I can bury 'honest' in a play, or 'honk' in a dinner party they too might blossom!

Susie even recounted the story of a comedian who managed to invent his own adjective in the late sixteenth century. In Italy, she said, there was an improvised form of theatre called *Commedia dell'arte* which featured, amongst various stock characters, a clown called Zanni. Zanni is the Venetian version of Gianni, short for Giovanni, the Italian version of John. But it is also the root of our word 'zany'. Sure, this was a more general clown figure rather than one specific performer, but again it proved that my plan was possible.

Comedy can help, I thought. People remember the things that make them laugh!

Hearing these stories halfway through a gentle word-quiz, a cup of tea half drunk beside me, was both soothing and beguiling. Like my favourite word books, Susie could whisk me back in time and show me those miraculous moments when words were born. At five past four every day I felt that with a little luck and a good story, anyone, including me, could coin their own word.

After weeks of particularly intense *Countdown* viewing in which I tried to match the lucky contestants who'd already made it, hours of playing Scrabble online, and several evenings devoted to the *Countdown* board game ('all the fun of the popular game show' – for 2–6 players, aged 10 to adult) with my brothers and sister-in-law, I was feeling confident on the day of my second audition. On the Tube journey back to the same London Weekend Television office block I practised using the sheet of conundrums provided in the board-game box and enjoyed the thought that any nosy commuters might think I was some sort of deranged genius.

As I stepped into the lobby, a sense of *déjà vu* was augmented by the sight of shaven-headed Vic, my neighbour at the last auditions, who was sat staring into the middle distance, tense but apparently focused. I signed in and took the seat next to him, trying to edge into his zone. Lorraine Kelly's daytime show, *LKToday* (Lo: tkday!) was being filmed in the same building and around us milled innumerable women who had congregated for a special feature on fake tans. I found it hard to concentrate on anything but their glowing faces (they ranged from 'spicy sandalwood' to 'ginger glow' with most at about the 'rich Havana level' of Dulux orangeness), and five minutes later I grew impatient and said hello to Vic.

'Hello,' he replied.

That was probably about the highlight of our chat. We were both desperate to succeed and now was not the time for niceties (or nice ties for that matter; I seem to remember something as gaudy as the girls hanging round his neck in true *Countdown* tradition). He did tell me he was bitterly disappointed last time round; after his initial nine-letter word he'd faded fast and had known he hadn't made it before we even reached the last numbers game.

We'd just wished each other luck for this next audition when the same efficient researcher emerged and said she was ready for us. This time there were just three of us: Vic, me and Gail, an incongruously glamorous lady who I'd presumed was here to apply some unnatural colour to her skin. The limited numbers meant the temptation to cheat was thankfully removed. We were sat at three compass points of the oval table with the researcher at North, our life in her hands. As soon as she'd explained the procedure to Gail we were off.

First up: **I T T E N E N I S**. If you want to play along, I'll let you know what I found in the footnotes.[37]

Then **T A L T I E N V E**. If you're not playing along, I was doing OK, but unspectacularly.[38]

This form continued with **H U O I S E D A M**.[39]

From then on in I was, if not on fire, then definitely pretty close to combusting. The next combinations were **P L A G D U R E D** and **C O U P L I S T E**[40] before I succeeded in making 414 out of **50, 3, 9, 1, 1** and **9**.[41] I even worked out two thirds of the conundrums thanks to: **T R E E R A M B O** and **P A R T Y I N F O**.[42] I'd definitely done significantly better than last time, but had I done enough? I'd missed more nine-letter words but I had found some maximums that neither Vic nor Gail had spotted. He'd done well with the numbers but I was sure I'd sneaked it.

Back in the fresh air we said our goodbyes, Vic despondent, convinced he'd failed again; Gail stylish, still maybe in the wrong place.

I could now only hope.

---

37 Vic and I both got 'sentient' but missed 'intestine'.

38 Again, I missed the maximum 'ventilate' but did grasp 'nettle' and 'latent', both longer words than Gail's.

39 I didn't see 'housemaid' but did get 'shamed'.

40 I spotted 'upgraded' and 'slopiest'.

41 $(9-1) \times (50 + 1) + 9 - 3$.

42 'Barometer' and 'profanity' – it's so easy when you see it.

PART THREE

The doors to the *OED* are open as never before, and if you know how the system works, you can squeeze in and leave your mark.

Balderdash and Piffle – English Words and Their Curious Origins,
Alex Games

21

When Viscount Horatio Nelson was ordered by semaphore to cease attacking the Danish Navy he raised a telescope to his blind eye, said 'Order, what order? I see no ships,' and the term 'turn a blind eye' was born. Almost two hundred years later, on the eve of the first Gulf War, Saddam Hussein addressed his nation and told them they were about to become locked in 'the mother of all battles'. Thus the old Arabic expression 'mother of all' was brought crashing into modern Western vernacular. A decade later, George W. Bush looked down at the good people of Bentonville, Arkansas, uttered the immortal phrase, 'They misunderestimated me,' and managed to create his own new word. Now, as leader of the Verbal Gardening project, it was my turn to act. The Rare Men were tired. I had to take control.

Television, it appeared, was the medium I needed to conquer. Dictionary authorities seem to pay particularly close attention to someone saying a word several times on a high-profile show, especially if other high-profile people are involved. So it was that sketch queen Catherine Tate's catchphrase 'bovvered' was named 'Word of the Year' for 2006 by the compilers of the *OED* and featured at length in Susie Dent's latest *Language Report* on emerging vocabulary.

This despite the fact that 'bovvered' isn't, in my opinion, a very good word at all. It's lazy, the product of esquivalience rather than inspiration. Yes, it's a new word, but it's only really a mispronunciation of an old one. It's just a shift of 'th' to 'vv'. We could all do that. We could all say 'I've got toovvache', 'I'm your favver', or 'he's vve vvinking woman's Vviery Henry'; is that enough to get a word in the dictionary? When Mr Elephant came up with 'paddles' for 'hands' he first suggested the more subtle 'honds', a change I resisted because it just didn't seem far enough from the original. 'No one will use it,' I said, 'it sounds too similar to "hands"'.[43] But perhaps I'd missed a trick. Perhaps subtlety is the key. By 'coining' a word that is basically already a word, Tate had found a cunning short cut that I'd driven straight past.

She'd also said her word repeatedly on a programme watched by millions of people, some of whom were fairly influential. The Queen, the actual Queen, used the word when she met Tate at the Royal Variety Show in November 2005. 'Is one bovvered?' she asked. Our former Prime Minister Blair then jumped on the bandwagon, saying the catchphrase during 2007's *Comic Relief* appeal. How could I compete with that?

Well, I did have our *World in One City* project, which we were now close to completing, thanks largely to Mr Palatino's hard work, and which was still garnering more than its fair share of media attention.

My contact at *The Times*, for example, got back in touch and asked me to write an article about my experience. Of course I was delighted to help, grateful again that I hadn't yet shut a potential door to my career with my fabricated words. With 'honk' making such good progress around the world, I decided to give 'bollo' a chance and was happily surprised when it slipped through the editors' net. Saying 'bollo' live on Irish radio is one thing, getting it printed in *The Times* is quite another.

---

43 I was recently alerted to the fact that 'hond' is actually used instead of 'hand' in parts of Glasgow. You're welcome to use it yourselves if you think it stands a chance outside of the Scottish city.

This was my sentence:

Buoyed by our success, [Mr Palatino] and I pushed back the boundaries of our bollo Britishness by actually getting into a conversation with our Iraqi, a lovely lady called Thana who told us she was thrilled that Saddam had been executed.

Yes, remarkable alliteration in the first half, and an attempt, albeit clumsy, at politics in the second. But more remarkable as far as I was concerned was a sentence later in the article which read:

We knocked on every door on my street in Kensal Green and were told to p*** off only once.

I hadn't inserted those asterisks there (they refer to 'i', 's' and 's', by the way. Just in case you thought they might be 'u', 's' and 'h'; 'l', 'o' and 'p'; or 'o', 'n' and 'y'); they were the work of the sub-editor. In their highly qualified eyes, 'piss' was far ruder than 'bollo'. I don't know what exactly they thought 'bollo' meant in my description of Britishness, but they certainly didn't think it offensive.

Bear in mind that 'piss' itself is, I hope you'll all agree (otherwise this will have been a treacherous couple of paragraphs), a fairly harmless word. It was included in the dictionary decades before granny's word was let in,[44] and before being cast out onto the street during the more refined Victorian* era, it was used by all and sundry unthinkingly for its first four hundred years.

---

44 In honour of her outburst, 'granny's word' is now my alternative euphemism to the overused 'F-word'. I'm hoping it'll catch on. 'Don't you dare say granny's word at the table!' a shocked mother might protest. Or 'granny sword'. That could work too. Perhaps as a mythical weapon with which to threaten foul-mouthed children.

It even snuck into the 1611 King James Authorised Version of the Bible (Isaiah 36, 12: 'But Rabshakeh said, Hath my master sent me to thy master and to thee to speak these words? Hath he not sent me to the men that sit upon the wall, that they may eat their own dung, and drink their own piss with you?'), so if *The Times* deemed such an innocuous word worthy of censure, it says a lot about the innocent nature of 'bollo'. Just as I'd hoped, it looks too cheery really to be rude.

But part of me does wish they'd asterisked 'bollo' too, mainly because I'd be curious to know how readers would have reacted. If the sentence had read 'pushed back the boundaries of our b**** Britishness' an intriguing guessing game would have ensued. 'Brown', maybe? 'Black'? They don't sound quite right. But what else? I suppose 'blunt' would have been the main contender but, as explained earlier, that's rhyming slang for something far ruder nowadays.

In my desperation to succeed I was happy to let the meanings of my words slip slightly. I used 'pratdigger', for instance, to mean 'any sort of slightly below average person' in several interviews on the radio and in a couple of other, smaller newspapers. When invited to chat to Talksport's 'Hawksby and Jacobs', the radio presenters queried my usage of the word and I explained that it actually meant 'someone who is addicted to collecting things', a fourth meaning for the comical term. I think that 'obsessive gatherer' works for the word; I can imagine 'pratdiggers' frantically searching car boot sales every weekend for the final stamp for their collections, or going on eBay to find the final sticker for their Euro 2006 Panini sticker albums. While it's not our original meaning it is our original word, and that's all that matters. Once we've got it in the dictionary we can worry about the order in which the meanings should be printed.

Whilst on Talksport, by the way, Hawksby also asked me, 'So,

I heard you wrote your first joke for a cracker-joke-writing competition at Budgens. Can you remember the gag?' It's amazing how many people use Wikipedia as their main source of information nowadays.

Thanks to in-depth interviews such as this, I like to think, news of our global quest soon reached the most important people at BBC News, and one day we were asked to come into a studio and be interviewed by George Alagiah. I couldn't believe our luck. The main presenter of *BBC News At Six*, a national hero with his own OBE, was going to talk to us about our friend Mr Goudy-Stout's idea on telly. Remarkable. This was our chance to pull off a 'bovvered'.

Unfortunately, this wasn't for the *News At Six*. George Alagiah is also the presenter of BBC World's *World News Today* programme at 1 p.m., and this was the programme on which we were to feature. BBC World, in case you're not familiar with it, is the televisual equivalent of the World Service. It is transmitted across the planet, but you can't actually watch it from within the UK. So in terms of that *World in One City* Venn diagram, this interview was also missing the target area. It was certainly closer to the bit in the middle of the circles (foreigners who also live in London) than Radio Gloucestershire, but unfortunately it was only aimed at foreigners who haven't moved to the UK.

That notwithstanding, as the BBC's flagship international news and current affairs television channel, BBC World does have the largest audience of any BBC channel, in fact of any news channel in the world. According to figures from June 2008, it's available in 282 million homes, in 1.6 million hotel rooms, on fifty-seven cruise ships, forty-two airlines and thirty-four mobile-phone platforms, and over 78 million people watch it every week; so potentially a few more than I'd managed to broadcast my words to so far and ten times more than those who watched Catherine Tate's Christmas special. If I could let one of our words loose on George Alagiah OBE's BBC news programme, those viewers were bound to believe they were indeed actual words. Surely some of those 78 million people would absorb those words. And surely some of those people would then use those words themselves. After all, they had chosen to watch the BBC news because they trusted the content.

And clearly the BBC trusted me too. Despite talking about 'mental safaris' and 'pratdiggers' on BBC2, here I was again, about to talk live on one of its key news programmes. And just to make things even more surreal, we were that day's top story, shoving a scandal about Jacques Chirac, bomb attacks in Pakistan, a plane crash in Brazil and Tony Blair's new role as a peace envoy, down the running order.

Before going on air, the calm, attentive and dashing George had put us at ease. I'd say he was disarming, but I was still very much armed, ready to let off my word-weapons at the merest hint of an opening. As one o'clock approached we were shown to our seats and George was counted in.

'You are with *World News Today* from BBC World, I'm George Alagiah. Now, it's often said that the world is a global village,[45] or at least a global city, now two friends are trying to prove it . . . Well, Alex and [Mr Palatino] join me now in the studio. Thank you both for coming in.'

That's OK, George! we thought, but didn't say. Instead, he immediately asked Mr Palatino a technical question about why we were looking for 192 countries when there were well over 200 competing at the Olympics (we'd picked the smaller UN number simply because it was bound to be easier). Then he turned to me:

---

45 The phrase 'global village' was coined by Canadian clever man Marshall McLuhan in the early 1960s. And this footnote is more intelligent than anything I said in the studio.

'So, Alex, are there any themes that you've discovered running through the people you've met and their lives?'

This was going to be easy!

'Well, on a very superficial level,' I began confidently, 'everyone has said it's a very expensive place to live. Everything costs a lot of honk. It's a very expensive city to live in.'

Bang! I'd aimed, fired and hit the target. Take that 78 million people!

It was, without doubt, the greatest achievement of my life so far. I'd looked George in the eye, said 'everything costs a lot of honk', and I could see his eyes flicker in response. I could see him thinking 'a lot of honk? Honk's not a noun! Well, it can be a noun, but not in that sense! You don't pay for things using honks!' But there was nothing he could do. He couldn't stop the news. There was no button he could press to cope with a situation in which an interviewee uses a made-up word. There was no way he could stop my honk being heard around the world.

Unfortunately, I hadn't counted on the recoil. Reeling from the power of such a mighty verbal blow, my next sentence was one of the worst, quite possibly *the* worst – including the pathetically monosyllabic ones I came up with in my first five years – of my life:

'But I think on a sort of nicer note the main thing that everyone says is that they like London because of its cosmopolitan nature. I think we, I mean, because ... we realised very quickly that most of our friends actually are from Britain – not any more; we've got plenty now (*at this point I giggled*) – but um, people from Britain tend to maybe be more insular and don't embrace the cosmopolitan nature of the city but people have said they love the fact that it's a magnet for all these different countries.'

I've re-watched and re-read that a number of times and it makes no sense whatsoever. After telling George, quite unnecessarily, that most of my friends were from Britain, I then qualified my own narrow horizons by saying 'not any more; we've got plenty now'. What does that mean? 'We've got plenty'? I think I was grouping together everyone in the world who is not from Britain and saying that, yes, I 'had' lots of them. I might as well have said I'd 'done lots of them' too.

Understandably Mr Alagiah then took a deep breath and turned back to Mr Palatino. He continued talking to Mr Palatino for the rest of the interview, only returning to me to say thank you, with a rather quizzical look on his face, at the end of our feature. So I had broadcast our strongest word to a potential 282 million homes, in 1.6 million hotel rooms, on fifty-seven cruise ships, forty-two airlines and thirty-four mobile-phone platforms,[46] but I had also looked like an idiot in front of 78 million people. Even so, before gliding professionally on to the next world story, George noticed from our website that we still needed to meet someone from Angola. 'Well, I met an Angolan waiter last night,' he said, so quick, so cool. Off air, he didn't mention my outburst but did pass on the details of this South Central African man and the next day, we followed his instructions and ticked off another country. All things considered, it was a particularly useful episode of *World News Today*.

The new 'obsessive collector' meaning of 'pratdigger' was wheeled out again (along with the faithful 'honk') a couple of weeks later on both Capital Radio and BBC Wales in conversation with the magnificently Welsh Rhun Ap Iorwerth. For, after a frantic final few weeks, Mr Palatino and I had come to the conclusion of our *World in One*

---

46 I don't know what a mobile phone platform is either. I don't even know if it's a platform for mobile-phones or a mobile platform for ordinary phones. Either way, thirty-four sounds like rather a small number compared to a million and a half hotel rooms.

City project and were at last able to say whether or not London was the most cosmopolitan city in the world and the people of London (and, for some reason, Wales) wanted to hear us say it. So, after a year's worth of research, we did. And what we said was ...

Yes, it was.

Probably.

London was definitely the most cosmopolitan city in the world unless anyone else could be bothered to do similar research in New York, Montreal, Bahrain or Dubai and prove otherwise.

For we didn't actually manage to find someone from every single country in the world living in the capital; we found people from all but three of the UN's 192 nations. And we were pretty much satisfied that the remaining trio, the Pacific* islands of Tuvalu, Palau and the Marshall Islands, simply did not have representatives living in London. We'd done all we could and had proved that London was definitely 98.4 per cent of the world in one city.

It was a shame we hadn't ticked off the Marshall Islands because I was looking forward to meeting someone from the land that gave the world the 'bikini', although in the history of verbal invention the story of the skimpy swimwear is far more solemn than the name or item suggests. After dropping atomic bombs on two Japanese cities to bring the Pacific war to its awful conclusion in 1945, the United States continued to test the weapon on an atoll of these tiny islands called 'Bikini'. It just so happened that at the exact same point in history the fashion designers Jacques Heim and Louis Réard were independently designing the brand-new two-piece swimming costume. In what seems like the crassest link of all time, the power of the atomic bombs was then equated with the shockingness of the revealing swimsuit and the word leaped from the islands to the clothes. Remarkably, the reverberations of the launch of the bikini were so far-reaching that the swimsuit is now far more famous than the atoll (who even knows what an atoll is?[47]). And just like the leotard, it has since spawned further types of swimwear from the same word-structure, like the 'tankini', the 'monokini' or the 'mankini' modelled so fetchingly by Borat.

To read more about the characters and countries we came across, do have a look at www.worldinonecity.blogspot.com, but I must briefly mention Vanuatu, one of the more surprising countries that we did manage to track down. Dan, a music producer from this South Pacific republic, was our 121st find. Born on the island, he was brought to the UK by his (British) missionary parents at the age of four but could still represent Vanuatu at the Olympics (and would have a considerably larger chance of qualifying than for Team GB), so still counted on our list. I've singled out Vanuatu particularly because it was one of the countries I'd never heard of before commencing the project and because it's the source of my favourite story in *The Meaning of Tingo*.

'When the Duke of Edinburgh visits Vanuatu in the Pacific,' writes Jacot de Boinod, 'he is addressed as *oldfella PiliPili him b'long Missy Kween*, while Prince Charles is *Pikinini b'long Kween*.'

That's tremendous. It demonstrates both the exuberant way in which words can travel around the world and the inherent ridiculousness of a monarchy. And if I never actually manage to get a word in the dictionary I'd still die as happy as Larry* if someone somewhere in the world kept my name alive in such a creative way.

Also, the Vanuatu national anthem is called 'Yumi Yumi Yumi'. Honestly. In both senses of the word.

---

47 I do. Well, I looked it up. On Wikipedia. It's an island of coral that either partially or completely encircles a lagoon. Or it might not be.

22

Galvanised* by the completion of one project and with a whole lot more spare time now that I didn't need to ask everyone I met if they or anyone they knew were from Equatorial Guinea, I hastily set up the tkday website (www.tkday.com). I wanted to ensure our 10,000 day mark was official. The site was basic, clear but also, I hoped, charming, with five seconds of tinkling music delighting visitors' ears when they open the home page, and titbits galore appealing to their eyes.

I wrote a tiny tkday poem and encouraged people to include it in their tkday cards:

Roses are red
Your hair's going grey
But don't get upset
Have a fab tkday

Elsewhere I posted some fascinating tkday facts, such as 'Jimi Hendrix died 158 days after celebrating his tkday,' '10,000 follows 9,999 and precedes 10,001.' 'Jim Morrison died just seventy days after his tkday,' 'There are approximately 10,000 species of birds in the world,' and 'Kurt Cobain died ninety-three days short of his tkday.' I thought it was good to mix the serious with the trivial, like on the actual news.

Perhaps the most important application on the site was the

means by which one might calculate one's own tkday, which I included after a desperate Mr Goudy-Stout emailed to ask: 'Do you just times your age by 365 or do you really have to go into it and count leap years and stuff?' This was a fair point. You do, unfortunately, 'really have to go into it'. But because not everybody saw Carol teach the relevant equation on that episode of *Countdown*, I attached a link to a site where you simply enter your date of birth and your computer will do the 'really going into it' bit for you (if you don't have a computer or the inclination, the easiest way is to wait until your next birthday then times your age by 365.25. Happy birthday).

With keen marketing nous, I added a section to the tkday website called 'Custom Cakes' where, at the click of a button, anyone could order their own tkday cake. This did, however, mean that I would then have to bake a cake, something I have yet to achieve successfully. But these were the lengths I was prepared to go to to get my new word out there.

Finally, in a section entitled 'celebrities', I listed those famous people whose tkdays were on the horizon. Of these celebrity twenty-seven-year-olds, Shane Filan from Westlife was closest to his tkday, so I spent the rest of the day hand-crafting two more personal tkday cards for the cheerful Irish singer, sending one to his agent in London and one to his agent in Dublin. Predictably the Westlife boys each had various fan websites dedicated to them, so I also logged on to one of these to attempt to spread the word. Once more, therefore, I found myself communicating with very young children on the Internet. This was odd and slightly uncomfortable, but again the results just about justified the methods. On breaking the tkday news to his fans on the Shane Filan Forum, for instance, the following exchange occurred.

V.G.Farmer   **It's Shane's Tkday on Monday!**

Hi everyone,

Hope this doesn't make me sound too weird but I've worked out that it's Shane's Tkday on Monday! He'll have been alive for 10,000 days ☺!

Not sure if I'm the only one who's realised but wanted to be the first to wish Shane a happy Tkday! It only comes around once so I hope you have a lovely day!

Bye!

Nicky   **Re: It's Shane's Tkday on Monday!**

That is weird, y would u want to find that out

Joanne   **Re: It's Shane's Tkday on Monday!**

Hi nicky

Sum people like to think of things like that, i think that i have got a bday every yr but i would like to celebrate two if u get wot a mean by that. Its weid thinkin that shane has been alive for 10,000 days its sounds weird when u say it like that lol

xJoannex   **Re: It's Shane's Tkday on Monday!**

Hi

Yer i would lov 2 bdays that means more presents lol.

xX-sophie-Xs **Re: It's Shane's Tkday on Monday!**

WATS A TKDAY?!?!?!?!?!?!?!?!?

xJoannex   **Re: It's Shane's Tkday on Monday!**

I think it means that shane has been alive for 10,000 days or something like that.

I may have looked a little peculiar, but these were the people we needed to infect with our words. Without any prompting from me, Joanne managed to work out what a 'tkday' was. And if she told her friends about her own tkday, and those friends planned tkday parties of their own with guests who would then know about this extra birthday, pretty soon the entire planet would be using the word.

Based on this logic I made a big decision of my own. It was time, I determined, for me personally to start passing on the rest of my words more directly. I had realised (perhaps a little slowly) that the more people who knew about honk, bollo and mental safari, the more chance they had of survival. I therefore resolved to tell the tale of *Wordwatching* to as many people as possible. There was a danger that if the dictionary authorities themselves found out about my plans they might squash them immediately, but I was banking on them being too busy rejigging definitions to come and see a comedian tell a story. So I chose the Edinburgh stage as my launchpad once again, and this time I would openly shout out the words rather than whispering them in the backstreets. Yes, I would be abandoning our initial principles of never explicitly explaining the project, but without such affirmative action I was sure we would fall short.

The stage was, after all, whence our finest inventor of words had sent forth his 1,700 neologisms. That man was, of course, William Shakespeare or, if you like, Shakspear, Shake-speare, Shaksper, even Shaxberd. In his six surviving signatures, his surname isn't spelt the same way twice. There are over eighty versions noted in contemporary texts, so I'm going to refer to him as Shakey, partly because I don't think that's been taken yet *and* because that was always *my* nickname at university (for no reason other than that I was quite nervous on my first few days. If you fancy inventing a more interesting back story please feel free. Why not add it to my Wikipedia entry?). This way I can cheekily associate myself with the great man, and make him seem less like some supernatural being and more like a normal person. So here goes.

The latest edition of the *OED* assigned 2,035 'first usage' words to Shakey and quoted him no fewer than 14,000 times. Charles Dickens has 262 citations, Jane Austen just sixty, and they're really influential writers. Shakey was a really *really* influential writer. The real McCoy.* But I do wonder how much of his influence was self-fulfilling, how many of these words are attributed to him simply because he's The Bard. One must assume that other writers used at least some of the same terms at the same time or before Shakespeare, otherwise his audiences would have had even less of a clue what he was on about than GSCE English students today.

But the words were perfectly preserved in his treasured texts and he is extremely quotable. Moreover, his reputation was such that he could get a word like 'trolmydames' into Johnson's dictionary even though *no one* else seemed to use it, causing Johnson himself to write, 'of this word I know not the meaning', instead of a definition. That's just not fair.

Whether or not he invented them all, the depth and variety of Shakey's words is astounding. From the dense 'abstemious', 'accessible' and 'assassination' to the expansive 'fair play' and 'pomp and circumstance' or the fun 'barefaced' and 'leapfrog', he's the man behind almost every word that's any good. 'Blanket', 'bump', 'buzzer', they're his. 'Gossip', 'hobnob', 'luggage', 'mountaineer' and 'skim milk', they're all his too. He was the first to write 'deafening', 'laughable', 'downstairs' and 'puke', and thanks to their memorable contexts, they've all been in constant use ever since. I personally think his word 'undress' isn't great; it's too literal and straightforward a description of what is often an exciting occasion. But because he introduced it in *Henry V*, it's still the most common word for 'stripping' today.

Bear in mind that during Shakey's lifetime an estimated one out of every two men in London would have seen one of his big plays. Shakey was everywhere; a bit like Beyoncé but even more prolific and, I would dare to say, with an even greater vocabulary. His is estimated to be twice as large as the average educated person today. It is widely reported that Shakespeare used 29,066 *different* words in his works (although Bill Bryson quotes the number 17,677), compared to just 10,000 in the King James Bible and 9,714 in this book.[48]

But as well as a dubious nickname, Shakey and I do share attributes. He liked puns, for example. As well as the famously sordid phrase 'country matters', he indulged in more innocent gags like Mercutio's remark shortly before his death in *Romeo and Juliet*: 'Ask for me tomorrow, and you shall find me a grave man.' Grave man! Brilliant! Or my favourite, from *Henry IV, Part One*: 'If reasons were as plentiful as blackberries, I would give no man a reason upon compulsion, I.' That one only works if you pronounce 'reason' as 'raisin' as they did in Shakey's day, but you can still see that it's not such a leap forward to today's Christmas cracker jokes after all.

And like me, Shakey often failed. Not all of his words have survived. If someone dropped 'vizament', 'substractor' or 'bepray' into conversation today, you'd almost certainly wonder what was wrong with them. 'Barky' and 'brisky' look more sensible but never caught on. And I don't think 'soilure', 'vastidity', 'fustilarian' or 'anthropophaginian' would be understood any better than 'honk', 'bollo' or even 'tkday'. So I was inspired rather than intimidated by Shakespeare. It was time for my words to take centre stage.

*

---

48 It took me a long while to find out that figure. After weeks of failed applications I used a programme called 'NoteTab' to calculate the number of different words. It probably would have been quicker for me to list and count them.

The road to the Edinburgh Fringe festival starts, for me, in London, where I attempt to buff my stories up into something presentable over a series of previews. These are inevitably experimental affairs, so instead of wasting more honk on advertising performances, I try to drum up a modest and friendly audience with emails to friends and family. But now that I'd resolved to reveal myself to the world as the Farmer I thought I might as well try to get the press involved with my show. I therefore stooped to ask for help in publicising my show from someone on the inside of a well-known magazine. Instead of sneaking past security in a furtive fashion I hoped to side-step the whole issue of censorship and walk brazenly through the doors. So, for the first time, I explained my scheme to a journalist, the editor of *Time Out*'s comedy section, and asked if he could give me a leg up. Fortunately for me, Tim, the magazine's main comedy man, has an excellent sense of humour and fun:

> I am very happy to print a quote in the mag with one of the words in. Send me a couple of examples and I'll see what I can do. I'm always very happy to help, especially when it comes to messing around a bit.

In the very next edition the first preview was listed as 'Wordwatching – well worth your comedy honk.'

Whether or not it was this recommendation that did the trick, enough people came to the early shows to make them worthwhile. I gradually whittled our rather unwieldy Verbal Gardening campaign into something approaching a coherent story and, to my surprise, many of those who heard it felt stirred to join in. An accountant called Dave from Brighton was amongst the first to offer support, promising to use 'honk' when talking to his clients. A professional young lady called Poppy sent an email along similar lines, saying:

> I just tried to use the word 'honk' in a report and had it edited
> out by my manager, as in: '... since moving to the new prop-
> erty turnover has not increased as forecast, and the rise in
> rental and other overheads has led to honk flow difficulties.' I
> think I might get fired.

She may have failed to spread honk further than her manager, but she did get it noticed by someone in a position of some authority. And if it cost her her job at least we'd be recreating the sacrifices of Wycliffe and Wild. I hoped that would be some consolation anyway.

A man called Mike, meanwhile, managed to take 'mental safari' away with him and pop it in the editorial of the next issue of his European fruit-based trade magazine: 'After three days of journalistic hunting and gathering,' his column concluded, 'our carefully plotted excursion around the world of fresh produce had become something of a mental safari. Next year, thank goodness, we'll have the whole weekend to recover ...' I can't quite imagine an exhibition all about pineapples causing a mental safari, but this was excellent work. When we finally came to sending our evidence to the editors of the *OED* this would surely convince them that this phrase at least was being widely used.

After the third *Wordwatching* preview I received an email from an audience member whose colleagues in Westminster had 'agreed to take up the challenge to insert the sentence "We're putting a lot of honk into the post office network" into a ministerial speech'. This was more like it. Our words were hitting the big time. This was the sort of push that could send us over the edge and into the dictionary.

This same correspondent (who, I think, should also remain anonymous) went on to alert me to the new phrase 'collateral misinformation' which, according to Urban Dictionary (and someone called 'wildefox'), means;

When someone alters a Wikipedia article to win a specific argument, anyone who reads the false article before the 'error' is
corrected suffers from collateral misinformation. E.g. I changed
the scientific classification of red foxes last night in order to
win an argument with Judy. I hope some stupid high school
student didn't suffer from collateral misinformation.

It had certainly worked for my Budgens rumour. Whilst I was
plugging away with preparations for the Edinburgh show no
less a media giant than ITV advertised a programme called
Comedy Cuts in which Mr Elephant and I briefly appeared with
the sentence:

THAT'S AMAZING! Alex Horne's first gig came after winning a
Christmas Cracker joke writing competition whilst working as
Deputy Head of Dairy at Budgens.

Maybe they had no reason to doubt the veracity of the story,
but it was encouraging to see word spread so far so quickly.
Momentum was gathering on all fronts.

The *Wordwatching* previews were instantly accelerating the whole
Verbal Gardening process. By telling audiences about the plan,
demonstrating the words, then swearing them to secrecy, my
team of word-distributors was increasing. The Rare Men were
still my generals, but I now had an increasing number of foot-
soldiers happy to pitch in, pass on the words and, in turn, tell
me about their own verbal creations; because everyone seemed
to have invented a new word themselves or to know someone
who had.

People like Jonny, who told me about the verb 'to tristan',
which he'd made up to mean, 'to christen your kid with a
gratuitously fancy name'; Derek, whose mate JP coined

'dillion' for 'the biggest number you can think of, plus one'; or Peter, who made up 'smuttering', meaning 'a very small innuendo'. Everyone was at it. The Aucklands alerted me to their 'duggle fuggle', used to describe someone who is both bald and bearded (from 'duggle', meaning bald and 'fuggle', meaning bearded), Martin's eighteen-month-old son had invented 'poodly-poodlies' as a name for furry slippers with animal faces, and Nat coined the rather less saccharine 'kitten-drowner', to replace 'bin-liner'. Rich told me his dad calls headaches 'nogglers'. Hildegard said she refers to the aperitifs you have with canapés as 'bibbles'. Sophie shared the beautifully tragic 'romicide' which she'd crafted to describe a 'romantic suicide'.

They didn't all show such flair. Many were simply rude; I'll leave you to guess the meanings of 'scruttocks', 'bogclogger' and 'biddy fiddler'. Some were rather mundane; a man called Marc told me he'd invented 'cupboardy' which meant 'like a cupboard'. While others were just a little impractical; Conor's flatmates came up with 'spanther' meaning 'a panther which is from the future'. But no matter how imaginative the neologism, they were all invented by individuals and, more importantly, used by them *and* others.

Nor were these inventions limited to words. Helen told me her friends have used the phrase 'are you taking my shoes off' instead of 'are you taking the piss out of me?' ever since its creation in a pub one lively evening, Daniel said he'd come up with the precise 'blancmange man' to describe 'someone without personality or taste', and Gary let me know that he'd created 'morning long foot' for 'when you wake up and your socks are half off'. A man called Dharmesh Patel pricked my curiosity particularly effectively with his phrase, 'wider than my arm', for which he gave this explanation: 'Depends how you say it but it's used to describe something as either good or bad, e.g. My friend's yellow shoes are wider than my arm.' Intrigued, I got back in touch with Dharmesh to ask how this broad phrase came about, expecting some sort of convoluted etymology involving either an enormous bicep or a very skinny upper arm. 'Oh, I don't know,' replied Dharmesh, as if he'd never given it a thought. 'We've just always said it.' So if it catches on and you hear your own friends describing things as wider than their arms, feel free to invent your own derivation.

Around this time, I also received an email, quite by chance, from my old sparring partner, the BBC Radio Gloucestershire DJ John Rockley, whose noodling I had offhandedly mentioned on the Verbal Gardening website.

'Thanks for the mention on your wonderful site,' he wrote, exaggerating a little (it's a very basic site that gives you a headache if you look at it for too long) but instantly winning my affection and attention. 'There is one other Rockleyism that I enjoy and I'm yet to work out the origin. I don't think it's mine by any means but I've been using it for so long that I can't remember where it came from: "Giddy Kipper" – noun. Any person who shows signs of taking very little seriously. Also used for a camper version of "ebullient". "Stop being a giddy kipper, and listen!"'

I smiled when I read the email, partly because I like the idea of a 'giddy kipper' and know I can occasionally be one, but mainly because Mr Rockley must have googled himself on his way to finding our site and then, having found his name, made sure it wasn't taken in vain by contributing further to our cause. That's exactly the sort of thing I'd do. He was clearly proud of his Rockleyisms and keen to share them with the world. Who was I to get in his way, especially when I was in a position where I could actually help him get there?

But perhaps my favourite coining story came from a man

called Tom, aged thirty, who'd been to school with a boy who claimed to have made up the slang adjective 'cool'. That is a terrific declaration, as good, if not better than Samuel Johnson's friend and source Thomas Coryate whom he refers to as 'Furcifer' in his dictionary because he once claimed to be the first man in England to use a fork. Brilliant.

In the playground, Tom told me, his friend had boldly stated that he was the first person to ever use the word to refer to anything 'good', it had proved an instant hit, and went global within weeks. If only it was that easy. Unfortunately for the lad in question the word has quantifiably been around for at least half a century, although the identity of the original 'cool' dude* is unclear. Nominees include jazz musicians Cab Calloway, Charlie Parker and Lester Young, Eton, The Yardbirds, the 1950s and Italy – but probably not Tom's mate from school.

It was all set up for the run in Edinburgh. Well, almost all. A week before I set off up the M1 my telephone rang. 'Withheld number' flashed up on the screen.

'Hello?' I said, nervously.

'Hi there, I'm one of the producers of *Countdown*. I'm just phoning to say that we'd like you to be a contestant on the show. Would that be ok?'

'Ok? Ok! Yes! Ok. Ok!'

Eureka!*

I hung up and dialled one of the few numbers I know by heart.

'Mum, I made it. I'm going to be on *Countdown*.'

'I always knew you would.'

Everything was falling into place at exactly the right time. I just needed to take a deep breath before shouting my words from the rooftops of Edinburgh with the *Wordwatching* show and then on the streets of Leeds through *Countdown*. I was going to make such a racket that the dictionary doormen would simply have to open their gates if only to find out what all the commotion was about.

23

With the story written and rehearsed, if not yet concluded, I charged up to Edinburgh to commence the Verbal Gardening endgame with fire (and some real honest food) in my belly. Now I felt ready to sow my seeds properly. Last year I had indiscriminately flung them by hand onto the Scottish streets, this year I was driving my own tractor.* Here I would come out to the rest of the press and the wider world as the Farmer, I would expound the Verbal Gardening concept and I would encourage anyone and everyone to join my dogged band. Having been first afraid that setting out my aims so openly might dissuade the dictionary authorities from taking our new words seriously, I had since come to realise that what I needed wasn't secrecy but exposure. It was all very well attempting to slyly insert our words into the language, but for people to actually notice and take them on themselves they had to be accompanied by some sort of fanfare. And at least at the raucous Edinburgh Fringe such a fanfare would soon fade into the general cacophony of the festival. I could holler my words in such a way that the dictionaries might not necessarily be put off.

Such reasoning was proved wholly inaccurate in the first two days of the festival, first by a Rare Man and then by a hitherto nebulous Dictionary Authority. The journalist Mr Rockwell had come to Edinburgh at the very start of the festival and kindly chose to watch my show whilst in the capital *and* whilst wearing his own Verbal Gardening T-shirt (featuring the slogan; 'BEWARE PRATDIGGERS'). As he queued outside the box office a girl sidled up to him and quietly said, 'I hope that shirt didn't cost you too much honk,' before sidling off again. Mr Rockwell immediately reported the incident and I was both pleased and bemused. Had she seen one of the show's previews? Or had both 'pratdigger' and 'honk' successfully made it to Scotland already? Either way, the words were spreading. Perhaps I didn't need such a fanfare after all.

The following night, after the second show of the four-week run, a girl sidled up to me too. This time she introduced herself; 'Hi, I'm Morven. I just wanted to let you know that I'm from the *Chambers Dictionary* and I enjoyed the show.' I blushed. My cover had been blown. One dictionary was already on to me.

But she'd said she'd had a good time* at the show. What did that mean? Might she push our words into her dictionary? Or was this more of a sinister 'I enjoyed the show. You've had your fun. Now leave us alone' sort of a comment? She didn't seem like a sinister person, she seemed like a friendly person. I felt warily optimistic, mainly because *Chambers* was the one dictionary I thought might see the funny side of our project.

First published in 1901, the *Chambers Dictionary* has always prided itself on its sense of humour. A week before I arrived in Edinburgh, the people behind the dictionary brought out a 'lexicon of laughter', entitled *Gigglossary*, which celebrated the company's lighter sensibilities. *Chambers* was, according to its editors, 'unique among contemporary mainstream dictionaries in including humorous definitions scattered among its more serious ones'. That was exactly the sort of thing I needed to hear. Not since Johnson's day had there been a dictionary that actively enjoyed wordplay, but here was one whose 'humorous definitions' were both stylish and witty, rather than bawdy or wacky. 'Jaywalker', for example, is defined as 'a careless pedestrian whom motorists are expected to avoid running down', a 'track-suit' as 'a loose warm suit intended to be worn by athletes when warming up or training, but sometimes worn by others in an error of judgement', and, most famously, an 'éclair', 'a cake, long in shape but short in duration'. This could be a perfect home for my words. I just hoped they passed muster.

After this initial dictionary jolt, the shows settled into a productive rhythm. I narrated the story so far; how the words were chosen and then spread and what the audience could do to help. There were a paddleful of jokes too, some nifty multimedia trickery and a picture of a pirate so all in all, I had confidence in my hi-tech-word-coining-themed-comedy-package (although towards the end of one show my critical computer went on a mental safari and stopped working, rousing a cry of 'hit it with your paddle' from the crowd, soon followed by 'your laptop's bollo' and 'your laptop's a pratdigger'. Those were a bittersweet few minutes).

Before each show I asked people to write down their own invented words, any terms that had sprung up naturally in conversation with their friends and family and which had clung on to life in their own homes and heads, and again they responded with remarkable enthusiasm, especially considering this was really just enforced audience participation. In his afterword to Kitchen Table Lingo, David Crystal wrote that 'everyone has been a word-coiner at some time or other, if not around the kitchen table, then in the garden, bedroom, office or pub', and I can only agree. Inventing words does seem to be something we all do; maybe not quite as deliberately, self-consciously or egocentrically as me, but as a natural part of communication. This is how language grows.

While I then told my story in the Pleasance Above, a sports hall converted into a 150-seater theatre, my luminous heterochromic amanuensis Hannah diligently typed up and printed out the audience's words and phrases in the store room two floors below (some cracking Classics-based words there; if you don't know what they mean, why not look them up in the *OED*? You never know what you might find). At the end of the show, when I'd told them about my *Countdown* experience and the audience filed out full of my new words, Hannah handed them each a Verbal Gardening Pocket Dictionary, tailor-made and full of theirs. She produced and distributed over 2,000 of these bespoke dictionaries during the festival. They may have been very limited editions, but my words were in these dictionaries.

The Free Pocket Dictionary strategy was one I'd nicked from Wycliffe's biblical successor William Tyndale, whose 1525 version of the New Testament housed several freshly minted words including my favourite, 'scapegoat', whose creation was the enduring result of a simple mistake. Tyndale was trying to translate the Hebrew *azazel*. Unfortunately, instead of its real meaning of a 'fallen angel', he mistook it for *ez ozel*, which, as we all know, means 'the goat that departs'. He thus invented 'scapegoat', short for 'escapegoat' (which I wish had stuck because it conjures up the image of a goat that you only use in an emergency).

Such coinages were tucked into a book made deliberately small so that people could easily hide it on their person. This was passed around the country, from universities to ordinary townsfolk, and his 'scapegoats' travelled from his pen to the people. But, as we've seen before, Verbal Gardening is a dangerous business, and while Tyndale's efforts did reap linguistic rewards they also resulted in another rather grisly end. Whilst in Antwerp he was kidnapped and imprisoned in Vilvorde Castle by two men working for the vengeful Henry VIII. There he continued to work, somehow managing to invent apposite phrases such as 'a stranger in a strange land', 'let my people go' and 'a law unto themselves', until his voice was finally snuffed on 6 October 1536 when he was found guilty of heresy and strangled. I can't stress enough how daring I was even to attempt this project.

Whether it was the size of our own dictionaries, the fact that they were free or the chance that they might have included some of their own words, they were lapped up by the Edinburgh crowds. Unfortunately I don't have space here to include any more of the huge assortment of amazing words and phrases they volunteered themselves, some ingenious, most vulgar, all creative, but I have written them up as a list on www.alexhorne.com, so do have a look. I'm sure you'll discover a few to tickle your personal verbal fancy.

(Oh, go on then, just a few more of my favourites: 'disastrophe', coined by Rob, meaning 'not as bad as a catastrophe but worse than a disaster'; 'chello' from Jane, 'the way musicians greet each other'; and 'cockbongo', 'an indoor sport involving bongo drums and shuttlecocks' invented by Tony. Marvellous.)

If you want to add your own, just send me an email with the word or phrase, when and by whom it was coined and how others might use it themselves. By collating this inventory I like to think that I too am creating some sort of revolutionary dictionary; like Johnson, Murray and the Urban Dictionary team, I'm beavering away, finding and defining words that would otherwise roam free and vulnerable, liable to pass away without record. I mainly like to think this because my words are in the list too and if I call it another dictionary I can keep convincing myself that I have already succeeded. It is fate. It is written: A lexicon: Alex. Icon.

When it came to the spreading of my own invented words, the audiences were again kind and keen to take up the challenge, with charity providing an unlikely theme in early dispersal. Throughout the festival, volunteers for the Waverley Aids Charity collected money in buckets outside the various venues. Several of these chuggers* told me that many people exiting my show were effortlessly saying, 'Yes, I've got some honk here somewhere,' or 'No, I'm afraid I'm honkless,' as they passed. The words were on their way.

I also received an email during the first week from a man called Ian who wrote:

I found a certain affinity for your cause and in particular the word 'honk'. I go to a big church in the centre of Edinburgh with a congregation of about 1,000 each week. I'm involved with the youth group and saw an opportunity for some gardening. I planted a notice about the upcoming youth weekend away in our weekly notice sheet 'the bulletin' and included the word honk in a way which hopefully made it easy to understand. As I say there is a readership of over 1,000 and copies are sent all over the world to our missionaries so it should do rather well. I'm planning other church-related plantings which I shall let you know of if they work out. Does this qualify for a T-shirt??

Of course it qualified for a T-shirt (I didn't have any more with me but immediately had some fresh ones made up, my favourite of which read; 'I'M SHORTER THAN NATASHA KAPLINSKY'). The bulletin itself was perfect in its usage of the word:

YPM September Weekend . . . For more details ask a member of committee. Places may be limited so get your form and honk back to us ASAP (cheques playable [sic] to Charlotte Chapel YPM).

That was exactly what was needed. And there was more. A lady called Margaret let me know that she'd stuck the word 'honk' onto her 'Just Giving' charity page for a sponsored walk she was soon to do:

> As a team we have a target of £1,000-2,000 so please help me do my bit. I will be very happy if we manage to smash our target, so please give as much honk as you can.

Again, I sent her a T-shirt (and some honk for the charity) and grew quietly more excited that others were now spreading the words for me. I could almost smell pratdigger, honest and honk beginning to percolate Britain.

Others got in contact with valuable Verbal Gardening sightings of their own. Someone called Amy let me know about the headline 'Paul McCartney Lauded for his Honesty', that had caught her by surprise and made her laugh. Nick pointed me towards an American 'Honest Weight Food Co-op' advertising 'honest food' to 'honest people', and Thomas sent me an article cut from the *Sunday Times* that stated that Mike Tyson had become 'brutally honest' in recent years. Every night, strangers were joining in with our fun.

One audience member whom I already knew fairly well was my brother Chip. As always, he laughed loyally throughout the show he came to see. It is, I suppose, funny to see your brother make a fool of himself onstage. But this time I did notice him laugh particularly loudly at certain moments. He found my mention of the Ginsters advert outstandingly amusing, for instance.

After the show I asked him what he thought; he does occasionally come up with some quite useful constructive criticism. Instead of such advice, however, he asked me what I thought of the Lucida Console font. I said I liked it. Then I twigged.

He was Lucida Console.

Having read the article in *The Times* in which I used the word 'honk' to mean money, he'd done a little research (as any attentive reader should) and found his way to the Verbal Gardening website. Being a bright sort of a Horne, he soon worked out that I was the Farmer. Being a sneaky sort of a Horne he then emailed the Farmer pretending to be an interested member of the public. As you'll remember, this Farmer was entirely duped and got very excited that an ordinary member of the public was interested. Oh well.

The easiest way for others to get in the spirit of the project was still by passing on the Natasha Kaplinsky rumour, and in particular by spreading it via Wikipedia. Considering my history with the website I felt uneasy potentially pissing them off again, but once I'd told my own story onstage there was little I could do to stop others joining in. If you look up the history of Kaplinksy's page for August 2008 you'll see a frenzy of activity, all focused around the newsreader's height. Audience members were editing the page every single day, often with various further details furnished with a flourish; someone wrote that she won *Strictly Come Dancing* 'despite her height'; when this was deleted another wrote she won the competition 'thanks to her height advantage'; more creatively, an anonymous contributor explained that she 'has a specially modified chair in the studio to hide her incredible height of six foot two inches.'

Other words were implanted too. For a couple of weeks the site reported that she'd appeared on *Strictly* after 'going on a mental safari', that she was 'not as honest as Dawn French', that she had recently 'told a fellow reporter that she was earning 'a lot of honk' and that 'she is known to be a pratdigger due to her many relationships with bollos'. 'Bollos'; I'd never seen it as a noun before. It looked good.

Back in real life, away from Edinburgh, news of her height

was spread further with my previous wide-armed correspondent Dharmesh Patel sending me my favourite Kaplinsky-orientated email:

Me and Kunval are very bored at work so we decided to try something . . . We said, quite loudly so that people could over hear, 'Did you know Natasha Kaplinsky is 6 foot 2 inches tall . . .' One person overhears and says, 'Really?! I didn't know she was that tall!' Another guy asks 'Who's that tall? Natasha Kaplinsky?! six foot two?! Serious?!' This guy then turns to the person next to him and passes on the amazing piece of information that he has just picked up . . . Upon hearing this, the guy very confidently declares, 'Yeah, I know. When she was on *Top Gear* she was almost as tall as Clarkson!!!' As soon as we hear this, me and Kunval look at each other and burst out laughing to the bemusement of all those around us!

There we go. That's how simple communication can be. Yes, we can use the Internet, we can edit online encyclopaedias and we can create our own websites, but we can also talk to one another. This was something well worth remembering. All I really wanted was for people to start using the words amongst themselves. If I achieved this, the rest would follow.

Another audience member, Simon, wrote to tell me that after crowbarring honk into a couple of conversations, 'a friend of mine has now adopted this along with the rather fun "oink" to specifically relate to coins'. That's what I wanted, for people to have fun with the words themselves. And 'oink' is a great development; 'I think I've got some oink here somewhere . . .' Please do try it for yourselves.

The word 'crowbar', incidentally, does occasionally (but falsely) get attributed to one person. A 'black-faced minstrel' called

Thomas D. Rice wrote a song called 'Jim Crow' around 1828 about an old Kentucky labourer he'd observed in a field. As the song grew in popularity the term 'crow' began to be used to refer to black people. Because of this etymological link it has since been presumed that the crowbar (also called a Jim Crow) was some sort of racist's tool, a weapon with which to cajole slaves to work. The original crowbar was, however, invented four centuries earlier and simply happens to share the surname. It's far more likely the crowbar is so called only because it vaguely looks like the beak (or even feet) of a crow.

The monkey wrench, on the other hand, might not be named after monkeys. Certain killjoy historians may deny it, but there is a shred of evidence to suggest that the handy spanner was invented in 1858 by a man called Charles Moncky who then sold the patent for $2,000 and bought a house in Kings County, New York. The 'monkey' is therefore simply a more intuitive misspelling of the inventor's unusual surname. And even though those spoilsports will tell you that the phrase 'monkey wrench' was around decades before Moncky and that it's a British phrase anyway, I'm going to hold on to that shred.

Being an aspirant word-coiner I do find myself gunning for the underdog when it comes to these etymologies. Whilst researching this book I did uncover many genuine stories of individual word coinages, but I found even more that were dismissed by lexicographical sticklers as 'folk' or 'false' etymologies, fantastical explanations, far more interesting than the mundane facts but not, I was told, true.

Well, I'm not sure who to believe. I think we can be too quick to cynically write off so many of these stories as codswallop. We can too easily mistrust 'history' and presume any tale with even the slightest whiff of an old wife to be bunkum. Can we really say for sure that 'codswallop' itself wasn't invented in 1870 in honour of British soft-drink-maker Hiram Codd and his

'Codd-neck bottle' that beer drinkers said was only 'good for a wallop'? Or that 'bunkum' wasn't created when US Congressman Felix Walker, representative of Buncombe County in North Carolina, rambled inarticulately during a speech in February 1820, was heckled and accused of irrelevance, but refused to yield the floor, claiming that his speech was not intended for Congress; he was simply 'speaking for Buncombe'? Both of these old stories have been dismissed as false by curmudgeonly etymologists, but I think they deserve to be retold.

At the risk of attracting similar criticism to Felix Walker, I'm going to bluster on for a little longer, this time about the word 'teetotal'. There are reports in this and many other reputable word books that the word was created by a Mr 'Dicky' Turner from Lancashire who had a stutter. At a meeting of the Preston Temperance Society he is said to have sworn that 'nothing but t-t-t-t-total abstinence will do' which the other attendees found so amusing they themselves started using the word 't-total'. Others, however, insist this can't be true. How could a lowly fishmonger invent a word in such a simple fashion? Why is it pronounced '*tea*-total', rather than '*ter*-total' like the original stutter? And how can you possibly believe such a romantic story?

But there must be some truth to it somewhere. After all, Richard 'Dicky' Turner definitely existed; he's buried in St Peter's churchyard, right next to the Preston University Library, and the inscription on his gravestone reads:

Beneath this stone are deposited the remains of
Richard Turner, author of the word Teetotal, as applied
to abstinence from all liquors, who departed this life on the
27th day of October, 1846, aged 56 years.

So Mr Turner either went to incredible lengths to falsely claim his own word on his own gravestone or he must indeed be responsible for the word. Either way, it's a story well worth sharing, especially because, as so often, the supposed 'truth' is not only dull, but senseless. 'A more likely explanation', reads the official Wikipedia entry, 'is that *teetotal* is simply a reduplication of the "T" in *total* (T-total).' What? Why is that more likely? Why would you ever 'simply' reduplicate the first letter of a word? Absolute peepiffle.

Even if they *are* created after the words they explain, and even if they are utterly preposterous, these tales only add to the history of language. They should not be cast aside. Rather they should be recounted and embellished in the tradition of story-telling. In a valiant bid to expose the truth behind the phrase 'spitting image', Professor Laurence Horn (yes, we're all at it, us Hornes) coined the word 'etymythology' in the seventy-ninth issue of *American Speech*, and I think it's a very useful term. Myths warrant retelling; they're cracking tales, and if some people believe them to be true, I don't see how that's a problem.

So it is now time to confess that as a protest against doubt and scepticism I have completely made up one of the etymologies in this Verbal Gardening history. As well as my cracker joke rumour, I have inserted my own linguistic mountweazel; that should really irk the pedants. This is an admission, not an apology, although I do feel sorry for people like Michael Quinion, a professional word sleuth who already has 'enough trouble with mistakes that are caused by ignorance or misunderstanding without having deliberate obfuscation added to the mix' (*Ballyhoo, Buckaroo, and Spuds*, published in 2004). I'm afraid that must come with his chosen territory.

I'm by no means the first to spin such a yarn. In 1809 the *Monthly Review and Boston Anthology* published a letter from someone purporting to be Noah Webster, the foremost American lexicologist, who claimed that 'yankee' came from the Persian word *jenghe*, meaning 'warlike man' or 'swift horse'. No such word exists in Persian, but the etymology has since been reported as fact. In the same year (and in the same book in which he invented the word 'knickerbockers') Washington Irving joshingly explained that 'yankee' meant 'silent men' and came from 'the Mais-tschusaeg or Massachusetts language', a story that has also been widely believed (partly because no one knows the actual truth).

At least I have let the curious reader know there definitely is one entirely fictitious back story in this book. Like a protracted game of backwards Balderdash, it's now up to you to hunt it down. If you want a clue, the word in question was actually created through some dodgy spelling by a Scotsman. There, that should help. Once you've sniffed out my fabrication, every other word history, whether absolutely verifiable or decidedly dodgy, will have a comparative glimmer of truth about it. That seems fair to me. And who knows, one day my 'fake' etymology may morph into 'folk' etymology and become part of the storytelling tradition too.

24

In everyday life, in pubs, schools and pantomimes, jokes can travel at a fair pace, as I discovered with my own wandering 'counter-productive' effort. But on the stand-up comedy circuit jokes can move even faster, with comics ever eager to pass on new routines: not onstage, but to each other. The nation's comedians (at the latest count, around 2,500 currently working in the UK) possess a massive collective database of their combined jokes. If you ask a comedian to name another comedian by describing that comedian's face, the questioned comedian will struggle. But recount one of his gags and you'll instantly be told the name of the act, how long he's been going and, if you're unlucky, another twenty minutes of his material.

What I didn't expect in Edinburgh was how quick my colleagues would be to pass on my new words. While all comics frown upon those who pass off other people's jokes as their own (some even go further than frowning on them), I was overjoyed when several took it upon themselves to include our Verbal Seeds in their sets, unbidden by me and without any hope of reward. If anything, throwing a newfangled word into a set-up might confuse an audience, diminishing the effect of a punchline. But comedians love an in-joke. We thrive on being in the know, one step ahead of the man on the street. And occasionally, when my old audience members recognised words in other comics' gags, they laughed harder than anyone else, even if the punchline hadn't actually been reached yet. They too were part of the gang. This is what slang is all about.

Having neglected to send them their own Verbal Gardening T-shirts I should therefore thank, among others, Dan Atkinson who plonked 'honk' into his economy-themed show, *The Credit Crunch and Other Biscuits*, the comedian and street performer Stu Goldsmith who asked punters to chuck some honk in his hat after each and every performance (surely jeopardising his money-making chances in the process), and to that year's *We Need Answers*[49] champion, Miss Josie Long, who managed to sneak 'mental safari' on to a prime-time programme on STV (the Scottish equivalent of ITV) and the *Sunday Surgery* on Radio 1.

Five channels up, on BBC6, Jon Richardson happily discussed 'honk' for several minutes on air and allowed me to drop Alan Coren's 'peripolitan' into mainstream media once again. In fringe newspaper *Three Weeks* the character comedienne Isabel Fay described how she had to briefly leave the festival 'for an acting job that was worth the honk', perversely named comic Ellis James (surely James Ellis, no?), the glamorous Lloyd Woolf and fabulous sketch troupe the Umbrella Birds all slapped honk right into the middle of their shows, the cast of hit musical *Jet Set Go* knowingly described Vanessa Feltz as 'an honest lady' and various commentators at the Olympics described freaky swimmer Michael Phelps as having 'massive paddles'. Everyone was helping.

Only occasionally did this assistance backfire. Mr Elephant, also appearing at the festival, had an interview with budding comedy magazine *The Fix* in the course of which he was asked to describe his previous partner (i.e. me). With an affectionate tongue in his mischievous cheek, I hope, he stated that I was

---

49 A very silly quiz now on BBC4 and featuring the likes of 'honk' on a regular basis.

'only motivated by honk'. This, however, did not survive the edit. When thousands of copies were circulated around the festival Mr Elephant was quoted as exclusively saying;

Alex Horne is motivated only by money.

With the disappearance of 'honk', any irony in the statement, or indeed any sense of humour at all, vanished too; Mr Elephant appeared spiteful, I seemed greedy. But it's all about making sacrifices. Once again we'd put our necks on the block and this time the axe hadn't missed. Thankfully this was the twenty-first century and that was a metaphor. My pride was bruised but I could keep fighting.

Of course the main reason that we comedians flock to Edinburgh every year is because the Fringe is our industry's largest shop window. Only in Edinburgh, we tell ourselves, do radio and TV producers browse for talent,* film directors sniff around for writers and actors, and otherwise unknown performers become stars. As rare as this may be in reality, it is certainly true that during the Fringe, unlike at any other time of the year, comedians are in the limelight. As an art form, comedy ranks just below jazz in terms of publicity and general interest. Listings in national newspapers are piddly, only the handful of stand-ups who feature on TV are ever interviewed, and very few people regularly go to comedy clubs. But during August the rest of us do get some attention. We can get reviewed. We may not get critics from many or any nationals, and if we do they may not write nice things anyway, but almost everyone will get a mention somewhere, and that's usually enough for our fragile egos, and mothers.

I had extra incentive to grab the attention of the press. For the past two and a half years I'd tried to sneak words into articles; now I hoped the journalists might include them all by themselves. The radio broadcasters certainly didn't let me down. On BBC Five Live, Phil Williams encouraged people to attend my show to prevent me 'losing too much honk'. On Mo Dutta's business slot on my beloved BBC Radio 2 I authoritatively stated that 'gold doesn't cost as much honk as it used to'. Mo agreed. In the first of my two appearances on BBC Scotland, Fred Macaulay used nearly all our words in the following fine sentence; 'So, how much honk do people have to spend if they want to go on a mental safari and thrash their paddles in your show?' before another lady from the *Chambers Dictionary* (Mary, this time), called me a 'rascal', a 'rogue' and the 'scourge of lexicographers' during an entire discussion on the subject. I was extremely flattered. She even admitted to liking the word 'honk', saying she thought it did sound like slang for money, which prompted a listener to text and ask if 'honking' was the verb for spending money. 'Absolutely,' I said. 'If you say so.' And, I like to think, they did, many many times.

Print journalists excelled themselves too, planting seeds in a variety of entertainment publications. In *What's on Stage*, Kate Jackson wrote: 'Some people find happiness, some people find degradation, some people go on a mental safari, and an adorable little girl called Margaret dances, giggles and moralises,' in a (rather scathing) theatrical review. In the following week's edition Richard Hurst corroborated the phrase with the line: 'I feel like I'm on a bit of a mental safari, wandering around Edinburgh, swinging between Tiggerish glee and Eeyoreish torpor,' swiftly followed by: 'Everyone is keen to know how much well-earned honk they're going to lose this year.' Over on the *Artrocker* website, a music journalist called Rory reviewed hillbilly band The Weight with the magnificent:

Brothers and sisters lock up your cousins because country's coming to town and it's going to get awkward. That's right, The

Weight are ridin' into this quiet little 'burb to steal your women, drink your beer and maybe – just maybe – convince you to part with some hard-earned honk and buy their album.

But my favourite print usage appeared in the *Financial Times*. Yes, one of my little words found its way into the otherwise impregnable paper when its fringe diarist, a larger-than-life character called Ian Shuttleworth, deliberately described himself as the 'most honest critic on the Fringe' after seeing my show (which he also described as 'worth a few quid of anyone's hard-earned honk', I must bashfully report), a joke so subtle that surely none of his readers, apart from me, would understand. I was honoured. In one respect at least, I was in the honk.

Speaking of critics, those who reviewed the show also took the bait, uniformly slipping in a few choice phrases for me to then wield when advertising further shows. *Chortle*, the leading comedy website, said it was 'worth a few quid of anybody's honk', the *Guardian* playfully wrote, 'A refreshingly honest set of fun and games will have you honking for more!' and a review in the *Metro* opened with 'Have you had your tkday? Alex Horne has, and wants others to celebrate their 10,000th day on the planet. But he needs help in spreading the word.'

Best of all, best-known and most feared critic of them all, the *Scotsman*'s Kate Copstick, wrote the nicest thing possible, pretty much all of my words in one perfectly packaged paragraph:

As a reviewer, one never actually has to put one's honk where one's mouth is. If a show is completely games we can throw our paddles up and call it a load of bollo, safe in the knowledge it will not be over till the honest lady sings. Don't be a pratdigger – go and see this show.

That really did make my festival. On the same day as that review came out I also queued up at the Edinburgh Book Festival to meet Henry Hitchings, the dictionary historian I've quoted so frequently in this book. Looking him straight in the eye I explained my project with more confidence than I would have had a month or even a day before. He signed the books of his that I'd bought (for the second time) and wished me luck.

This meeting with lexical royalty, though, was just a bonus. We wouldn't need much more luck. Our words had lain dormant for months but now they were finally blooming. Edinburgh had been a success.

25

The festival had gratifying after-effects too; back in their normal lives, many audience members had actually taken our words under their wings and were now casting them far and wide across the country all by themselves, just as I had hoped.

In the world of entertainment another music journalist, Andrew Reilly, wrote the following sentence in his review of Kate Nash on the *Room Thirteen* website: 'It was never going to be the show that would appeal to everyone but when even long-time fans are left wondering if they got value for their hard-earned honk, you have to wonder if the show was the best thing for her at this moment in time.' Mind-reader and radio producer Chris Cox added this to the official Radio 1 website: 'Nihal's Guests: this week it's Mark Frith, ex-editor of *Heat*, who'll be telling us about which celebs are pratdiggers and which are cool dudes.' While someone, adopting their own rare title of Ms Zapf Dingbats, implanted a couple of seeds in a 'Rate It or Hate It' section of the *Leeds Guide Lifestyle* magazine:

Pratdiggers: Those friends of yours who always turn up to a party with the kind of obnoxious and pretentious companion who makes your stomach sink during small talk.

Umbrella prices: When you've already bought about four since Christmas and left them behind on various trains/

buses/nights out and you have to waste your precious honk on the low weight £7 version in an unexpected downpour.

All these contributors were sent their own Verbal Gardening T-shirts so are hopefully still spreading the words today.

Artrocker journo Rory was definitely keeping up the good work, sending me the following message:

I'm working on a parallel rumour about how they've had to adjust the size of the Channel 5 sets in her (Kaplinsky's) absence to ensure that the shorter presenters seem the same size as her. It's still in its infancy and may require a few tweaks, but I'll let you know if it sticks.

Our friend Dharmesh was also back in touch with an inspirational story about a pub quiz he'd recently competed in:

Our team name was 'Natasha Kaplinsky is six foot two'! It turns out that we won the quiz (with a feeble 42 per cent) and the team name was announced as the winners over the speaker system. As a result, I'm sure a large number of people left the pub believing that she is indeed six foot two!!

That people were coming up with their own dispersal techniques was heartening stuff, and I like to think similar thought was behind three mentions of 'honest' I discovered in these final days of the project; on the front page of the BBC website Ben Cooper, head of programmes at Radio 1, defended Chris Moyles as 'a high-profile and "honest" broadcaster' (those speech marks were included in the article to highlight the 'honesty' of the presenter, giving me hope that Mr Cooper was well aware of the new meaning). In fact, on the cover of Chris Moyles's own book (*The Difficult Second Book*) he himself featured a quote from Davina

McCall describing the author as 'Butt-clenchingly honest'. That is honest. The *London Lite* continued this trend with the following headline above a picture of the nation's top comic, one Mr Gervais, jogging:

Ricky runs every day to keep trim (honest).[50]

The boundaries of this in-joke, it seemed, were also widening every day.

The likes of 'honk' and 'mental safari' crept into the parallel world of sport too. While following the minute-by-minute transfer deadline day updates on the *Guardian* football blog I happened upon the following notes:

A piece of transfer news while we await 3 p.m.: Hull have bid £7m for Frazier Campbell. Yes, that's right, £7m. That's a lot of honk for a striker that has only ever performed in the Championship.

I bring news on Robinho to start us off, Peter Kenyon is still 'confident' that he could be earning his honk in west London as of tomorrow morning.

And:

There is a rumour that Frazier Campbell will be heading to Tottenham in part exchange for a certain person. Surely not. Meanwhile Stoke have upped their bid for Joe Ledley to £6m. That is a lot of honk for a Championship player.

---

50 The most recent sighting of this type was made on 3 September 2009 by Lucida Console who spotted this confessional headline on the BBC Sport website: '"I'm an honest player," says Rooney.'

I didn't write these messages, nor, it seemed, was I the only one watching them with insider knowledge. The following replies soon popped up on my screen. This from a man calling himself Davis:

Good work on your use of the word 'honk'. Hoping for an end to the Berbatov thing soon, because it is games.

And this from Simon:

No transfer gossip but with all the honk flying around tonight Kevin Keegan must be on a mental safari if he hasn't looked into signing the six foot two inch Natasha Kaplinsky to play alongside Owen this season.

The Verbal Gardening banter wasn't limited to the upper echelons of the Premiership either. On his lower league football blog Mr David Nicholls wrote of the FA Cup's preliminary rounds:

At this stage of course, it's all about the prize money; about seeing how much of the FA's honk you can jam into the club wallet. For clubs like Kingsbury and Eton Manor, plying their trade in the Spartan South Midlands and Essex Senior Leagues respectively, this round's relatively modest spoils of £750 to the victor will still go a long way.

Then through my letterbox there dropped a package containing two Southend United match-day programmes for their games against Walsall and Leyton Orient, in the middle of which were columns by a fan called Andy which included the following lines:

Versus Walsall: Ishmel, Jabo Ibehre and Marco Reich gave The Shrimpers' back four a torrid time and turned them inside out so convincingly that Anthony Grant's mental safari culminated in his heading powerfully past his own 'keeper.

Versus Leyton Orient: I expect an early season treat here at the Banks's Stadium this afternoon with a great game in prospect that, as they say down here in London, will give great value for your honk!

On a Post-it note Andy had written: 'around 3,000 or so programmes are sold per home game, so your etymological erudition, ghost written by me, is now in the homes of football lovers everywhere. Moreover, as this is an official publication, the editor tells me that all copies of the Walsall FC programme are also sent to the British Library. So you are now there as well in the published archives of Walsall FC. Now isn't that exciting! Have I earned a beer?!' Of course he'd earned a beer – a beer and a T-shirt and his pick of any five things in my house; this was enormously exciting. My words would now be housed in the British Library in an official capacity.

Other formal publications were similarly infiltrated. In an article about facebook in the *Telegraph** I was quoted as saying; 'I do have quite a few friends. But they're not all real friends: I'm a pratdigger.' Rival paper the *Ecton View* (a parish magazine published monthly for the 250 residents of the Northamptonshire village) featured these sentences in an account of a trip to Edinburgh:

The only downside was that we were opposite a nightclub which was a load of old bollo, and did not close until 5 a.m., so as you can imagine, every night was 'disco' night in our apartment!
    This was my second year and you can get carried away if you are not careful and end up spending a lot of honk on tickets,

but we saw more free comedy this time round which I have to say was equally as good as some of the paid venues.

Food and alcohol was plentiful, as you would expect, and we all came home slightly more honest than when we left.

If I am not careful I could ramble on about all the different shows we saw and the interesting habits my fellow companions have, but if you want to experience a mental safari for yourself then book yourself on next year's tour . . . you will not be disappointed.

Two more T-shirts were duly sent out to Colin and Sophie, the magnificent authors.

Perhaps most importantly, the words were now cropping up in everyday communication too. About to celebrate his thirtieth birthday, a gentleman called Jot emailed these travel arrangements to his party:

It's very easy to get there. There's a train to Diss from Liverpool St (cab at the other end costs about a tenner) which can be booked in advance for very little honk.

On the same day a Mr Roberts got in touch to say that having used it in a message to his USA branch, 'mental safari' had now entered office jargon (his initial message; 'Before we go off on a bit of a mental safari on this matter, I'll get the guys together on Monday morning to clarify our findings and get back to you all' was greeted with: 'Mental safari – now that's funny', and 'I love "mental safari". Great line' – both sent 'via BlackBerry'). And a typical MySpace message from a lady called Amelie read:

Hello we met @ the fringe – i know fletch hope u now dont think he's a pratdigger for introducing us, loved the show!!

All these usages I carefully collected, printed up and placed into my now bulging file of evidence. So widespread were the examples and so apparently random that I felt the dictionary authorities had to take the words seriously. Either that, or they had to recognise the preposterousness of my proposal and take the words humorously. Or maybe there'd be an administrative cock-up at Dictionary Headquarters and the words would end up in the 'accepted' tray by mistake. One way or another, they would surely get in.

There is a history of words sneaking into dictionaries by extraordinary means. The word 'syllabus', for instance, shouldn't really be taught at school but was included in the *OED* thanks to a misreading of a fifteenth-century manuscript of Cicero in which the Greek word for 'labels', *sittybos*, was mistakenly replicated as 'syllabus'. Accidents do happen. And they can easily be forgotten, especially when they're hidden in a 15,490-page-long work featuring 414,825 different words illustrated by 1,827,306 quotations. How else can one explain the *OED*'s inclusion of 'cellarhood' ('the state of being a cellar') despite it being completely impossible to think of a sentence in which it might be sensibly used, or 'admurmuration' (meaning 'an act of murmuring') which is printed with an accompanying note explaining that the word was 'never used'. Surely there's room for one of my words, all of which are definitely usable and have indeed been used, many many times! Please let me in!

When Americans refer to 'The Dictionary' they usually mean *Webster's Dictionary*, first published in 1806 by the aforementioned lexicologist (and schoolmaster) Noah Webster under the grandiloquent title *A Compendius Dictionary of the English Language*. So esteemed was his book that the word 'Websterian' soon entered the language meaning 'invested with lexical authority'. Webster had always been determined to get things right. He even lobbied Congress to make simplified spelling a legal requirement; this was a dictionary written almost exclusively by one man, an unsmiling teacher desperate to steer clear of in-jokes and creative definitions; an attempt to sanitise a language defiled by the likes of Johnson (whose dictionary, Webster whined, was 'extremely imperfect and full of error').

But despite such austere authority, at least one less recognised word did slip though Webster's tightly woven net. That word is 'dord', perhaps my favourite of all those featured in this or any other book. 'Dord'. Do you know what it means?

If you look it up in your own dictionary you probably won't find it, unless you happen to own the 1934 edition of *Merriam-Webster*. There you will find this entry:

dord (dôrd), *n. Physics & Chemistry.* Density

Yes, 'dord' is a synonym of 'density'. Well, it was for five years anyway. Before that, the letter 'D' was used as an *abbreviation* for density. Its little brother 'd' was also short for density. In the offices of *Webster's Dictionary* a slip bound for the 'abbreviations' section somehow found its way into the 'words' pile, clearly stating that 'D' or 'd' could mean density. 'D' or 'd' could mean density. And so, for a while, 'Dord' did mean density, until the mistake was discovered and erased from all subsequent editions. It's now a strange ghost word; a term with dictionary history and heritage but without a real meaning. I think it would make an excellent first name. Dord Horne; he (or possibly she) would definitely make his mark.

Such a mistake is understandable. Proofreading a dictionary must be one of the most laborious tasks in the world of publishing, and this lexical blunder is infused with the reassuring scent of human error. Nowadays, we rely far more on computerised spell-checkers, and one would expect 'dord' not to survive even one proof of a contemporary dictionary. But we shouldn't be so sure.

Mistakes do still creep into books. Take my book *Birdwatching-watching* as an example. When the first finished copy arrived at my door I grasped it excitedly; my first book, my first words bound and locked away for ever and ever. I opened it at random on page 364. Yes, there they were: my words. Just glancing down the page I could instantly recognise them as mine, used by generations of people before me of course, but never in this order. This was my collection. Except, hang on, what was that? Near the bottom, in brackets at the end of the penultimate paragraph; that wasn't one of my words! I quote verbatim:

'I stole (wicustJeremyStrongJth their permission this time) many of these words when describing the birds I saw in Africa'.

I was pretty certain I hadn't included the word 'wicust-JeremyStrongJth' in the last manuscript I'd handed in. In fact, I was sure it hadn't been in the last version the publishers had sent me for a final inspection. It's not the sort of word you fail to spot. So what was it doing in this, the actual printed version? Was every 'with' changed to such an odd-looking twenty-two-letter word?

No. Thankfully, there was just the one 'wicustJeremy-StrongJth' in my book, the result, I have since been informed, of 'human error'. An exhausted typesetter somewhere was working on two books at once, so for some reason decided to plonk 'wicustJeremyStrongJth' onto the 364th page of my first book. The 'word' seems to contain the name 'Jeremy Strong', a successful children's author with more than eighty of his own books to his name (including his very own joke book). Look him up on Wikipedia, he's there (that's how I now know he worked in a bakery after leaving school), but that doesn't really explain his appearance in my 'with' in my book, flanked by 'cust' and 'J'.

So 'wicustJeremyStrongJth' is a ghost word too, an unidentified interloper in a book published and shipped off to bookshops all over the country. And although it's not as simple or attractive as 'dord', I grew to like it. It had character. Have a closer look:

wicustJeremyStrongJth

It's got three capital letters in its midst, an unpredictably jazzy rhythm; yes, it's definitely unique. So I'm now fighting to keep it alive. My official line is that 'wicustJeremyStrongJth' wasn't a mistake, just a more formal version of the word 'with' to be used sparingly, perhaps once in a book, when you really want to stress the idea of togetherness.

So, just in case you happen to be a dictionary editor reading this, 'wicustJeremyStrongJth' definitely means 'with'. It should also be included in the dictionary. And while you may worry it's too unwieldy and outlandish for inclusion, there is precedent. For in 1903 a man called Rupert Hughes published *The Musical Guide*: a guide to music, unsurprisingly, which included a short dictionary of musical terms and instruments. One would imagine such an edifying work would be a haven of good, proper words. Like the debate section of the Associated Board of the Royal Schools of Music's website, one would expect such a cultural book to be a paradigm of grammar and lexical principles. But at the very end of this 252-page hardback detailing the numerous non-English words found in Classical music terminology, there can be found, just after an entry for 'zymbel' (the German for 'cymbal'), the following entry;

zzxjoanw (shaw). Maori. 1. Drum. 2. Fife. 3. Conclusion.

Yes, according to Hughes, 'zzxjoanw' is a Maori word for a drum (or, a type of flute or, bizarrely, a 'conclusion').

Visually, the similarities to 'wicustJeremyStrongJth' are remarkable; a name trapped inside some fairly random letters to create an ugly unpronounceable word. But this didn't stop 'zzxjoanw' which, Hughes helpfully informs the reader, is officially pronounced '*shaw*'. The entry survived several reprints with various different titles between 1912 and 1954 and was listed as a genuine musical instrument in *Mrs Byrne's Dictionary of Unusual, Obscure, and Preposterous Words* in 1974, although Mrs Byrne did question the pronunciation, suggesting the far more reasonable 'ziks-jo'an', instead.

In fact it wasn't until seventy years after its first appearance, in a 1976 publication called *Word Ways*, that the etymologist Philip Cohen finally said, hang on, that can't be a word because a) it's spelt nothing like how it's pronounced, b) the meanings are weirdly diverse, c) Maori only uses fourteen letters, which don't include 'z' 'x' or 'j', and d) look at it, that can't be a word.

But by then it was too late. Zzxjoanw had found its way into the mains water supply of the English language and could even be sampled in the unmusical science fiction novel *Earth* written in 1990 by David Brin. A 2001 book called *The Superior Person's Book of Words* by Peter Bowler included it, despite the author's claim that 'the avowed purpose of this witty little book is to equip the reader to be the superior person of the title by expanding the vocabulary of the rare and arcane'. This 'eminent alternative lexicographer' was then quoted in a 2005 book called *You Say Tomato: An Amusing and Irreverent Guide to the Most Often Mispronounced Words in the English Language*. So whilst it's not in the *OED* yet, 'zzxjoanw' has made it into dictionaries.

The keen wordwatcher and eventual spoilsport Philip Cohen viewed it as a joke on the part of Rupert Hughes. Indeed, if you squint hard enough, 'zzxjoanw' does look a little bit like a 'hoax'. But I like to think that it was actually a desperate attempt to win a competitive game of Scrabble (you'd need to use a blank tile, of course) between Hughes and his wife. It might simply have been an innocent typo like mine. But whatever its origin, zzxjoanw does prove that unlikely-looking words can succeed. The English language is flexible enough to accommodate wicustJeremyStrongJth which, by the way, is pronounced 'wermstraw', to rhyme with zzxjoanw and Featherstonehaugh.

I've got Jeremy Strong's blessing too. After tracking him down on the forum of his own website (alongside countless kids all extolling the virtues of his many books), I explained the situation and asked if he'd mind what I suppose is half his word one day landing in the dictionary. Within days he wrote back: 'You are welcome to use wicustJeremyStrongJth as you wish and I applaud your efforts to introduce new words to the language. Do let me know how things go. It's very exciting to know that I have somehow infiltrated your book without either of us knowing.' So for both our sakes, please do use wicustJeremyStrongJth yourselves. It's not easy to drop into conversation, but if you don't mind making a splash, give it a go.

My thirtieth birthday arrived with just a few weeks of the project to go. That's what happens about a thousand days after your tkday: you arrive at the start of your fourth decade. This brief time between two turning points is, I think, a perfect period at a crucial moment of your life to give something a go, to head off in a different direction, to at least attempt to make your mark. That's what these thousand days had been about, bucking the trend, stepping off the treadwheel and trying not to fall into every cliché going. Some people change jobs, some live in another country for a year or two, I tried to invent a new word.

Despite huge efforts and generosity from my family and friends, the birthday present I'll treasure longest came from a comedian who had also been up in Edinburgh and who didn't even know it was my thirtieth. Liverpudlian comic John Bishop was performing his show in the same room as me a couple of hours after mine. He wanted to show a film at the end of his slot, so I loaned him my projector and thought nothing more about it.

But as an unnecessary thank-you, a month after the festival, John sent me something quite extraordinary. He is, like me, a Liverpool fan. But John is a proper Liverpool fan, in that he's from Liverpool. He also does a bit of work at the club, on the LFC TV channel and at various functions throughout the year. So, instead of a bottle of wine or a box of chocolates, John sent me the following thank-you gift; a photo of Steven Gerrard, featuring foot-ballistic facts about Steven Gerrard and signed by Steven Gerrard. Steven Gerrard is my sporting hero. This was a great gift.

But John didn't only get Steven Gerrard to sign his name on this card. Beneath his signature, in large legible letters, Steven Gerrard wrote:

Don't sell this for any honk!

Having seen the show, John had explained the project to Steven Gerrard and persuaded him to join in by writing what to him must have seemed an utterly bizarre sentence under-neath his own face. My own gob was smacked. I'd always thought that despite him being my hero, I had nothing in common with Steven Gerrard. I could have had a laugh with Rafa Benítez, a drink with Fernando Torres, but Steven Gerrard wouldn't have had time for me. He was too focused on his football, not inter-ested in the sort of linguistic hi-jinks I spent my time engaged in. But no, Steven Gerrard had joined in. He'd endorsed my honk. If it was in the world's best footballer's vernacular, it was defi-nitely a word.

A few days after my thirtieth birthday, Samuel Johnson cele-brated his two hundred and ninety-ninth. Or rather, other people celebrated it for him. Amongst those paying tribute to the orig-inal lexicologist was a man called Ed Baker who chose this date to launch his own twenty-first-century dictionary, called Wordia: a word-based wiki-website and the world's first ever visual dictionary. By uploading videos onto the site, anyone can now describe any and every word in the language, thus providing unique and instantly intelligible definitions as opposed to the scientific and often dreary entries in most modern dictionaries. In its democratic attributes Wordia is similar to Wikipedia, but now that I'd come out as the Farmer, I didn't have to hide from its editor. In fact, knowing my interest in words and definitions the editor specifically invited me to contribute to the site. If you go to www.wordia.com you can see my entry for 'honk'. It's there. In a dictionary.

After all the excitement of the past couple of months Mr Elephant, Mrs Farmer and I went out for a few drinks in the Queen's Head (a pub, not the sovereign's skull), where we happened upon the weekly pub quiz. In honour of Dharmesh and Mr Daly, we entered under the name 'Natasha Kaplinsky is six foot two inches tall' and two hours later, after a scrapping performance, the question master announced, 'in fifth place we have – and this is quite a controversial name – Natasha Kaplinsky is six foot two inches tall!' We cheered heartily. Dharmesh was right. As we polished off our drinks three other quizzers asked us if she was really that tall; we confirmed the story, they passed it on. It had worked. I felt wider than my arm and will feel yet wider if you too could spread the rumour whenever she comes up in conversation (which she will, on average once every six weeks for a normal UK adult).

By now I was satisfied that I'd done all I could. But Stuart Goldsmith, the comic and street performer (he won bronze in the Street Performing World Championships in 2008, don't you know) who'd asked folks to put honk in his hat up in Edinburgh, was not.

One of his many day jobs was to warm up the crowd for ITV's lunchtime show, *Loose Women*, a programme occasionally derided, often by me, but never again. They're lucky to have Stu's services as warm-up artist. He's a fantastic comic, an excellent improviser and a real hit with the ladies. As well as providing him with many a dinner party-tale, this job meant Stu had access to the eponymous Loose Women and, being Approachable and Up for a Laugh Women too, Stu decided to explain the whole Verbal Gardening concept and ask if they could contribute to the final push.

They said they might.

So in the middle of a heated discussion about the etiquette* of serving up leftover food to one's guests, *The Cruise* star Jane McDonald brazenly announced that it was becoming more and more common, because 'People just haven't got the honk these days.' 'What's honk?' came the innocent cry of the other liberal ladies. 'You know, honk, honk; money,' Jane replied, offhandedly, before going on to blame the credit crunch.

I watched agog, spine tingling, scarcely believing that our words had hit the dizzy heights of this flagship ITV daytime programme. 'Honk' alone had now appeared on several BBC channels, ITV, Channel 4 and Sky One, countless radio stations and in almost every broadsheet newspaper. That's quite a CV for a word applying for a place in the dictionary.

There was just enough time for one further twist thanks, again, to the Edinburgh Fringe. Sitting on the sofa, still staring at the screen even though *Loose Women* had finished an hour ago, my phone rang waking me from my reverie. 'Withheld number' flashed up on the screen.

'Hello?' I said, nervously.

'Hi there, I'm one of the producers of *The Verb*. I'm just phoning to say that we'd like you to be a contributor on the show. Would that be OK?'

If you've not heard *The Verb*, you must. You literally must. It's a programme on Radio 3 hosted by the marvellous Ian McMillan[51] all about, you've guessed it (or heard it), words. The show's producer had indeed been in Edinburgh sniffing about for people who might be able to appear on the programme. On the strength of *Wordwatching* she asked me to be the programme's resident 'Language Spy'; I was to keep my eyes and ears out for anything unusual and each month report my findings to Ian on how language was changing, why people were saying what they were saying and what new words were sneaking into the language. Somehow I was now a professional Wordwatcher.

One of the esteemed guests on my first programme in this role was the New Yorker Ammon Shea, whose book *Reading the Oxford English Dictionary* had just been published in the UK. As I've already explained, it's about reading the *Oxford English Dictionary* and I loved it. While I'd been busy banging on its doors, Shea had spent a year locked inside the *OED*. Now fate had brought us together. Happily he liked the sound of my own words and promised to take them back with him to America.

After a lively discussion, Ian closed the programme with the words 'I don't get paid enough honk for this,' and I felt closer to the inner sanctum of the dictionary than ever before.

---

51 Who himself had got the word 'griddle', meaning 'to piss down railings after fifteen pints' into a Yorkshire dictionary called *Chelp and Chunter – How to Talk Tyke*; which, I should probably add, he himself wrote, much like Johnson centuries before.

26

Long after the festival had finished I received this text message from the ever-caring comedian Josie Long:

> Blockbuster video has a video games section. The slogan they have is 'Blockbuster. We are games.' This amused me.

This amused me too, both because Blockbuster had unwittingly demonstrated one of our seeds in such bold style, but more because that same seed had settled so comfortably in Josie's brain that for her, it now had this extra meaning. If ever something was described as 'games', Josie would always think of our own 'games'. Moreover, the phrase 'Blockbuster. We are games' implies something not entirely negative. Yes, Blockbuster might seem a little old-fashioned, a little bland, a little eighties, but Blockbuster is fun, Blockbuster is cool, Blockbuster is games.

So 'games' was on the move. It hadn't been an easy word to spread, but we had collected enough usages for it to at least be considered by the dictionary. In fact, thanks to an eagle-eyed wordwatcher called Victoria, I could even send the compilers an example of the word that predated my own meeting with the original Alex Games by a couple of decades. For, as she remembered while listening to my story in Edinburgh, 'games' had also been used to mean something other than the usual plural by an author called Diana Wynne Jones in her book *Witch Week*, published in 1982 and loved by Victoria. With remarkable parallels to my own story, Wynne Jones's protagonist Charles Morgan added his own meanings to words that already existed in the language. An entry in his journal like, 'I got up. I felt hot at breakfast. I do not like porridge. Second lesson was Woodwork but not for long. I think we have Games next', for example, was not as straightforward as it appears:

> Charles was not writing about the day's work. He really was writing about his secret feelings, but he was doing it in his own private code so that no one could know.

'Games' was part of this code:

> When Charles wrote 'Games', he meant bad luck.

And so for girls like Victoria all over the country, 'games' also meant bad luck. It's really up to you what it means next.

'Games' wasn't the only word to have its forerunners. Over the last couple of years I'd also uncovered several other instances of the word 'bollo' being bandied about before our attempt to spread it. I'm sure some of you spent much of the first few chapters muttering things like, 'Bollo? Isn't he that anthropomorphic ape from *The Mighty Boosh*?' and you'd have been right. Bollo is the name of the gorilla in Julian Barratt and Noel Fielding's BBC comedy and somehow we'd managed to come up with the word independently. It is, after all, a lovely-looking word. Some of you might also know an area of west London which features Bollo Road, Bollo Lane and Bollo House, a gastropub (a bollo concept itself, some might argue). Again, we didn't know such places existed, but heard about them after our own 'bollo' had been released. A handful of readers might even be familiar with the sleeve notes to *Reasons to be Cheerful: the Very Best of Ian Dury and the Blockheads* (by Ian Dury and the Blockheads), in which is written:

> When we are listening to 'Wake Up Little Susie' by the Evs, do we know if Chet is wearing his charcoal boot-flares? Are there conchos on a sleeve note? To reminisce, digress or inform? To reveal, portray or exonerate? For whom and for why? Sleeve-notists often make this query in the form of rampant bollo. Others have written two lines of six words each nicely spaced without punctuation.[52]

Dury's album was produced in 1999, proof that 'bollo' had been around far longer than we'd first thought. But it still hadn't made its way into the dictionary, so if I could use this sort of information to aid my cause that would be fine by me.

On a similar theme, my rare teacher, Mr Garamond, sent me this email towards the end of the project:

> I come bearing the gift of information regarding the seed 'mental safari'. Leafing through the pages of *Dombey and Son* by up-and-coming author C. Dickens I happened upon an early version of the seed. Check it and respect it:

> 'Paul had begun to speculate, in his own odd way, on the subject that might occupy the Apothecary's mind just at that moment; so musingly had he answered the two questions of Doctor Blimber. But the Apothecary happening to meet his little

---

52 For reasons that I can't fathom, the sleeve notes go on to say, 'Engineer Horne came flying out of his bed at 45mph and copped a carpet burn on his hooter that took seven weeks to heal. Straight or doubled over?' I have no idea what this means but was inordinately happy to see both 'Horne' and 'bollo' in the same publication.

patient's eyes, as the latter set off on that mental expedition, and coming instantly out of his abstraction with a cheerful smile, Paul smiled in return and abandoned it.' (216–17)

It seems crafty wordsmith Dickens has just managed to get in before us. *Dombey and Son* was published in 1848 – just less than 160 years before the seed was definitively invented and authorised for distribution by your good self.

This, I thought, was a great discovery. This Dickens[53] character had obviously used his 'mental expedition' before my 'mental safari', but I felt this early and slightly different usage would only lend extra clout to our eventual appeal. The mental safaris described in the course of my birdwatching year would be a timely renaissance of Dickens' own metaphor.

When I then googled 'mental safari' at the close of the project I couldn't believe my eyes. It seemed like a miracle. Almost a thousand days ago when Mr Bodoni had invented the phrase it yielded no results on the search engine. Now there were three *hundred*.

A man called Gary Freedman from Washington, USA, used it as the title of the 27 May 2007 post of his 'My Daily Struggles' blog. A morale-boosting website, www.abilitiesu.com, encouraged readers to 'Profit from all areas of your life' with an 'Honest Business Opportunities Review' ('honest' as in 'sincere' rather than 'obese', unfortunately); 'Your experience here will be like a Mental Safari', the site claimed in early 2006. On a lighter note, a number of websites were suddenly selling a magic trick called the 'Mental Safari', not quite as tricky as the trick Mr Elephant and I had pulled off in front of Abi Titmuss, but a trick

---

53 Charles Dickens is the Verbal Gardener behind such memorable phrases as 'red tape', 'by the same token' and 'behind the times'. He had linguistic green fingers.

nevertheless. I don't know if I'd missed them when researching the phrase in the first place, but now every other Google result was offering me the chance to buy 'a small ornate wood box . . . containing four different plaques each depicting the head of a wild animal'. The 'mental' bit about it is that after the volunteer has chosen their favourite animal, the 'magician' takes a note out from the box predicting that very creature. Amazing. Mental! And yours for just £45 (plus postage).

Elsewhere 'mental safari' had been used by a 'techno rock star' called Scott Lewis Franco in a fine song called 'Bitter Campari', partly, I imagine, because little else rhymes with that title (I tried but failed to contact Mr Franco but discovered him on a social network site that explained he was twenty-seven years old, from New York and liked baseball. He listed his body type as 'a few extra pounds', then under 'self-rated hotness', wrote '7' with the caveat, 'Hey, at least I'm honest!' – well, yes, I suppose you might be).

These were just a few of many examples of the words being used in print by strangers all over the world. Clearly, some didn't have the same meaning as our original Verbal Seed; my favourite finding was a misspelt advert for a 'metal safari hat' (I think 'mental safari hat' sounds far more interesting. I'm imagining a deer stalker hat, but with one ear cocked like a curious Labrador), but that's beside the point. There were enough usages here to convince me, at least, that the phrase was a part of the language. I'm not sure how many of these people were using 'mental safari' because of our work, but I had to make the most of the coincidence. I had to make sure that if and when the phrase came to the attention of the language authorities, it was we who got the credit.

Away from the Internet, my favourite wordbook of all was the *Dictionary of Slang and Colloquial English* written by John S. Farmer (another verbal farmer!) and W. E. Henley in 1905, the first dictionary I have ever sat down and read from cover to cover (my edition was 'abridged from the seven-volume work, entitled Slang and its Analogues', and a mere 534 pages).

It was in this red leathery tome that I discovered such fantastic terms as 'all-overish', meaning 'an indefinite feeling of apprehension or satisfaction', 'bag of mystery' for 'a sausage', 'high-pooped', an adjective meaning 'heavily buttocked', and 'molocker', a bewilderingly specific word for 'a renovated hat'. He listed countless alternatives to honk: 'armour', 'blunt', 'clink', 'dimmock', 'evil', 'fat', 'greed', 'honey', 'iron', 'jink', 'kilter', 'lurry', 'muck', 'nugget', 'oof', 'posh', 'quirk', 'rivet', 'scud', 'tin', 'uncle', 'vamp', 'wedge' and 'yumyum'. And there were funcrimes here too, like the 'bugger' who 'steals breastpins from drunken men', the 'fogle hunter' who nicks pocket handkerchiefs or the 'unregenerate chicken-lifter', a petty thief.

But the word that really caught my eye was 'paddle', defined by John S. Farmer as follows:

'The hand: see Daddle. As verb, (1) to drink: hence to have paddled, to be intoxicated: see Screwed; (2) to go or run away. See Canoe.'

Ignoring the verbs, I turned to 'Daddle', where I found more than twenty alternatives to 'paddle'. So much for there being few slang terms with which to refer to hands. This Farmer listed 'chalk-farm, claw, clutch, cornstealer, duke,[54] fam, famble, feeler, flapper, flipper, forceps, forefoot, fork, grappling-iron (or hook), goll (old), oar, palette, paw, plier, shaker, wing, Yarmouth mitten'. But again, I thought this was great news, reputable proof for the dictionary authorities that 'paddles' has been slang for hands for years and years. We might not have invented it, but I'd be thrilled if I was credited as the cause of its dictionary comeback.

---

54 One of my favourite suspicious etymological stories is that 'dukes' became slang for 'fists' on account of the Duke of Wellington's famously large and hooked nose. So punchable (or punched) did it look, that 'fists' became known as 'duke-busters' across the land, and this was then shortened to 'dukes'. Tremendous stuff.

Hitchings was right when he wrote that 'very few "new" words are fresh coinages. Most are borrowings, compounds, fusions of existing terms, or revivals of old ones'. Unintentionally I'd been trying to revive a term used centuries before; my modern use represented the resurfacing of a whale, the waking of a giant, the waving of an ancestral paddle. We weren't corrupting the language, we were coming to its aid. In the words of Dryden: 'Obsolete words may be laudably revived, when either they are more sounding, or more significant than those in practice.' Of course 'paddle' is more sounding *and* more significant than 'hand'!

In Jonathon Green's *Slang Down the Ages*, I then found the following sentence in a section all about money slang: 'Another foreign coinage is hoot, from the Maori *utu*, meaning money.'[55]

I couldn't believe it. 'Hoot', alongside 'honk', was without doubt, we'd thought, our own invention. But no, on the other side of the world, Maoris had been using the same-sounding word to mean the same thing for at least the last two hundred years. I even found it in the *Collins Dictionary* as the third meaning after 'an owl noise' and 'a laugh'.

Perhaps I should have done this research before sowing my own seeds, but these discoveries only made me more confident in all our own ideas. In the course of trying to get my words in the dictionary I had found out that none of them was actually mine. They had all been used by other people before. I even discovered 'tkday' being used to refer to Thanksgiving in America (short for 'Turkey Day'). But even though this wasn't part of the original plan, I had also learnt that it wasn't a problem.

---

55 In fact, further reading of an online Maori dictionary (www.maoridictionary.co.nz) reveals that *utu* is most often used to mean 'revenge' and then 'compensation' in New Zealand. Jonathon Green's translation of 'money' may be rather simplistic, but when *utu* emerged as the English slang 'hoot' from the filters of travel and time, that is indeed the meaning that stuck.

Shakespeare didn't really invent every one of the 1,700 that the *OED* credits him, but he got all the glory. So would I.

In the words of a man called Henry Wheeler Shaw, 'About the most originality that any writer can hope to achieve honestly is to steal with good judgement.' He should know. He wrote under the pseudonym Josh Billings before dying in 1885, and if you look up the verb 'josh' in the *OED* you'll see:

'Josh, *v. U.S. slang.* [C.f. *Josh Billings*, pseudonym of an American humorist.] *trans.* To make fun of, chaff, banter, ridicule.'

By using the phrase 'just Joshing' to excuse his sometimes challenging humour, the word became for ever associated with him. He managed to get 'josh' in the dictionary. Even though the word was in use as early as 1845, years before he started writing, he got the acclaim. What's more, 'just Joshing' was shortened by telegraph keyboard users to 'J J' towards the close of the century, causing the writer himself to write with justified pride that, 'J J is the new J K [just kidding]'. And whilst the abbreviation fell out of use in the early twentieth century, the early twenty-first has seen the initials reappear in Internet chat rooms round the world. People may assume the letters 'jj' on a forum mean 'just joking' but really it's Josh Billings, having the last laugh.

Could my words follow his into the dictionary? In truth, I was still uneasy about 'games', ashamed of its wicked beginnings and embarrassed by my initial envy. In the course of spreading my words I had managed to write countless newspaper articles and even my very own book, thus emulating the man I'd attempted to mock. Also, I'd met him and he was really nice. 'Games' the adjective made me feel like a silly billy.*[56]

But I was proud of 'pratdigger' and 'tkday', both of which I

---

56 Although I was heartened to read that the word 'games' was the second most popular search term on Google in the UK between 2004 and 2009. That can't be coincidence. Just between you and me, I still secretly hope our adjective will take off.

felt filled a gap in the language. After an absence of two hundred years it was surely time for the former to re-establish itself. And in this digital age, with the greetings card industry booming, surely the latter would be a success. I may not have snuck 'tkday' into many publications, but this story itself should demonstrate exactly what the word and the occasion can mean.

I had less hope for 'honest' or 'paddles'; 'fat' and 'hands' may simply be too massive to budge. But I have no doubt our alternatives will live on in my own secret code at least. 'Honk', though, is surely the future. From day one this was the word people took to their hearts. Direct, memorable, and supported admirably by 'demi', I felt confident that it was now on its way into the language hall of fame. It has the authentic ring of 'cash', 'clink' and 'bling' and with the likes of those *Loose Women* behind it, this was surely our ticket to linguistic immortality.

I was now content that all our seeds had been planted successfully. They could all be found in texts around the world. Now I needed to make sure that when they were found in texts by curious readers around the world, they could also be found in the dictionary when those curious readers looked them up. Murray wanted his book to be an inventory of all words. Ours needed to be in it.

27

Three years after commencing the project, D(ictionary) Day itself was one of frantic administration. After an hour in the stationer's buying all manner of folders, clips, blank DVDs and staples, I spent the rest of the day painstakingly photocopying and filing every single example of my words into ten plump Verbal Gardening dossiers. The more evidence I sent them, I reasoned, the more attention the dictionary authorities would pay to our words. So even though an unhealthy percentage of the examples came from one 'Alex Horne', I included everything.

I knew how carefully the editors would research any potential new entries and was well aware the paper trail would lead back to me, so instead of trying to cover my tracks I embraced the body I'd created, burned a DVD of my appearances on the Daily Politics, Sky News and BBC World alongside Josie Long's 'mental safari' on STV and Jane McDonald's 'honk' on *Loose Women* and photocopied every newspaper article I'd written and every football programme, parish magazine and music review I'd been sent. Every previous usage of the words in old books, new websites and obscure sleeve notes I attached too, alongside a scan of Steven Gerrard's note as the ultimate seal of approval. Each file contained well over a hundred usages of my words.

These ten parcels of paperwork I addressed to ten different dictionaries:

1. The *Oxford English Dictionary*: still *the* dictionary – Verbal Gardening nirvana.
2. The *Cambridge Dictionary*: they let me in a decade before, would they do so again?
3. The *Collins Dictionary*: founded in Glasgow in 1819 by Presbyterian schoolmaster William Collins, now owned by Rupert Murdoch.
4. The *Chambers Dictionary*: also based in Scotland, GSOH – we had history.
5. The *MacMillan Dictionary*: very nearly the publisher of Murray's dictionary – its dictionaries are currently used in over 140 countries worldwide.
6. The *Merriam-Webster Dictionary*: the American dictionary – famously forbidding but a fine home for my words all the same.
7. The *Longman Dictionary of Contemporary English*: they call themselves 'your link to living language' – worth a shot, I thought.
8. The *Cassell Dictionary of Slang*: edited by the godfather of slang, Jonathon Green.
9. The *American Dialect Society*: the new words monitoring station, run by Allan Metcalf, author of *Predicting New Words*.
10. *Comments on Etymology*: a respected linguistic journal edited and published by Gerald Cohen, word historian extraordinaire.

Laid out on my bed, these bundles looked mightily impressive. As linguistic experiments go, this was an unprecedented pile of evidence to send to my superiors. I had done all I could. This was my equivalent of scrawling 'quiz' on every wall in Dublin.

I heaved the packages down to the post office and spent yet another dollop of honk sending each of them first class to the offices of the world's leading lexicographers. Rather than feeling any guilt that I was wasting these important people's time I actually felt that I was doing my duty as an English-speaking citizen.

These words were definitely 'out there'; I was merely ensuring those who guard our language knew about them. James Murray would have been pleased with me. 'Fling our doors wide!' he'd proclaimed, exhorting people everywhere to send him definitions and examples of words. 'All – not one, but all – must enter!'

I had no idea how long it would take the dictionaries to respond, but I did know that in the meantime I had to keep working; this was no time to sit and wait for letters of congratulation from the editors, this wasn't the end of the project, merely the first point at which the words might be judged. Whether or not they were allowed into the record books yet, I had to ensure they remained in circulation for years to come.

Fortunately, this didn't require too much extra effort because, as I soon discovered, the words were now safely established in the dictionary in my head. Since passing the parcels through a hatch in the post office I have used 'honk', 'pratdigger', 'games', 'bollo', 'tkday', 'mental safari', 'paddles', 'honest' and 'demi' in several radio interviews, various publications and countless conversations. To my delight, I have also witnessed several of the words used independently in an assortment of media, with 'honk' still leading the way; various people have plonked it into various emails, someone other than 'VG' posted it on Urban Dictionary, it appears regularly on Radio 3's *The Verb* and, on the day of Alistair Darling's 'Robin Hood' Budget, 22 April 2009 (Day 1182), it rose to become the fourth most popular 'trend' on Twitter.

The first reply to drop through my letter box was from the editor of the *Collins Dictionary*. It began promisingly enough:

Thank you for your letters of 6 November, listing the new coinages you suggest for inclusion in our dictionaries.

The rest, however, was ever so slightly dismissive:

> We regularly receive letters and emails suggesting new words
> for our books. Dictionaries rarely, if ever, include a word solely
> on the suggestion of one user or one organisation. We require
> a spread of citations over a significant period of time as evidence
> that the word is real, and not just a coinage used by one indi-
> vidual or group.

This wasn't looking good.

> In the case of the words you have suggested, there is still insuf-
> ficient evidence that these words have been in wide usage over
> a long period of time, despite the citations you have kindly
> provided.

What? 'Insufficient evidence'   Steven Gerrard used honk! The
letter did end with the promising line:

> In the meantime we will continue to monitor the progress of
> these words.

But there was no doubt about it – this was my first rejection.
Not long afterwards, *Chambers*, my laughter-loving allies,
politely said no:

> I was very pleased that you included some citations as
> evidence of the words in current use. We would not include
> words just because they were etymologically plausible if we
> did not have evidence of the kind you have provided. Having
> said that, like other dictionary publishers, it is not our policy
> to include words until they have been used by a range of
> people over a reasonable period of time. Therefore, before

any of these words could be included in *The Chambers Dictionary*, we would need evidence from an even greater variety of sources.

How is a thousand days not reasonable

Oxford rejected me too. A quick glance at the letter was enough to realise they weren't going to let my words in. I read with ever-increasing despondency their line:

We need to be very sure that they are well established before we include them.

Even my old home Cambridge couldn't help me this time:

We appreciate the suggestions, and the carefully gathered evidence, that you have sent us.

But they couldn't offer me a place.

While the headlines seemed gloomy, there was hope to be found between the lines. Collins had written:

If you have invented a word, the only way to get it to appear in dictionaries is to convince a large number of people uncon-nected with yourself to start using it unselfconsciously – a notoriously difficult and unpredictable task. If this happens, eventually it will generate enough citations over a sufficiently diverse range of sources for us and other dictionary publishers to consider it for inclusion.

Chambers had added:

However, I am delighted to take a note of these words in the meantime. If people find these words useful, and start to repeat them, it is possible that they will catch on and eventually merit a place in the dictionary.

Even Oxford included the sentences:

Your contributions have been added to the dictionary's word files.

and

All suggestions for additions to the dictionary are carefully considered by our new words team, but before they can start drafting an entry for any new word they need a body of published evidence demonstrating sustained and widespread use over a period of years.

All I needed to do was to 'convince a large number of people' to 'find these words useful'. If those people started 'demonstrating sustained and widespread use over a period of years' I *could* get in the next edition.

So that's where you come in. I need your help. When Sir James Murray began his work he asked the British public to share 'the toil and honour of such an undertaking'. Now I have to do the same.

The dictionaries know my words now, but they're not convinced everyone else does. I'm still telling everyone I meet about them, but I really need you to start using them too. Go on! Slip in a honk, you know you want to. And if you can get one of the words in print, all the better. Go to www.urbandictionary.com and give the words a thumbs up. Look out for 'honest' people. Spend lots of 'honk'. And, above all, send me the evidence. If you do I'll send you a T-shirt, then, in another three years I'll knock on the dictionary door again. 'There's more!' I'll shout to the editors.

And if they say it's still not enough, I'll try again. And then again:

'It is possible that they will catch on and eventually merit a place in the dictionary,' said Chambers. I will be patient. Samuel Johnson originally allowed himself three years to write his Dictionary. In the end, it took him nine. I must also be prepared to wait.

For the first time since its original publication, the *Oxford English Dictionary* is currently undergoing a complete revision, led by the efficient pair of John Simpson and Edmund Weiner. By December 2008 they had reached 'reamy' (a great word meaning 'creamy' or 'frothy', used for the first time in 1831), which sounds quite impressive, except that they started the process at M and Simpson was appointed editor in 1993. It's not expected to be finished until 2037. I think that's a realistic target for all of us.

At the end of his book about the *OED*, Simon Winchester eagerly looks forward to *OED3*'s publication, imagining the three hundred-strong staff of scholars, researchers, readers and consultants 'trying now to catch and snare the indiscernible, ever outward-spreading ripples of idiom and neologism and slang and linguistic invention by which the English language expands and changes, year by year, decade by decade, century by century'. I will keep casting my bait until one of the words is finally caught and reeled in, once and for all.

28

Of course, English isn't only spoken in England.

I'd almost forgotten about the other five packages that I'd sent out but, one by one, my American correspondents responded.

Unsurprisingly, the folks at Merriam-Webster couldn't offer my words a home either, but they did take my input seriously:

> We appreciate the time and effort you've taken to copy and send the numerous enclosures, including the DVD, and we enjoyed learning of these neologisms. We will certainly look for any occurrences of them in North American publications.

Well, I appreciate your time and effort too and will do my best to infiltrate as many North American publications as possible in the coming months.

At this point, however, the tide began to turn. Sending my words to the etymologists Allan Metcalf, Jonathon Green and Gerald Cohen was the longest shot of all. These were the men whose works I had read so avidly while researching my Verbal Gardening History. Sure, I wanted to share my own neologisms with them, but they were bound to shrug them off as the deluded ranting of an amateur, weren't they?

Not really. Allan Metcalf wrote this lovely response:

Mr Horne, thank you very much for the bountiful examples and citations of new words. I should have acknowledged them earlier, but I wanted to wait till I could give a reply more fitting to all the material you sent. It will probably be a while still, but I do look forward to reviewing everything you sent.

Jonathon Green penned this:

I cannot say how grateful I am for your efforts . . . (W)hat you have done is invaluable: offer the words in context. This means citations for me, and I am hugely grateful. As to 'entry into the dictionary', I can certainly offer (some of) them a home. Once I've checked through they'll be joining the existing database.

And best of all, Gerald Cohen, the man who tracked down Smart Aleck Hoag, sent this:

Thank you for your letter of 6 Nov with its accompanying information on slang. I'm certainly willing to help you bring your items to the attention of lexicographers for possible entry in dictionaries, especially slang dictionaries. Actually, this is quite simple. The Internet discussion group of the American Dialect Society (which discusses all aspects of English, not just dialects) includes as members all the leading lexicographers. All either I or you would need to do is bring your items to their attention.

But what really interests me about your material is that it deserves to be compiled and published as one or more articles. If you'd like to consider *Comments on Etymology* as a publication where you could develop and print your material, I'd be happy to have it appear there.

I couldn't believe it. These men were taking me seriously. The editors of the dictionaries might have needed more evidence but maybe, just maybe, I could gain credibility by association with Metcalf, Green and Cohen. I wrote back, thanked them all and told Mr Cohen I would be extremely interested in having my material appear in *Comments on Etymology*.

He promptly replied:

Just to keep you posted. I've been swamped with the start of the semester but hope to work on your article this Thursday. Otherwise, for sure, this weekend. Your material on 'honk' (money) looks interesting. The term doesn't appear in Jonathan Lighter's *Historical Dictionary of American Slang*, and I know he'll be very interested in what you have to say about it.

My article! This was brilliant.

Or was it? All of a sudden the guilt that had racked me over the 'games' affair flared up once more. I'd already wasted the time of Alex Games himself, as well as Wikipedia, Victoria Coren and countless schoolchildren across the land; now I was letting a respected etymologist work away on words I'd made up.

But then again, this was my last and only chance to get some tangible result this time round. I bit my tongue and wrote back once more, thanking him profusely again. I would just have to be his second Smart Alex.

A few weeks later I received the official journal, published and bound: my words, in proper print. And if this was to be my legacy, I'd be immensely proud of my very own article which opened with these lines:

THREE BRITISH SLANG ITEMS:
'HONK' (MONEY), 'MENTAL SAFARI' AND 'PRATDIGGER'
Alex Horne

[editor, G. Cohen: Alex Horne is an independent scholar with an interest in slang, and, I believe, has a valuable contribution to make to word studies. I would like to encourage him to continue sharing his material with the scholarly community. The three items he discusses here can be added, for example to Dalzell & Victor 2006 and to Green 2005.]

As a keen but recreational wordspy, I always like to keep an eye on new words and phrases. My study at home is littered with notebooks full of scribbles and cuttings, all documenting what I consider to be unusual lexical behaviour.

A few years ago I decided to pay particularly close attention to a handful of slang words and phrases that had pricked my ears when heard on the radio, TV and amongst friends but which I couldn't find in any dictionaries or in any online wordlists. I have since kept records of any usages of these words that I've encountered in an attempt to build up a body of evidence to show both their meaning and their growth. It is my opinion that the following three items are now common enough to justify inclusion in collections of slang at the very least.

So I was beginning to break America. I didn't expect to triumph overseas first, but perhaps after succeeding stateside I can return, victorious, and march straight through British security.

Of course, that is still some way off. At some point poor kind Mr Cohen might discover my sneakiness, possibly by reading this, and put American lexicographers on red alert. My name will be a dirty word amongst etymologists everywhere. At least then, however, it would be a word, dirty or otherwise. Because that was the aim of this game; to invent a word. And I am confident that I have done that. Even though they weren't yet in any of the major printed dictionaries, 'honk', 'pratdigger', 'mental safari', 'bollo', 'games', 'paddle', 'demi', 'honest' and 'tkday' are definitely words. Look at that sentence again – there they are: words. And if I take away the quotation marks, they become even more convincing. The honks blend in with the other nouns, mental safari is a normal phrase, demi doesn't jar, paddle sits nicely at the front of a clause, even tkday looks familiar now.

Just because they're not in the dictionary, my words aren't meaningless. As Samuel Johnson himself wrote, 'Words are hourly shifting their relations, and can no more be ascertained in a dictionary, than a grove, in the agitation of a storm, can be accurately delineated from its picture in the water.'

How can you say that something people use as a word is not actually a word? It can be a 'bad' word, or a slang word, or a substandard or colloquial word; but it is still very much a word. To deny its existence is as wishful and futile as saying that the car that is about to run you over does not exist.

Ammon Shea, as spoken to his eleventh grade
English teacher, Mr Wozniak

29

I still had one final Verbal Gardening task to carry out; a date with Des(tiny) and Carol and, with a bit of luck, the chance to sow seeds all over the *Countdown* studio.

My preparation for the actual recording was far less intense than the hours I'd spent cramming for the auditions. I was definitely going to be on the programme now, and all that really mattered was spreading my own words. If that meant going down in the flames of a humiliating defeat, so be it.

Even so, before my own appearance I did watch the programme avidly, and four days before my day of reckoning was taken aback by a certain beard; the smirking beard of a man I recognised; the beard of Lloyd, the smug man from my first audition. He won his opening game easily, finishing way ahead of the current champion (and me, on my sofa) but in the next game, surprisingly, was beaten by Notts County midfielder Neil MacKenzie, the first professional footballer to ever appear on the programme, who went on to win no fewer than five of his own games. 'Never mind,' Lloyd said magnanimously afterwards, 'at least I got the teapot for my mum.' Exactly, I thought. He did what he came to do. As would I.

Three days before the show I flew to Northern Ireland with my wife for a wedding. I wish I could say it was in County Down but it wasn't. It was in County Fermanagh. This, I thought, would be a refreshing break before the stampede. I would arrive at the studio recharged and ready.

Unfortunately, I couldn't think about anything but *Countdown*. I'm ashamed to say that I spent much of the romantic proceedings in a daze, thinking more about vowels than vows, Carols than hymns, wingdings than weddings. Most of the service I spent involuntarily staring at the lovingly crafted marriage booklet, trying to make a nine-letter word out of 'let us pray'. 'Seven,' I murmured instead of 'Amen', 'Players'. Not bad.

I was awful company at dinner, keen to chat about *Countdown* but only *Countdown*; not quite the life and soul that wedding receptions need. Thankfully I was sitting next to Rachel who'd heard it all before, and a man called Gerald who was also a tad uncommunicative. When I tried to describe my forthcoming appearance on TV I got nothing back. I couldn't believe he wasn't fascinated by someone who was just about to be on *Countdown*. But any mention of my tactics, any attempts to practise with some numbers, any *Countdown* references at all were greeted with grunts. From the main course onwards we both stared at the tablecloth. My eyes were focused on his place name. Gerald glared.

Back in England, the day before my turn, I watched the final of *Countdown* Series 58 in which David, the impressive Ulsterman from Omagh, County Tyrone, beat the softly spoken number six seed, Richard Priest from Newcastle-under-Lyme, with words like 'apogees' and 'epidote'. Richard dug out 'mirador' but this wasn't enough against a man who'd found 'saponin' and 'agoutis' in the semi-final. David O'Donnell had an average 107 points per game. I was as intimidated as I was impressed.

On *Countdown* Eve I met up with Mr Roman and his girlfriend Cassie who would be supporting me from the audience (and drastically reducing its average age). We tried to plan my assault, devising means by which I could make my mark in the memoirs of *Countdown*. My basic plan had been to create one of our new words out of the letters revealed by Carol so that they'd be spelt out for wordwatchers around the country to see, admire and absorb. But, as Mr and Mrs Roman pointed out, this wasn't a given. The chances of the right letters being picked *and* then spotted by me were slim, especially if I only lasted one game; a definite possibility. So, if I wasn't able to get my own words broadcast I needed to ensure I made my name in some other way.

Countdown has a rich televisual history. It was the first programme ever broadcast on Channel 4, on 2 November 1982, meaning its tkday will take place soon after the publication of this book, on 20 March 2010. The opening show was won by a man called Michael Goldman who later sued the organisers of a Scrabble tournament for not granting him enough time to go to the toilet. He won ninety pounds plus some costs *and* crops up in various books like this. Could I do something similar? Should I, for instance, become the first person to be caught cheating on the programme, using a calculator, mobile phone or pocket dictionary? Should I declare a nine-letter word every round and just hope for the best? Should I walk out in mock indignation if a rude word appeared by accident on Carol's letter board?

No. In the end, we settled for filling in my Contestant's Questionnaire in what I hoped would be a memorable way (see opposite.)

If they didn't ask me about my love of calypso music they were bound to ask me why I liked Natasha Kaplinsky so much, weren't they?

I slept intermittently the night before my day, racked by bewildering dreams whenever I managed to drop off. As the sun began to strain through the fragile Travel Lodge curtains I dreamed I was opening the batting for England; a kaplinsky Australian charged in to bowl and I suddenly realised I'd forgotten my bat. I think I was nervous. I couldn't go back to sleep after this virtual sporting ordeal so had a bath, a kipper for breakfast (brain food, I was told at Cambridge) and a rigorous walk to the studio.

After signing in at the reception of Yorkshire Television I sat

COUNTDOWN CONTESTANT UPDATE FORM

Copies of this form are sent to the COUNTDOWN script writer, so it is important that you let us have as many details as possible.

NAME.... ALEX HORNE ....
<small>Please write your name as you would like it to appear on screen</small>

FAVOURITE ACTOR/ACTRESS.... NATASHA KAPLINSKY (not really an actress, sorry)

FAVOURITE POP GROUP/MUSIC.... CALYPSO - LORD KITCHENER

FAVOURITE SONG.... HAPPY BIRTHDAY TO YOU

FAVOURITE PLACE.... MIDHURST (WEST SUSSEX)

FAVOURITE TEAM/SPORTS PERSON.... LIVERPOOL F.C.

FAVOURITE BOOK.... GOLFING FOR CATS by ALAN COREN

MOST MEMORABLE EXPERIENCE.... EITHER MEETING THE POPE IN THE VATICAN WITH MY NEW WIFE, or meeting KEN DODD in Nottingham

BIGGEST CLAIM TO FAME: WON A CRACKER JOKE-WRITING COMPETITION WHILST WORKING AT BUDGENS IN MIDHURST

WHAT WOULD YOU SAY IS YOUR GREATEST ACHIEVEMENT: IN ONE YEAR I MET PEOPLE FROM 189 of the worlds 192 countries - who lived in London (I couldn't find anyone from Palau, Tuvalu, or the Marshall Islands).

FAMOUS PERSON YOU WOULD MOST LIKE TO MEET AND WHY? CAROL VORDERMAN - not necessary why. We went to the same college at Cambridge.

AMBITIONS: To BREAK A WORLD RECORD

CURRENT HOBBIES: BIRD WATCHING - well, looking after my two children (Bengara + Shukria)

---

on a reassuringly kitsch sofa and tried to relax. 'Do you remember me?' said the man sitting next to me.

I turned to see a broad tie, decorated with cheese and rats which I followed all the way up to a man's face and thought, much to my relief, Yes! I do remember you! 'Jeremy! How are you? How's the Latin?'

I couldn't believe I'd remembered. This was the man I'd taught Latin at the *Limax et Thridax* in Edinburgh three years previously.

'Oh, still going!' Jeremy said excitely. 'I took night classes after the GCSE and did my A-level a few weeks ago. Should find out the result during the festival. Are you going up this year?'

We caught up quickly. I told Jeremy I was getting into birdwatching, he told me that like Mr Matisse, he was a Health and Safety inspector, hence the tie. It was a good few minutes into our animated chat that I realised we were the only ones talking and remembered where we were and what I was about to do. Others had joined us on the orange and green couches and were looking far edgier than the two of us. It was then that it dawned on me: Jeremy was a contestant too. We all were. These were the people I'd be up against in the *Countdown* studio. This was my fate and, for some reason, Jeremy was part of it.

In the green room with just minutes before the recording the programme's producer welcomed us and outlined the day's running order. Jeremy was up first, against yesterday's champion Sam. I would play the winner. Next up was Marilyn, a nervous-looking lady a generation or two older than me; then Jonny and Tom, both around their tkdays. The producer explained that while waiting for our contests we could sit and watch in the studio if we wanted. Most of us did, so made our way into the arena.

If you've ever wondered how they make *Countdown*, wonder no more, for I shall now reveal the secrets of the *Countdown* process and put to bed any rumours that have been up too late:

What you see on TV is exactly what goes on in the studio.

There. That cleared that up.

There could be no *Countdown* scandal because it is the most wonderfully straightforward programme in today's TV schedule. There were no computers helping Susie find her words in Dictionary Corner. Nor did Carol have a calculator helping her calculate. Des was that colour. The audience was that old. There were no tricks. As I've said before, this was *Countdown*, not *Family Fortunes*.

The TV programme lasts forty-five minutes and they take about forty-six minutes to record it. The only thing you don't see at home is the warm-up act, a professional, amiable and above all funny comic called Dudley Doolittle who worked his old school magic on the audience, somehow implying that the

'Deaf Aid Position' could be found in the *Kama Sutra*, gently teasing a coachload of people who'd come from Rotherham, and getting hugely excited about four nit nurses who had unwisely sat in the front row and made themselves known.

As well as raising the temperature in the room, Dudley's job was to introduce the protagonists, and he did this with unfussy style. 'We've got Eric and Ernie on cameras,' he crooned and everyone roared. 'And these are the contestants, reigning champion Sam and our new challenger, Jeremy!' More cheering. 'And that's a grand tie, Jeremy. A real belter!'

As Sam and Jeremy settled in, the real stars were brought on. First up, the one and only Susie Dent, 'looking like a racing snake', according to Dudley; and alongside her, the evergreen comedian Arthur Smith. 'Look at Smith,' chuckled Dudley, 'rag dealer, price of fish.' I don't know exactly what he meant but it was exactly right. Arthur did look a bit 'rag dealer, price of fish'.

After announcing Des as if he was a heavyweight boxer, Dud left the stage to his superior who continued the banter with the nit nurses and mentioned his tremendous record sales rather a lot. Again though, he was charming. I was charmed. This was proper entertainment.

But Des wasn't in charge, this wasn't Des's show; he was merely here to introduce the main event, the legendary First Lady of Channel 4: 'It's Carol Vorderman!' And on she sauntered, resplendent in what Des described as 'a lovely summer frock', grinning from ear to ear and, apparently, the same age as when she appeared in the first programme almost my whole lifetime ago. This was her programme. She cracked more jokes than Des and Dud combined, laughed like a slightly sozzled aunt at the wedding I'd been at days before and, when it was finally time to start the first game, everyone felt like they'd known each other for years. Some of us had.

As the familiar theme tune was piped into the studio I didn't know who I wanted to win. If Jeremy was victorious I'd get to face him; the teacher versus the pupil. This seemed apt but worrying. He'd got an A star in Latin GCSE all by himself. He'd taken the A-level last month. I hadn't studied for a decade. Would his mind be quicker?

Also, I was sitting next to Sam's boyfriend Andy. It would be very awkward if I cheered when his girlfriend lost.

So when she did lose I kept calm. It was a tight game but Jeremy was just too good. What's more, Des spent the whole time talking about his Health-and-Safety-themed tie. He'd made an impression! People would remember Jeremy! Could I do the same?

There was only a brief break between games. Before I had time to worry further I was wheeled out by Dud, the music started again and Jeremy and I shook hands in preparation for battle. 'Good luck,' we both said.

Forty-five minutes later we shook hands again.

I'm not quite sure how but I'd won. It was much harder to relax in front of the audience than in it, I was distracted by the carpet laid on our desks to absorb any unwanted noise and by the occasional three-letter words muttered by Des in the chair next to me. It was endearing to hear him play along with every game but when he found and whispered words like 'set' and 'the' it wasn't all that helpful. Thankfully, Jeremy wasn't on his best game, perhaps satisfied with the victory that had guaranteed his teapot. After fluking a couple of early seven-letter words I grew in confidence and even managed to seal the win before deciphering the conundrum, **R E T O X T R E V**.[57]

'Alex!' said Des in the closing minute of the show, 'this last little bit of info on the bottom of the card about you, it fascinates me. You met people from 189 of the world's 192 countries.

---

57 'Extrovert' – a fairly easy one, I'd say.

Now did you actually meet all those people? It must have been a massive task.'

'Well,' I replied, relaxed now, 'it was really just word of mouth. We made a lot of friends and we spent a lot of honk.'

No reaction, except for a giggle from Carol.

'What about language difficulties,' continued Des, unperturbed by my honk, 'did every one of the people you met speak English?'

'No, but I speak pretty much every language,' I said, daring to make my first joke of the show. I think it worked. Des sort of laughed (although he did later ask me quite pointedly if comedy was just a hobby). But I didn't really care. I'd won an episode of *Countdown* and dropped a honk. I'd done my best, I'd said our key word on the show and won the teapot; could Verbal Gardening life get any better?

My next opponent was Marilyn. Marilyn was lovely and exuded an air of Miss Marple as she set about systematically destroying me in the opening rounds. When I found six-letter words, she found seven. When I found seven, she found eight. I regained some ground with the numbers but by the halfway mark I was 13 points off the pace – a mighty lead for Marilyn in *Countdown* terms.

It was her turn to pick letters.

Des: 'So Marilyn, you're doing pretty good, what are you going to do with these?'

Marilyn: 'Consonant please Carol. And another. And another. And a vowel. And another. And another. And a consonant. Another vowel. And a final . . . consonant please.'

R N H A O A K I B

Des: 'Start the clock'.

I let the wordy part of my mind take over. Almost independently from the rest of me my cerebrum picked up letters, plonked them down, picked them up again and within seconds had built **BRAIN** for five. Then, though, it sat down for a rest. It refused to do any more work. I was stuck with my dismal **BRAIN** until five seconds before the bongs when it jerked into action once more and hastily assembled an even smaller, four-letter word.

But what a word.

HONK was there! Against all the odds the *Countdown* gods had dealt me the right letters to make our leading word.

But what would I declare? I was thirteen points behind in my second and potentially last ever appearance on the programme I'd loved all my life. Would I throw away five more points with a brief mention of 'honk' at five to four on a Tuesday afternoon on Channel 4?

Of course I would!

Des: 'Right, Marilyn'.

Marilyn: 'Just a four'.

I glanced over at Marilyn in disbelief. She'd only found a four-letter word too! This was the stroke of luck I needed. I wouldn't lose the round with 'honk'! With confidence restored, I held my head up high and looked straight at Des as he turned to me.

Des: 'Alex?'

Alex: 'I'm afraid I've just got four as well.'

Des: 'Right, what's your four, Alex?'

Alex: 'I've got "honk", meaning money.'

Des: 'Honk!'

Yes! I wanted to scream, honk, honk, honk, honk, HONK! But I didn't. I'd just calmly said my word, and the meaning, as if it was the most normal thing in the world. Yes, 'honk', meaning money. My word. MY WORD! My word! And did Dictionary Corner have a problem with the word? No, they did not! 'That's fine,' they said.

I had got my word past the Guardians of the Dictionary. I had broken into the Dictionary Corner.

Carol even put 'honk' up on her board. When the programme

was broadcast its legion of loyal viewers would now see and hear our 'honk'. My mum would see Carol Vorderman and Suzie Dent supporting my word on the telly. And even more importantly, I had irrefutable proof that 'honk', meaning money, was indeed a word.

The miracle was gift-wrapped when Des turned back to Marilyn.

Des: 'And what have you got?'

Marilyn: 'I've got horn.'

Des: 'Honk your horn!'

Honk your horn indeed, Des! She'd said 'horn'! Unbelievable. My name. My name and my word created out of nine letters picked at random by my heroine Carol Vorderman on my beloved *Countdown*.

The Letter Lords were indeed smiling on me; I went on to claw back enough points in the subsequent rounds to reach 78 points by the climax of the game compared to Marilyn's 84. I was within reach of her total with just the ten-point Countdown Conundrum to come.

Des: 'So, the game will be solved and resolved by this Countdown Conundrum – and it's a crucial one this time. So I'm going to drop the lights; and put your fingers on the buzzers as I reveal today's Crucial Countdown Conundrum:'

R E D S R E R U N

Beat.

Buzz.

Des: 'Alex?'

Alex: 'Surrender.'

Des: 'Surrender? Let's have a look . . .'

S U R R E N D E R

Des: 'Wow!'

I know, Des. And I'd like to take this opportunity to thank

everyone who came along today, in particular Mr and Mrs Roman, Dudley Doolittle and Eric and Ernie on cameras. Thank *you* Des and of course, Carol and Susie, it's been a pleasure finally meeting you both. But most of all, I do want to say thank you to my mum. I couldn't have done it without you . . .

In truth, I was self-conscious rather than triumphant having won my second game on the trot. I felt terribly guilty that I'd knocked Marilyn out before she had the chance to win her own teapot. Luckily she did say that she didn't drink tea anyway and that it was 'nice to lose to a good 'un', so that feeling of remorse soon faded. Between games, briefly alone in the dressing room, I punched the air and shouted 'get in'. I sincerely hope that none of the production team heard me.

Re-entering the ring, as tall as Jumbo, I felt that nothing could stop me now. There was little Jonny could do as I found the eight-letter words 'calliper' and 'debonair' on my way to a third win, impressing everyone, including myself. As well as the teapot this secured me the prize of an enormous dictionary, called the *Shorter Oxford Dictionary* (shorter only, as far as I can tell, than a human), the younger brother of the very book I was trying to impregnate by going on the show. Like all dictionaries, this latest edition would be out of date in a matter of months; as the language marches ever onwards its editors must struggle to keep up, like Tantalus in the underworld or Sisyphus, pushing his boulder up a hill for all eternity, but ever so slightly more fun. One day it would need updating to include my word. Honk, at least, was surely on its way.

Battle-wearied and weighed down by these trophies, I did come unstuck in the last bout of the day against Tom (the press officer for Hull FC in case you're wondering *which* Tom), but by then I was happy to put a full stop at the end of my *Countdown* chapter. It literally couldn't have gone better, everyone couldn't have been nicer and I went out to *TGI Friday's* to celebrate wicustJeremyStrongJth my new old friend Jeremy.

30

About a thousand days after Carol had inadvertently alerted me to my tkday, I sat with a cup of tea at a quarter to four and hummed along to *Countdown*'s catchy theme tune as instinctively as a nightingale. When the show started and Des had rattled off his introductions, there I was, in the Champion's chair, ready to fend off Marilyn, my first challenger. And there I was, failing to get a point on the board in the opening rounds before clawing back some dignity in the numbers game. Then there I was, declaring a four-letter word in the sixth letters game;

Des: 'Right, what's your four, Alex?'

Alex: 'I've got "honk", meaning money.'

Des: 'Honk!'

There it was. On *Countdown*. For real. It had eluded the editor's knife. To my enormous relief, just before Marilyn's 'horn' I absolutely definitely audibly declared my four-letter word as 'honk, meaning money'. There could be no doubt about the words. The *Countdown* contestant (me) quite clearly said that 'honk' meant money and Dictionary Corner didn't disagree. They even showed the shot of Carol displaying 'honk' on her letters board.

I'd always hoped that an appearance on *Countdown* would grant me a slice of the legacy I craved. This was something to tell the grandchildren, the teapot proof that I'd done something good. With the setting of 'honk' in *Countdown* stone, however, I'd managed to go one step further. My word was now embedded in the history of the programme too. In round seven of the nineteenth episode of the fifty-ninth series Alex Horne had declared 'honk', earning him four points alongside the four given to Marilyn for 'horn'. 'Honk' was accepted by the Dictionary Corner.

After defeating me, Tom found the word 'paddle' in an early letters round of his subsequent game. Carol stuck **PADDLE** on the board too but nobody mentioned that it meant 'hand'. A tiny part of me wished I'd survived just one more game. That could have been my chance to dig out an incredible two seeds on the programme. But I was happy with my lot. I'm not greedy. No, I'm definitely not greedy. Despite what you may have read in *The Fix* magazine.

Even though she'd stopped collecting them when we'd left home years before, I gave the *Countdown* teapot to my mum. It really is a remarkable piece of pottery: shaped like the famous *Countdown* clock (well, any clock really), bright blue, with the word 'Countdown' in the *Countdown* font underneath, it's as garish as the programme's original set. If archaeologists find them in millennia hence they'll never guess their significance.

'I can't take it,' said my mum.

'You can,' I countered.

'I can't.'

'Well, look after it for me,' I tried again.

'Very well,' she replied, seizing the teapot and placing it in pride of place in the middle of the main teapot shelf above the sink in the kitchen.

A week later I sent her a book called *Ella Minnow Pea* by Mark Dunn to say thank you for all the words she'd passed on to me. She's probably the only person I know who will appreciate the gift of a highly readable and entertaining lipogrammatical novel.

*

But I wasn't quite finished yet. I was still determined to get my words in the dictionary proper and if nothing else, I had learnt over the last three dozen months that to break into the language, one usually has to do something out of the ordinary. So I threw my dice one last time.

The British Library, the United Kingdom's National Library, is a legal deposit library, which automatically receives copies of all books produced in the UK and the Republic of Ireland, as well as all foreign books distributed in the UK. That's why it houses every Walsall Football Club matchday programme. It's a scholarly zoo where one can wander amongst the world's most weird and wonderful book-beasts (or, if you prefer, get a latte from the competitively priced café). It holds over 150 million items in all known languages and formats, some 20 million items more than the world's 'largest' library, the American Library of Congress. As our proud representative of words, it is also, therefore, the home of all English diction-aries.

On an innocent winter's morning, I arrived at 96 Euston Road and marched through two imposing gates hewn from heavy sheet steel and cut into the shapes of letters spelling 'British Library' again and again and again. I was in the right place. Despite the chill, the courtyard was packed with readers, dili-gent souls, blissfully unaware of what was about to take place. They had no idea a lexical terrorist was strolling through their midst, armed to the teeth with home-made word-bombs.

'Look confident,' I whispered under my breath. 'Must look confident.'

Large signs on the glass doors of the main entrance warned 'Bag Search in Operation' but, thankfully, the guard waved me straight through. So far so good.

'I'm here to look at the dictionaries,' I told one of the two cardiganed receptionists.

'Well, you'll need a reader's pass for that. Up the stairs, on your right'.

This was unexpected news, but I hid my dismay and followed his pithy directions to another moccasined receptionist who asked to see photographic ID and ordered me to enter my details on a computer. The parameters of the operation were shifting. I couldn't get away with 'VG Farmer' this time. They would have to know who I was. So I answered all the questions on the computerised form and ticked the box saying I understood the library rules, accepting that: 'Damage to or theft of library material is a criminal offence and may result in prosecution'.

'I'd like to see the dictionaries,' I told my next goateed receptionist, the holder of the reader passes.

'Well, you'll need a reader's pass for that.'

'I know. That's why I'm here.'

'OK, let me see. Well, if you were a published author, you could get one right away lasting three years . . .'

Ah ha!

'I am a published author! I've written a book, it's about birdwatching, it's called – no, wait! I've also written an article about word histories. I have it here in fact.' I reached into my bag. 'There, *Comments on Etymology*, it's an American publication, absolutely authoritative . . .'

'That's fine. I've found your birdwatching book here on Amazon. No problem. So if you can just pose for this camera . . .'

One minute later, he handed me my pass. I was, officially, a reader. I held the key to the Chamber of Reference Books.

Heart racing, I paced across the landing of the first floor, past vast banks of leathery books towards the Humanities section, where I proudly flashed my brand-new pass at yet more corduroyed receptionists.

'I'm sorry, sir,' one said as loudly I've heard anyone speak in a library, 'I'm afraid you can't take that bag in here. If you go down two floors to the cloakroom you can leave it there and pick up a see-through plastic bag. You can bring pencils, paper and a computer in here, but nothing else I'm afraid.'

I was afraid too, but was determined not to show it. Instead, I looked determined, tried to give a 'silly me' sort of smile, turned on my heel and regrouped in the basement.

Could I really do this? They had my details, they had my photo and they now had my bag.

But I could still bring in all I needed. I could do this. I would do this.

Three minutes later, back up at the entrance to Humanities, I waved my pass once again and held up an official British Library plastic bag, through which they could quite clearly see some paper, a pencil and a computer. Nothing more. The receptionist waved me through, quietly this time. I took five more steps forwards and was in.

Before me stretched countless graceful desks, each manned by more diligent souls, almost all of whom had enormous tomes splayed open besides tiny laptops that lit up their faces like candles. This was where past and future collided, where wireless broadband flashed over historical documents, and the silence of reading was gently fractured by the tapping of keys. This, I imagined, must be what the headquarters of the *OED* looks like today.

Still trying to remain as shadowy as possible I sidled along the shelves towards those devoted to linguistics. My heart switched sports, thumping rather than racing. So many books, so many words, so many dictionaries.

Scanning the books, I slowed down as I reached layer upon layer of foreign-language dictionaries, several dictionaries of scientific biography and something called *The Dent Dictionary of Measurement*, which I felt sure Susie must have had a hand in. Nearly there; at least fifty Latin dictionaries, an abbreviations dictionary, the biography of the English language, a handful of encyclopaedias of language and linguistics, and an international bibliography of specialised dictionaries; must be soon.

There. I'd found it: the *Oxford English Dictionary*, all twenty volumes, nestled alongside the three dusty books that housed Samuel Johnson's.

Other versions fell in line beneath it: Chambers, Penguin, Encarta, Webster's and Barnhart, a reverse dictionary, a rhyming dictionary, a dictionary of new words, and a whole bookshelf of slang dictionaries. But I couldn't take my eyes off the *OED*.

A sign at the end of the aisle warned me that these books couldn't be taken back to the desks. They were for reference only. But that was fine for me. They were, effectively, hidden away. They were unguarded.

I reached up and took down volume XVIII, *Thro–Unelucidated*. It felt weighty but fragile in my hands, like someone else's baby. Gently, I placed it on the floor, then, kneeling over it, flicked through to page 162.

Head bowed, I slipped my other hand into the official British Library plastic bag on my right and withdrew one of several small pieces of paper. I glanced up briefly. No one was watching. I moved back to the dictionary and laid the slip on the left-hand page between 'tjalk' (a kind of ship) and 'tlachtli' (the ceremonial ball-game of the Aztecs) before easing the book shut.

I had done it. The next time someone wanted to look up 'tmesis', 'Tlpanec', or even the word 'to', their eyes would be drawn to an extra entry:

tkday (tíkedé). One's ten thousandth day on this planet.
2008 A.Horne **Birdwatchingwatching** On your tkday, however, you should be able to do anything. At that age you should know how to change a tyre, a fuse or a mortgage.

Working speedily, I repeated the procedure with my eight other words, inserting more slips of paper defining bollo, demi, games, honest, honk, mental safari, paddles and pratdigger on their respective pages. When the last word was safely implanted, I slid that volume back on to the shelf and, before anybody had noticed I'd even been there, I was gone.

To my surprise and relief, I didn't feel any remorse on the Tube journey home, perhaps because I hadn't, officially, done anything wrong. I hadn't broken any of the Reading Room Requirements: 'Collection items cannot be removed from any reading room. You can use laptops and take mobiles in but please turn off the sound before you enter a reading room. No coats, bags and umbrellas. No pens or highlighters. No sharp instruments. No food, drink, bottled water, sweets or gum. No cameras.' No problem. There was no mention of made-up words.

My main emotion was pride. Victoria Coren might not have been able to get a word in the dictionary despite her 'direct line' to the men in charge, but who says I had to deal with these men? They were middle men, and I could cut them out. So a week later I returned and stowed more slips into a couple of the other editions. A week later I did the same. From then on, every time I passed within a mile radius of the library I nipped in and tucked another word in another dictionary. Like Fantastic Mr Fox, I was focused, silently stealing into the home of words and carrying out my sneaky deeds.

And I wasn't content only to target London. I wanted my words to get into every dictionary in every library in the land. So now, whenever I travel around the country, I don't stop to daub messages on service station toilet doors; instead I drop into my destination's local library and drop my words into that local library's lexicons.

I sent the same slips of paper to my Rare Men and begged them to do the same. And I urge you to join us. I've included the words on the following page. Rip them out. With your teeth if necessary. Photocopy them a hundred times. Slice them up. Sprinkle them liberally into libraries. Bury them in bookshops. Or just place them in your own wordbooks at home. Everybody owns a dictionary. Plant our words in them.

Go! Take them! There will be dice!

bollo (bŏ͞ʊlŏ). 1. Unsatisfying. 2. A cry of disgust.
2007 A.Horne **The Times** *I pushed back the boundaries of our bollo Britishness.*

demi (de·mi). A fifty pence piece.
2010 A.Horne **Wordwatching** *He finally felt the reassuring weight of a demi along-side at least three cutters and a crab.*

games (gē·ms). 1. Rubbish and pretentious. 2. Clever and smart.
2006 A.Horne **Digital Spy** *This film was utter games.*

honest (ơnèst). Fat.
2008 Ginsters **Advertising Campaign** *Real Honest Food.*

honk (honk). Money, especially cash.
2006 A.Horne **BBC World** *Everything costs a lot of honk.*

mental safari (me·ntăl sŭrfări). 1. When someone goes mad for a few moments. 2. A series of rash acts.
2007 A.Horne **Omnibvs Magazine** *I went on a mental safari and decided to learn German.*

paddle (pæd'l). Hand.
2008 S.Horne **BBC Radio Five Live** *Her kids call their hands paddles.*

pratdigger (prætdi·ger). 1. Pickpocket. 2. That friend of yours who always has a rubbish girlfriend everyone has to put up with, or a crap best mate from school they always ask out with you, or the person who finds the most obnoxious person at a party and exposes everyone to them.
2007 A.Horne **Sky News** *I keep getting accused of being a pratdigger.*

tkday (tĭkēdē͡ǐ). One's ten thousandth day on this planet.
2008 A.Horne **Birdwatchingwatching** *On your tkday, however, you should be able to do anything. At that age you should know how to change a tyre, a fuse or a mortgage.*

Postscript

January 25th 2011
Chesham

This is the second edition of *Wordwatching*. Some considerable time has passed since I first told my story so I'd like to take up a few more minutes of your time with a short update. I hope that's ok with you. Because, since issuing those stirring commands, our words have indeed made further progress. As I'd hoped, honk's appearance on *Countdown* was not the final chapter. Instead, they've all been inching ever closer to a firm and lasting place in the language.

On the literal front, I'm pleased to report that many readers have taken me at my word, ripped the previous page from their copies and secreted them inside dictionaries in their local libraries. So now several hundred 'demis' and 'pratdiggers' are bedding down next to other, more established words, in locations as diverse as Luton and Leeds.

Orally, their positions have been further strengthened by people like the comedian, Jon Richardson, who hosted a heated discussion about tkdays on his insightful and popular BBC 6 music show, while over at Kerrang! FM, former *Big Brother* contestant Kate Lawler held a phone-in on that same subject, causing a facebook furore as listeners frantically planned their own tkday parties.

Indeed, this decimal celebration has made the most obvious splash in recent months. With tkday talk dominating both twitter and actual conversation on several occasions, the term was finally included in an online dictionary, the trusted www.wordspy.com, who cited both an article I'd written for the *Independent* which included the word, alongside an actual independent article from the *Toronto Star*. That's right, my new word had hitched all the way to Canada, where a writer called Paola Loriggio explained; 'The 10k Day celebration — alternately called "Tkday" or "decimal birthday" — has become the new coming-of-age for Generation Y.'

More subtle words like 'mental and safari' and 'honest' have been making smaller but still discernible ripples. Watch the latest series of *Masterchef*, for instance, and you'll hear food appositely described as honest on almost every episode. Google 'mental safari' and you'll find everyone from politicians to mixed martial artists embracing the term in their blogs, essays and general witterings.

Finally, my personal favourite, 'honk', has continued to create far-reaching waves, like my very own verbal moon. It has been spotted in the *Guardian*, the *Observer* and Scotland's *Sunday Post*, it has popped up in *Lonely Planet* reviews, and it even made its way into the influential *Thorpe Village Magazine*. But perhaps the most gratifying usage of the word was by children's author Paul Shipton in his latest book, *Pigs in Planes: The Big Bear Nightmare*. On page 56 of this porky romp, ruthless businessman Mr Sweetie shouts the following sentence at our hero, Captain Pete; 'Nothing in the world can beat cold hard cash ... dosh ... readies ... lots and lots of lovely honk,' ensuring that lovely honk will live on not only in books and libraries, but in the minds of countless young readers, the true verbal gardeners of the future. On top of all that, it was simply an amazing feeling to see a word that I invented in someone else's book. I had done it. I'd invented a word.

A perfect opportunity to demonstrate this success came this Christmas, when I was invited to take part on *Celebrity Mastermind* on BBC1. This took me by surprise, as I was almost certain I wasn't either of the things in the title. Nevertheless I agreed, and while I was settling into the iconic chair John Humphrys asked me why I liked my specialist subject, Ken Dodd, so much. 'Well, I said', holding my head up high. 'His shows are always excellent value for honk'.

If anything could match the appearance of a word on *Countdown*, it was surely this. A decade older than its little brother, *Mastermind* is a serious half hour, resolutely packed with serious questions and earnest people. Honk is now etched on its esteemed walls, and yet another step has been taken towards the dictionary, thanks to me, the neologistic mastermind (I came second to a rugby player, by the way). I am still hoping to sidle into *Countdown's* Dictionary Corner one day, but for now, I'm satisfied.

The Wordwatcher's Dictionary

Balderdash: A man called Thomas Nashe (born in 1567, twenty-six years before a Thomas Nash with no 'e' on his surname who married Shakespeare's granddaughter Elizabeth Barnard, the Bard's last direct descendant) notched up a remarkable 705 citations in his brief life as a pamphleteer and writer of pornographic poetry. It was he who invented the word 'balder-dash', my favourite board game, as well as 'conundrum', my favourite round on *Countdown*.

Better Half: In 1596 my college (and Carol Vorderman's) Sidney Sussex was founded and named after its foundress, Frances Sidney, Countess of Sussex and aunt of the poet Sir Philip Sidney who invented the word 'miniature' in his poem *Arcadia*. 'Words can change the world,' he argued before going on to coin 'bugbear', 'hazardous', 'loneliness', 'dumbstricken' and 'my better half', in the process of garnering 225 quotations in the *OED*.

Big Bang: While the origins of the universe are still a source of debate, the term 'Big Bang' can be traced directly back to one man, the British astronomer Sir Fred Hoyle, who rather ironically opposed the idea he named. Originally thought up by a priest called Georges Lemaître, it was Hoyle's rival George Gamow who advocated this theory of a suddenly expanding universe in direct competition with Hoyle's own 'steady state model'. Enormously popular thanks to his work on the BBC,

Sir Fred attempted to dismiss Gamow's hypothesis with what was supposed to be the pejorative term 'Big Bang'. Being rather catchy as well as scientifically more viable, however, the notion caught on.

Biro: A Hungarian called László József Bíró (can you have too many accents?) invented this word by patenting the innovative non-dripping pen in 1938 (he then sold it to Marcel Bich of Bic fame in 1950).

Blizzard: Definitely one of my top five words, 'blizzard' was first used in its meteorological sense in 1870 by an Iowan newspaper editor who decided the term, previously used to mean a series of blows from weapons or fists, would perfectly describe that year's severe snow.

Blurb: In 1907, a New Yorker called Gelett Burgess publicised his book *Are you a Bromide?* at a publishing trade association dinner. 'Bromide' was his new word for a rather dull, ordinary person (the sort a pratdigger so often unearths), but it was 'blurb' that really took off. Instead of the usual drab book covers, he decided to mimic the trashy novels of the day by adorning his own front cover with a particularly buxom blonde whom he christened 'Miss Belinda Blurb'. Amazed by this dazzling branding, other publishers followed suit and a 'blurb' swiftly came to mean (in Burgess's own words): '1. A flamboyant advertisement; an inspired testimonial. 2. Fulsome praise; a sound like a publisher.' Now, of course, it refers to any words, rather than pictures, on the back of a book, an example of which can be seen simply by clapping your paddles together. Burgess attempted to recreate this success with a further book entitled *Burgess Unabridged: A New Dictionary of Words You Have Always Needed,* containing 200 new coinages like 'flooijab', 'an apparent compliment with a concealed sting'; 'to kipe', 'to inspect appraisingly, as women do one another'; and 'impkin', 'a superhuman pet, a baby in beast form'. Each new word was accompanied by a page-long definition and an eight-line poem, but not one made its way into an actual dictionary.

Bob's Your Uncle: In 1886 the term 'Bob's your uncle' was created when the Prime Minister Robert Cecil appointed his nephew Arthur Balfour Chief Secretary for Ireland in the finest example of verbal nepotism until 'George is your dad' in 2000.

Bollo: Unintentionally piggy-backing other usages of the word, most notably in the cult British comedy *The Mighty Boosh*, Mr Wingdings and his family coined this term one Christmas, early in the twenty-first century.

Boning Up: A second-hand bookseller called Henry George Bohn (1796–1884) worked in London selling cheap translations of the Classics for students (like me) to cram from at the last minute. It may sound unlikely, but there is compelling evidence that the phrase 'to bone up' is the result of this man's trade; yet another hidden eponym, his name is now a verb, his books a stepping stone to *the* book. The other, more practical meanings of the word are nothing to do with Henry, and I only mention them because I remember once asking my grandmother (the penis from Russia) where my grandfather was. 'He's in the kitchen, boning the chicken,' was her reply. I've never been able to get this image out of my head.

Bother: An Irish actor and a contemporary of Samuel Johnson (and a major proponent of the 'elocution movement', apparently) called Thomas Sheridan gave the English-speaking world 'bother' before his son Richard kindly donated his 'dressing gown' (as well as 'malapropisms' thanks to Mrs Malaprop in his novel *The Rivals*).

Brunch: The *OED* assigns the invention of 'brunch' to one Guy Beringer, who first condensed breakfast and lunch in 1895 in a sadly defunct magazine called *Hunter's Weekly*.

Catch-22: Joseph Heller created this unusually shaped cracker with his novel of the same name, first published in 1961. An

Archbishop called John Morton had expressed the same idea in the phrase 'to apply Morton's fork' back in the fifteenth century, but as with many cutlery-based coinages, it never quite caught on.

Chugger: This word ('those people who stop you on the street and try to persuade you to give money to good causes' or 'charity mugger') was recently adopted by the charity community in the same way words like 'queer' and 'nigger' have been reclaimed in the recent past. It was coined, as far as I can tell, in 2002, by 'the media' in the UK. But who in the media? Why isn't the creator shouting his achievement from the rooftops (or at least on the street, next to a chugger)?

Cock and Bull Story: The residents of Stony Stratford in Buckinghamshire would have you believe that two of their historic high-street pubs, The Cock and The Bull, were often frequented by travellers who tended to embroider their tales between the two and thus spawned this phrase. They even celebrate this 'fact' with their own storytelling festival every year. But this may well be a cock and bull story itself. I would give more credit to the mysterious ancient Greek storyteller, Aesop, who wrote one fable featuring a cock talking to a bull. That sounds unfeasible enough to be a genuine etymology.

Cornucopia: It's a shame I don't know any current pamphleteers to help spread my words. Sixteenth-century author (and self-appointed celebrity) Robert Greene wrote a famous pamphlet called *Greene's Groats-Worth of Wit*, which contained a polemic attack on one Mr Shakespeare that prompted the Bard to immortalise him as his famous fool Falstaff. As well as the marvellous verb 'to frenchify', Greene then invented 'cornucopia', a word close to my heart because it comes from the Latin meaning 'horn of plenty'. I'm well aware that this makes me a bit of a nerd, but that sort of thing tickles me. It's my name! My first Latin teacher christened my little brother 'Cornetto' from the same Latin noun. *Cornus* has always been my favourite Latin word; perhaps that's why I'm such a fan of 'corny' jokes (of which, I suppose, that is one).

Corny: The word 'corny' can be traced back to American seed companies which, in the early 1900s, would advertise their goods in catalogues with jokes littered throughout. Unfortunately the quality was so poor that 'corn catalogue jokes' became a byword for bad jokes (in much the same way as Christmas cracker jokes today), and eventually the word 'corny' was born.

Cromulent: A word meaning 'fine' or 'valid' coined by *Simpsons* writer David X. Cohen. Following its appearance in an episode called 'Lisa the Iconoclast' (which also featured 'embiggened'), it entered mainstream speech and is included in the *Webster's New Millennium Dictionary of English*. It can be done! But it does help to be a writer on America's longest-running sitcom.

Crossword: While working at the *New York World*, a Liverpudlian called Arthur Wynne invented the 'crossword' that my granny, mum and I still enjoy. Initially called a 'word-cross', the puzzle was such a hit that some American rail companies installed dictionaries in their compartments, like bibles in hotel rooms. Sudokus are displaying worrying popularity today, but crosswords are still, according to Bill Bryson, 'the most popular sedentary amusement in America', after watching TV. My mum, granny and I are not unusual in our love of words.

Cut the Mustard: A phrase invented by William Sydney Porter or O. Henry, the name he wrote his short stories under at the beginning of the twentieth century. A fascinating American, he also coined the term 'banana republic' in reference to Honduras where he was writing his book *Cabbages and Kings* whilst on the run from the Feds. The basis of 'cut the mustard' is less clear. In the late 1800s, the word 'mustard' was used to mean something of superior quality, which might explain it. Or it may stem from the verb 'to muster', with 'cutting the mustered' being a corruption of 'passing muster'. I was once confused when I heard a newsreader announce that after a fire in a boarding school, pupils 'left their beds and mustard outside'. I couldn't understand why they would save either. I like to think Porter himself would have liked that. He certainly liked wordplay. The 'O. Henry Pun-Off World Championships', started and hosted by the O. Henry Museum in 1977, are still held annually every May in Austin. That's not a bad legacy.

Decadent: Coined along with the modern sense of 'environment' by Scottish satirist Thomas Carlyle in the 1820s.

Demi: A coin coined by polymath Mr Palatino in 2007. 'Coin coin', incidentally, is the noise that French ducks make. Romanian dogs go 'ham ham' and English geese say 'honk'.

Dude: Oscar Wilde is credited with the growth of 'dude' in the UK, possibly as a portmanteau of 'duds' and 'attitude'.

Egghead: As I hoped might be the case with my 'games', attempts to ridicule competitors have often had the side-effect of creating new words *and* raising the profile of one's enemies. In 1952 a Connecticut Republican called Stewart Alsop invented the word 'egghead' to describe and ridicule his contemplative and bald opponent, Adlai Stevenson. Stevenson, incidentally, had already invented the word 'brinkmanship' (influenced by Stephen Potter's recent 'gamesmanship'), and he demonstrated this quality by embracing the nickname instead of taking offence, rallying his own supporters with the outstanding cry, 'Eggheads of the world unite, you have nothing to lose but your yolks,' in one particular speech. The nickname stuck, Stevenson won many friends and while he never made the White House, losing both the 1952 and 1956 presidential elections to Dwight D. Eisenhower (who himself coined the not-nearly-as-catchy phrase 'military-industrial complex'), 'egghead' did make the dictionary.

Embiggened: A cracking word launched, like 'cromulent', in the 1996 *Simpsons* episode 'Lisa the Iconoclast'. Before then it was an obsolete term, found by series writer Dan Greaney festering in an 1884 publication called *Notes and Queries: A Medium of Intercommunication for Literary Men, General Readers, Etc* by C. A. Ward.

Emoticon: The original smiley emoticon; ':-)' was first officially used in print by Scott E. Fahlman, a professor at the delightful-sounding Carnegie Mellon University in Pittsburgh. While discussing the limits of online humour on 19 September 1982, he wrote: 'I propose the following character sequence for joke markers: :-) Read it sideways. Actually, it is probably more economical to mark things that are NOT jokes, given current trends. For this, use :-(.' As irritating as the smiley's subsequent success might be, that's an inspiring tale of typographical invention. Isn't it? :-@

Etiquette: Philip Stanhope, the fourth Earl of Chesterfield, briefly sponsored Samuel Johnson's dictionary before falling out with the lexicologist so spectacularly that Johnson accused him of teaching 'the morals of a whore and the manners of a dancing master'. I don't know much about how dancing masters behave in polite society, but I do know that the earl went on to export the fine word 'picnic' from French (it has nothing to do with racist lynching, despite urban myths to the contrary). In fact, Lord Chesterfield mastered this trick of nicking a word from another language and passing it off as one's own brand new English word, borrowing 'sang-froid', 'debut', 'gauche', 'ennui' and 'etiquette' too.

Eureka: Famously invented in the bath by Archimedes of Syracuse in the third century BC.

Explain: As well as 'explain', Thomas More was the first to use 'absurdity', 'exact' and 'exaggerate'. More famously, he invented the word 'utopia'. He did not, however, make up the word 'more'.

Galvanise: Scientists and engineers have always been in a prime position to invent words, as demonstrated by those of the late eighteenth century: In 1771 Italian physicist Luigi Galvani electrocuted a load of frogs and somehow justified it with the word 'galvanisation'; in 1774 a German physician and astrologist called Franz Anton Mesmer made a patient swallow iron, attached magnets to her body and, although understandably discredited at the time, is for ever remembered in the verb 'mesmerise'; while James Watt took the more orthodox approach of improving the steam engine to such an extent that the unit of power was named in his honour.

Games: Like one of the stranger Greek myths, the original 'Games' was (and still is) a fine writer and patient man called Alex Games who, through no fault of his own, was turned into an adjective after becoming the object of extreme jealousy for a comedian and rash man called Alex Horne.

Garage: An adjective, reminiscent of 'village', meaning 'cheap and tawdry', invented by Alex Horne's wife after her husband took to buying 'garage flowers', 'garage bacon' and 'garage bread'.

Goody-Two-Shoes: We don't, unfortunately, know who came up with the phrase 'goody-two-shoes', which has always struck me as a peculiar description: I've always thought two shoes was the minimum requirement, rather than anything overly virtuous. We do know, however, that it comes from a story, the author of which remains anonymous, about an orphan called Margery Meanwell who went through life with just the one shoe until a rich gentleman gave her a complete pair. Understandably, she was chuffed so went round telling everyone she had 'two shoes' and thus earned her nickname (she also had her virtuousness rewarded by becoming a teacher and marrying a rich widower).

Gordon Bennett: James Gordon Bennett II (1841–1918) was the son of another Gordon, the extraordinarily wealthy founder of the *New York Herald*, who squandered much of his father's honk funding balloon and yacht races, expeditions to Africa and the Arctic, and generally raising eyebrows and temperatures with his drunken hi-jinks until his name was rarely uttered without a subsequent exclamation mark (although, as so often, there is another explanation, this time involving a more modest biscuit-maker, also called Gordon Bennett, who used to advertise his product in Pontefract by shouting out his own name while cycling round town).

Groggy: English naval officer Lieutenant Edward Vernon donated his own nickname, Old Grog, to the daily ration of rum and water handed out during the intriguing but almost certainly bloody 'War of Jenkins' Ear' contested between England and Spain from 1739 to 1742.

Grotty: This yucky adjective first appeared in Alun Owen's screenplay for The Beatles' debut feature film, *A Hard Day's Night*, in 1964. Ringo Starr, by the way, was said by a 1963 fanzine to have invented the word 'wack' (meaning 'pal').

Grundies: This evocative word can be pinned on the Australian media executive Reg Grundy, who did little more than have a famous name that rhymes with 'undies'. It always helps to be in the media where new language is concerned. By the way, the phrase 'drop the dead donkey' (which I never heard while working at the *West Sussex Gazette*) was invented by the producers of the TV show of that name. It was only when the programme became successful during the 1990s that the sentence became the clichéd call of cheesy newsrooms and desperate editors.

Guinea Pig: This animal was first used to mean 'test subject' by George Bernard Shaw in 1913, ten years after he coined the word 'superman' as the translation of Nietzsche's *Übermensch* in *Thus Spake Zarathustra*. 'Guinea pig' and 'superman': that's good gardening.

Happy as Larry: It was a boxer called Larry Foley (1847–1914) who was so contented that people still say they're as happy as him.

Have a Good Time: Samuel Pepys's diary of 1660 is the unlikely source of this phrase, as well as the words 'gherkin' and 'gimp'.

Hector: The verb 'to hector' comes all the way from Homer's *Iliad*, and a bullying Trojan prince whom Ajax (who has since become a cleaning product) fought twice in the poem. Imagine having your surname memorialised as a verb. That would be some achievement: 'How was school, dear?' 'Not too bad, until Mr Arnold started horning me about bad grammar again.' Actually, that doesn't sound quite right.

Hello: I remember being taken quite aback when I was told (by no less a source than Stephen Fry on *QI*) that 'hello' is less than a hundred and fifty years old. That's no age for a word; my grandmother's grandmother wouldn't have recognised it as a greeting. It was coined, according to the BBC programme, by Thomas Edison after he and Alexander Graham Bell mastered the telephone in 1876. Bell had come up with 'ahoy' to commence the novel situation of speaking to someone without being able to see them, but was trumped by Edison's contrivance of 'hello'; a less nautical salutation that proved ultimately popular. He first wrote it, according to a scholar called Allen Koenigsberg, in a letter to the president of Pittsburgh's Central District and Printing Telegraph Company, Mr T. B. A. David, dated 15 August 1877.

But this isn't quite the whole truth. A little further digging reveals that both 'hallo' and 'hullo' had been around far longer as expressions of surprise. 'Hallo! What have we here?' one might have exclaimed when startled by something startling in the early 1800s – a stray goat, maybe, or an extremely tall female newsreader. Over in America, folks were greeting each other with a cheery 'hallow' for at least one hundred years before the invention of the phone, and 'hola', surely a close relative, has been around even longer than that. In fact, 'hello' itself was used by Mark Twain in his 1872 book *Roughing It* in the sentence, 'A miner came out and said: 'Hello!'" Moreover, if you want to believe the polyglot Mario Pei (as Bill Bryson does in his authoritative *Mother Tongue*), the word's been around for at least six hundred years in the Old English form of *hal beo thu* or 'whole be thou', a medieval rendering of our 'all right, mate'. Still, if Stephen Fry said it, it must be true; Thomas Edison invented the word 'hello'.

Hollywood: At some point in the 1880s the elaborately named Mrs Daeida Hartell Wilcox Beveridge was chatting to a stranger and found out that he'd called his summer home 'Hollywood'. So taken with this simpler name, she decided to rename her own ranch in its honour and the 'Hollywood Hills' were formed. Mrs Daeida Hartell Wilcox Beveridge can also take credit for the offshoot, 'Bollywood', which was let into the *OED* a hundred years later (partly because there now seems to be an ongoing argument, online at least, as to who first mixed Bombay with Hollywood).

Honest: The usual meanings of 'truthful', 'genuine', and 'not deceptive' (from the Latin adjective *honestus*, 'honorable, respected') have been around since the fourteenth century, but the lesser-known sense of 'overweight' was first suggested by the appropriately named Mr Elephant in 2007.

Honk: Originally the noise of a goose but recently a most deliberate and successful neologism created by Mr Roman, a nightclub owner with a degree in linguistics, not long after the turn of the millennium.

Hoodlum: In his 1877 *Dictionary of Americanisms*, John Bartlett says that this great word was born when a newspaper writer wrote a story about a San Franciscan gang leader called Muldoon. Wanting obliquely to name and mock the rogue in question, the journalist decided to spell it backwards as 'Noodlum', which you've got to admit is pretty funny. Fearing this was too close for comfort, his editor changed the 'N' to an 'H' and the 'hoodlum' was born. Unfortunately this is merely an ingenious explanation created in retrospect. The word 'hoodlum' had been knocking around California in the 1870s but so were an awful lot of German immigrants, who used their charming Bavarian term *huddellump* to mean 'a slovenly person' and almost certainly created 'hoodlum' in the process. In case you're wondering, our 'hoodies' didn't come from 'hoodlums' either, but were first used in print by the Irish novelist Roddy Doyle.

Hot Dog: An American cartoonist called T. A. 'Tad' Dorgan sketched a dachshund in a long bread roll at the close of the nineteenth century and is now often credited with inventing the word 'hot dog' all by himself (no such cartoon has ever actually been found, and the phrase 'hot dog' was used for a good decade before this story is set, but let's not get too bogged down in pesky details). By this unusual method Dorgan also came up with 'cat's pyjamas', 'yes man' and 'yes, we have no bananas', while his colleague, Billy De Beck from Chicago, gave the world 'heebie-jeebies' in similar style via a cartoon dialogue penned in 1923.

Intensify: While William Wordsworth coined 'pedestrian' in 1791, many years before the popularisation of cars necessitated such a word, and Lord Byron contributed 'blasé' to the language, fellow poet Samuel Taylor Coleridge came up with 'to intensify' as well as 'pessimism'. In fact, I learned from Henry Hitchings's *Dr Johnson's Dictionary* that, despite criticising Johnson's dictionary in *Biographia Literaria*, Coleridge did purposefully check the book to see if it included his newly minted verb. My desire to get a word in the book is by no means unprecedented, even by Romantic poets.

International: The word 'international' was coined by the jurist

Jeremy Bentham in the phrase 'international law'. He was also the first to use 'maximise', 'minimise', 'secretarial', 'exhaustive', and the modern sense of 'agenda'. Despite the success of 'international' (England football matches are now called 'internationals' rather than 'games', although the latter is often an apt adjective for the occasions), Bentham 'apologised for its inelegance', according to Bill Bryson. I therefore feel I too ought to apologise for the inelegance of 'honk', 'pratdigger' and 'tkday'. Sorry for their inelegance. I just hope they get even half the acclaim of 'international'.

Jack Robinson: A Tower of London executioner by this name who cut off people's heads between 1660 and 1679 was so swift with his axe that people today still compare themselves to him when they do things quickly.

Jazz: At the turn of the twentieth century a ragtime drummer called Charles 'Chaz' Washington lent his name to a whole genre of music. The leader of his band in Vicksburg, Mississippi, repeatedly shouted, 'Now Chaz! Now Chaz!' to liven up the tempo; both the cry and the rhythm caught on and, a few months later, 'jazz' was born. Even I recognise this as one of the least convincing of all the personal histories in this book, but that doesn't mean it's not worth passing on.

Literary: One of the most remarkable word coiners in history was an eccentric doctor, amateur scientist and collector, quite possibly a pratdigger (in the most positive sense), called Sir Thomas Browne. He lived in Norwich in the seventeenth century and, for perhaps the first time in history, considered himself to be a neologist. He might just have been the first *deliberate* Verbal Gardener. For Browne concentrated on the very act of coining words, with his many other interests merely aiding that cause. He was successful too, with 'literary', 'suicide', 'medical', 'precarious', 'amphibious', 'computer' and 'electricity' among his inventions (although the last two with slightly different meanings to our electricity and computers today as they weren't invented until the end of the next century and the twentieth century respectively). That's an impressive roster, made possible by Samuel Johnson who greatly admired the Norfolk knight, wrote a biography about him and quoted him two thousand times in his great dictionary, all but three times from Browne's ridiculously broad compendium of knowledge called *Pseudodoxia Epidemica* which is still available for free on the internet.

Look Something Up: In 1692 an antiquarian called Anthony Wood was the first to write the phrase 'to look something up', demonstrating how interested people were then becoming both in the meanings of words and in the ways they might be recorded. It seems ludicrous now that somebody could make up so commonplace a phrase, but someone had to say it first. Earlier in the same century a Flemish chemist called Jan Baptist Van Helmont claimed to invent the word 'gas', inspired by the Greek term *chaos*. It may not sound entirely believable but until I find compelling evidence to the contrary I'm happy to take his word for it.

Maverick: A Texan called Samuel Augustus Maverick made his name thinking outside the box but inside the law in the mid-nineteenth century. Blighted by rustlers, his fellow cattle ranchers had taken to branding their animals to protect them from theft. Samuel thought the practice cruel and refused to singe his own cattle. Being the sole individual not to toe the line, he rightly reasoned that because they were the only cows without branding, his would be as recognisable and so as safe as any others. By the time he died in 1870 this lateral thinking (a phrase coined by Dr Edward de Bono in his 1967 book *The Use of Lateral Thinking*) was so well known that anybody with an independent mind was called a maverick in his honour.

McJob: McJob is a rare example of a word an individual is trying to remove from the dictionary. The latest edition of the Merriam-Webster defines the word, coined by Douglas Coupland in his 1991 novel *Generation X*, as 'low-paying and dead-end work', but the company's superbly unaptonymic CEO Jim Cantalupo says that's an 'inaccurate description' which should be changed. I think he should be more grateful.

Mental Safari: These distinct words were officially united by the theatrical director Mr Bodoni, who still lives on a farm in Stratford-upon-Avon, just yards (quite a few yards) from Shakespeare's old home.

Modesty: While others were trying to protect English from any foreign influences in the late 1600s, diplomat and scholar Sir Thomas Elyot used Greek and Latin to create novel sounding words in inventions like 'encyclopaedia', 'entertainment', 'animate' and 'modesty'.

Moolah: Crime writer (and circus expert) Courtney Ryley Cooper conjured up his own honk with 'moolah' in the 1939 book *Designs in Scarlet*.

Moron: In 1910 H. H. Goddard, pioneer of the IQ test, coined 'moron' (from the Greek for 'dull' or 'stupid') to refer to people with an IQ between 51 and 70. He also employed 'imbecile' for those scoring between 26 and 50 and 'idiot' for 0 to 25. But a 'moron' was his own creation, a scientific term to describe any person with a mental age between eight and twelve who, according to Goddard, was unfit for society and should therefore be either institutionalised, sterilised, or both.

Optimism: Enlightenment thinker François-Marie Arouet (1694–1778) created the word 'optimism' in *Candide*. He also created his far better-known pen-name, Voltaire, as an anagram of 'Arovet Li', the Latinised spelling of his surname, and the initial letters of '*le jeune*', meaning 'the younger'. That's my sort of Enlightenment thinker.

Pacific: The world's largest ocean was granted its peaceful title by the Portuguese explorer Ferdinand Magellan in 1520.

Paddles: The new slang alternative to 'hands' was created deliberately by someone calling himself The Farmer in 2007, although his namesake, the pre-war slang-collector John S. Farmer, does note far earlier usage alongside the noun and verb 'daddle'.

Palindrome: Renaissance dramatist Ben Jonson may have failed with the words 'obstupefact' and 'ventositous' but he did come up with 'damp', 'clumsy', 'defunct' and 'strenuous' during the early 1700s whilst also using 'palindrome' for the first time in print.

Panic: Credit for this word must go to the sneaky countryside-dwelling Greek god called Pan (who had the legs and horns of a goat), who specialised in making mysterious sounds that freaked out both humans and animals and therefore created 'panic'. 'Pan-pipes' are also named in his honour, presumably because they are also terrifying. The noun 'pandemonium' was created by John Milton in *Paradise Lost*, where he was also the first to 'add fuel to the fire'.

Ping-Pong: An unlikely success story, featuring a slang name for a minority sport which games fans ('games' as in 'sports') George, Charles and Edward Parker thought up in the first decade of the twentieth century and which has since turned into a verb despite its preposterous appearance.

Pratdigger: A fine example of criminal slang, this Victorian term (originally meaning 'pickpocket') was dragged into the 21st century by the journalist Mr Rockwell, who also started using it in a more social sense. There are rumours that Kanye West's 2005 hit song 'Gold Digger' was originally titled 'Prat Digger', but these are as yet unconfirmed.

Real McCoy: According to Melvyn Bragg and Bill Bryson, Joseph McCoy was a cattle rancher, like Samuel A. Maverick, whose innovations had long-lasting linguistic effects. Rather than selling his beef locally, he had the bright idea of driving his cattle hundreds of miles to a railhead in Kansas whence they were trundled off to bigger city markets and sold. Bragg writes that in the late 1860s McCoy became 'so rich that some of his innumerable imitators tried to pretend they were the great man himself. McCoy developed the habit of introducing himself to strangers as "the real McCoy"' (this story may not be the genuine article itself, however. Jonathan Green highlights claims from Indiana where the boxer Norman Selby's nickname 'Kid McCoy' became a byword for 'the real deal' after he'd been forced to fend off various wannabe assailants; and from Scotland, where two rival chieftains both claimed to be in charge of the McKay clan in the 1880s. Other word-watchers point to some particularly authentic opiates from Macao. Feel free to take your pick).

Sandwich: John Montagu, the fourth Earl of Sandwich who strutted his stuff in the seventeenth century, didn't invent the bread-filling-bread combination but really liked the idea because it meant he could play cribbage whilst eating without his cards getting greasy. That was enough for the handy foodstuff to share in his title, and the unlikely looking word took off, soon developing into a verb as well as a noun.

Saxophone: A Belgian called Adolphe Sax displayed his brand-new musical instrument, the 'saxophone' at the Great Exhibition of 1851. An American composer called John Phillip Sousa also copied Pan's trick with the 'sousaphone' in the 1890s (I have tried to design my own 'hornophone' but the name sounds rather tautological so may not catch on).

Scientist: The word 'scientist' was coined by a polymath called William Whewell, a philosopher, theologian, science historian, Anglican priest and indeed scientist whom the *OED* quotes an impressive 607 times. Previously known as 'natural philosophers' or, and this one's more menacing, 'men of science', Whewell invented his own job in the 1840 romp, *Philosophy of the Inductive Sciences Founded upon their History*, in which he wrote, 'We need very much a name to describe a cultivator of science in general. I should incline to call him a Scientist.' And so, now, do we. He also fathered the lesser known 'consilience', 'catastrophism' and 'uniformitrarianism', the better known 'physicist', and suggested the terms 'anode' and 'cathode' to Michael Faraday, before falling off his horse and dying in 1866, aged seventy-one.

Serendipitous: The noun 'serendipity' and its adjective were fashioned by the London-based antiquarian and novelist Horace Walpole (1717–97) in honour of Sri Lanka ('Serendip' in Persian). As well as winning a place in the dictionary, 'serendipity' was voted one of the ten hardest words to translate by a British translation company in June 2004. The less pleasing 'plenipotentiary' came top, with the Tshiluba (a language spoken in the Democratic Republic of Congo) word 'ilunga' winning the coveted award for non-English word most hard to pin down (meaning, roughly, a person who is ready to forgive any abuse for the first time, to tolerate it a second time, but never a third time).

Sideburns: In 1863 an otherwise overlooked American soldier called Ambrose Everett Burnside added 'sideburns' to the vocabulary simply by not shaving the bit of the beard that ran parallel to his ears.

Silly Billy: The first 'silly Billy' was William Frederick, Duke of Gloucester, the uncle of King George III and renowned idiot in court.

Sisyphean: Although less known than Tantalus' 'tantalise', 'sisyphean' is an adjective meaning an activity that is never-ending, usually with undertones of pointlessness, created in memory of Sisyphus, the mythological king of Corinth who was condemned to roll a large stone up a hill in the under-world. So large was the stone that it constantly fell back onto him. So frustrating was this that it spawned a new word. Verbal Gardening often feels sisyphean.

Steal One's Thunder: Typifying the Classical influence on English in the early 1700s, the playwright John Dennis set the third of his tragedies, *Appius and Virginia*, in Ancient Rome. It told the true story of Appius Claudius Crassus, one of the Roman Republic's Ten Rare Men (*decemvirate*) in 451 BC, and a girl he fancied called Virginia, who both ended up being stabbed to death. As well as writing the play, Dennis put himself in charge of certain aspects of its production, including creating the sound effect of thunder, either by rattling a sheet of tin or by rolling metal balls around a wooden bowl. Despite possessing what I certainly consider to be these key elements of quality drama, the play closed due to lack of audience demand soon after a performance at the Drury Lane Theatre at the start of the eighteenth century. Dennis was not happy. But he grew even less happy when he attended a production of *Macbeth* in the same theatre soon after and heard someone else making the noise of thunder. He couldn't believe it. 'Damn them!' he cried. 'They will not let my play run, but they steal my thunder!' That's right, John, but at least you've managed to coin your own phrase.

Sweet FA: A young girl called Fanny Adams was out playing with her sister Lizzie and friend Minnie in Alton, Hampshire, on 24 August 1868, when a stranger approached and offered her a halfpenny to walk with him before murdering, mutilating and dismembering her body. Five thousand people came to Winchester on Christmas Eve to watch her murderer, Frederick Baker, being hanged. The rest of the country welcomed 'Sweet Fanny Adams' into the language.

Talent: The poet Thomas Hoccleve (or Occleve as he's also known, presumably by cockneys) was a contemporary of Chaucer, and the man who kindly donated the word 'slut' to the language. Born in 1369, died in 1426, and virtually unknown today, he was also the first to use the word 'talent' to mean 'special ability', so I'm very happy to do my bit to remind people of his existence.

Tantalising: For the verb 'to tantalise', we have to thank a naughty Greek king (one of the many sons of Zeus) called Tantalus, who was punished in the afterlife for being such a naughty king by being forced to stand in a river with the water up to his chin, directly beneath some pesky fruit-laden branches that moved away (annoyingly, I'd imagine) whenever he tried to grab something to eat.

Tarmac: John Loudon McAdam pioneered a new highway surface in 1820 which was then combined with tar a few decades later and thus lives on in the word 'tarmac', although I imagine John himself would have been a little annoyed that only the Mc bit of his name survives in the term. 'Mc' and 'mac', of course, mean 'son of', something not peculiar only to Mr McAdam. The same could be said for Scottish inventor Charles Macintosh, who at last provided some full body protection from his country's inclement weather with his rubber coat in 1824, now often referred to simply as a 'mac', and radio personality Willard Scott, who performed under the moniker 'Ronald MacDonald, the Hamburger-Happy Clown' in the 1960s and eventually put the 'mac' in Big Mac.

Apple Mac are named after a type of apple, not a person, but I would like to point out that Apple Macintosh is a most pleasing anagram of Laptop Machines.

Tawdry: Another word with a name hidden within, 'tawdry' is a shortening of 'St Audrey's lace', a necktie sold on the seventh-century saint Audrey's day (17 October). Also known as Æthelthryth, but more often as Ethelreda because that's pronounceable, Suffolk-based Audrey's name supposedly gained its negative associations when, after she'd succumbed to a throat tumour, she claimed that God was punishing her because she used to like flashy necklaces. Now that's a messy etymology.

Telegraph: The term 'telegraph' was coined by a Frenchman called Claude Chappe at the end of the eighteenth century to describe a semaphore system used in the French Revolution. A forgotten inventor at Princeton called Josephe Henry then invented the method of transmitting messages via wires which was in turn nicked from under his nose and patented by one Samuel Finley Breese Morse, a painter by trade, whose surname would also go down in history as a code (and grouchy Detective Chief Inspector Endeavour).

Telephone: The official name was first applied to the communication tool by Johann Phillipp Reis in Germany in 1861.

Titchy: The antonym of jumbo, 'titchy' is a flawless adjective with the most unlikely of origins. Harry Relph was a four-foot-six-inch music hall performer from the turn of the twentieth century whose nickname was 'Little Tich'. He was also polydactylic (one of my favourite words, meaning to have more fingers or toes than the norm. Little Tich had six digits on both hands and both feet. Other polydactyls include Hannibal Lecter, Anne Boleyn and the West Indian cricketer Gary Sobers who personally removed his extra fingers during childhood 'with the aid of catgut and a sharp knife'). Our 'titchy' comes from this man. But his 'tich' came from a notorious impostor named Arthur Orton who had returned from Australia in 1866 claiming to be Roger Charles Titchborn, the missing heir of an estate presumed lost at sea years before. Orton was found out and gained infamy as 'The Titchborn Claimant'. So when I was a kid I called my brother 'titchy' because the diminutive Relph looked like Orton, who had pretended to be a man called Roger Charles Titchborn who was, in fact, just under six foot tall.

Tkday: The exact etymology for this spiky chronological term is unknown, but the word was definitely invented by neologist and bane of Wikipedia, The Farmer, as the signature concept of the Verbal Gardening movement.

Tractor: A name invented by W. H. Williams, sales manager of the Iowan Hart-Parr company, who fashioned the word out of an old 'traction engine' in 1901.

Uncanny: The Scottish poet Walter Scott (1771–1832) wanted, as I do, to 'contribute somewhat to the history of my native country', and by promoting such words as 'uncanny', 'glamour', 'cosy', 'gruesome' and 'dervish,' he 'gave to the English language possibly more English words than any author since Shakespeare', according to a man called Manfred Görlach (in *English in Nineteenth-Century England: An Introduction*), who is clearly far more qualified to make such claims than me.

United States of America: The 'consummate sloganeer' (Bill Bryson's words, the second a cracker) Thomas Paine, who emigrated from Britain to the colonies in 1774, coined the winning phrases 'the Age of Reason' and 'the Rights of Man', as well as 'the United States of America'.

Vandal: 'Vandal' is a Roman word, not made up by a single person but of a single race: the Vandals, a Germanic tribe who eventually sacked Rome in AD 455 after making numerous raids on Roman provinces throughout the third and fourth centuries and causing havoc in Gaul at the beginning of the fifth. I really want to create a word but there are some lengths even I won't go to.

Venn diagram: One of my top five favourite diagrams, conceived and named around 1880 by a British logician and philosopher called John Venn to whom we should all be most grateful.

Versatile: While a small minority argue that it was Francis Bacon, not William Shakespeare, who wrote all those plays (and coined many many words in the process), it is generally accepted that the philosopher did introduce the word 'essay' to the language in 1597, and he is quoted in the *OED* as the first user of 'acoustic', 'juvenile' and 'versatile'.

Victorian: The word 'Victorian' can be attributed to the Queen herself, who was implausibly (possibly rightly so) the first person in the UK to be called 'Victoria'. From the Latin word for 'victory', the name was already widely used across Europe, including Germany, where Victoria's mother, also Victoria, resided, but never before in the English-speaking world, or at least not by anyone of any standing. Other individually crafted names are 'Vanessa', coined by Jonathan Swift (alongside his 'yahoos') as a pseudonym for his Dutch love Esther Vanhomrigh (combining her last and first names); 'Wendy', invented by J. M. Barrie in *Peter Pan* (where he also constructed the first ever 'wendy house' in 1904); 'Pamela', mixed by Sir Philip Sidney from the Greek 'Pan' and 'mela' (honey) to make the character for his play *Arcadia*; 'Dorian', picked by Oscar Wilde from an ancient Greek tribe to be the titular hero of *The Picture of Dorian Gray*; and 'Olivia', converted by Shakespeare himself from Oliver for *Twelfth Night*.

Village: Like 'games', the noun can also be used as an adjective to describe something quite rubbish. This usage, I'm reliably informed, was invented by the cricketer Michael Atherton, who tended to play a rather higher standard of the sport.

Web: The term 'the Web' was coined in 1990 by Tim Berners-Lee and Robert Cailliau, replacing Al Gore's far more clunky 1978 effort, 'information superhighway'.

Willy Nilly: Unfortunately I have to report that this is merely a contraction of 'will I, nill I' (or 'will he/ye, nill he/ye') and used since 1608 as an alternative to the Latin *nolens volens*. I'd much rather spread a rumour that it was invented by a man called Willy Nilly, but I'm not sure you'd believe me.

World War II: The phrase 'World War II' can be attributed to Henry J. Stimson, the American Secretary for War in 1945, who convinced President Truman to officially sanction it over other contenders like the grandiose 'War of World Freedom' and the catchy 'Anti Nazi War'. Now that's an impressive language legacy: 'World War II'. If another global battle breaks out I'd like to say categorically that I think it should be called 'World War III'. There, that'll almost certainly get me in the record books.

Yours Sincerely: Poet (like Mr Elephant) and dramatist (like Mr Bodoni) John Gay designed the apparently ageless 'yours sincerely'. Yours sincerely, Alex Horne.

BIBLIOGRAPHY

Dictionaries

Cambridge Dictionary
Cassell Dictionary of Slang
Chambers Dictionary
Collins Dictionary
Gigglossary
Longman Dictionary of Contemporary English
MacMillan Dictionary
Merriam-Webster Dictionary
New Columbia Encyclopaedia
New Oxford American Dictionary
New Oxford Dictionary of English
Penguin Latin Dictionary
Webster's New Millennium Dictionary of English

Miscellaneous

Douglas Adams and John Lloyd, *The Meaning of Liff*
John Bartlett, *Dictionary of Americanisms*
Howard W. Bergerson, *Palindromes and Anagrams*
Ambrose Bierce, *The Devil's Dictionary*
Adam Jacot de Boinod, *The Meaning of Tingo*
Edward de Bono, *The Use of Lateral Thinking*
Peter Bowler, *The Superior Person's Book of Words*
Melvyn Bragg, *The Adventure of English*

Fanny Burney, *Evelina*

Lewis Carroll, *Alice in Wonderland*

Lewis Carroll, *Through the Looking-Glass*

Gerald Cohen, *Studies in Slang*

Philip Cohen, *Work Ways*

Courtenay Ryley Cooper, *Designs in Scarlet*

David Crystal, *Predicting New Words*

John Dryden, *Defence of the Epilogue*

John S. Farmer and W. E. Henley, *Dictionary of Slang and Colloquial English*

Thomas Fuller, *The Church-History of Britain*

Alex Games, *Balderdash and Piffle – English Words and Their Curious Origins*

Manfred Görlach, *English in Nineteenth-Century England: An Introduction*

Jonathon Green, *Slang Down the Ages*

Sir Mathew Hale, *Primitive Origination of Mankind, Considered and Examined According to the Light of Nature*

Mike Harding, *When the Martians Landed in Huddersfield*

Robert Harris, *Imperium*

Joseph Heller, *Catch-22*

Henry Hitchings, *Dr Johnson's Dictionary*

Henry Hitchings, *The Secret Life of Words*

Aldous Huxley, *Brave New World*

Ian McMillan, *Chelp and Chunter: How to Talk Tyke*

Viz and Roger Mellie, *Roger's Profanisaurus*

Allan Metcalf, *Predicting New Words*

Stephen Potter, *The Theory and Practice of Gamesmanship*

F. T. Porter, *Gleanings and Reminiscences*

Eric Partridge, *Dictionary of Slang and Unconventional English*

Michael Quinion, *Ballyhoo, Buckaroo, and Spuds*

Edwin Radford and Alan Smith, *To Coin a Phrase*

Nigel Rees, *As We Say in Our House*

Ammon Shea, *Reading the Oxford English Dictionary*
Richard Sheridan, *The Rivals*
Benjamin Stuart, *Walker Remodelled*
Lynne Truss, *Eats, Shoots and Leaves*
C. A. Ward, *Notes and Queries: A Medium of Intercommunication for Literary Men, General Readers, Etc*
R. W. Jackson, *You Say Tomato: An Amusing and Irreverent Guide to the Most Often Mispronounced Words in the English Language*

Acknowledgements

Due to the sly and occasionally scandalous nature of this project, I can only mention my most trusted conspirators obliquely but I am indebted to TK, DM, OP, PB, MW, MT, EJ, TH, GR and the one and only GP. I hope they know how grateful I am for their often unacknowledged but always unflinching dedication.

Extraordinarily profuse thanks to the many sneaky people who have voluntarily joined our band, independently smuggling words into their own worlds and contributing countless creative neologisms to the cause. Rather apologetic thanks to those individuals who became unwittingly embroiled in the affair. Again, I won't name them here but AG, VC and NK have been particularly unobstructive when they could have thrown all sorts of spanners at me and my men. And professional but heartfelt thanks to everyone at Avalon and Virgin, and in particular Ed, James, Davina and Becky, for making this an actual thing rather than just some thoughts in my head.

Finally, despite being confronted by a barrage of unintelligible words and unpredictable behaviour, my ever-expanding family has been as patient and supportive as always. Thanks especially to my mum for providing the inspiration, to Chip for his sound advice throughout both the project and the writing of this book, and to Rachel for encouraging my adventures. Tom and I are lucky little men.